THE WORK OF POVERTY

The Work of Poverty

SAMUEL BECKETT'S VAGABONDS
AND THE THEATER OF CRISIS

Lance Duerfahrd

THE OHIO STATE UNIVERSITY PRESS · COLUMBUS

Copyright © 2013 by The Ohio State University.
All rights reserved.

Library of Congress Cataloging-in-Publication Data
Duerfahrd, Lance Alfred, 1967–
  The work of poverty : Samuel Beckett's vagabonds and the theater of crisis / Lance Duerfahrd.
    p. cm.
  Includes bibliographical references and index.
  ISBN-13: 978-0-8142-1237-0 (cloth : alk. paper)
  ISBN-10: 0-8142-1237-9 (cloth : alk. paper)
  ISBN-13: 978-0-8142-9339-3 (cd-rom)
  ISBN-10: 0-8142-9339-5 (cd-rom)
  1. Beckett, Samuel, 1906–1989. En attendant Godot. English—Criticism and interpretation. 2. Beckett, Samuel, 1906–1989—Influence. I. Title.
  PQ2603.E378Z618 2013
  842'.914—dc23
                              2013022653

Cover design by Jennifery Shoffey-Forsythe
Text design by Juliet Williams
Type set in Palatino

∞ The paper used in this publication meets the minimum requirements of the American National Standard for Information Sciences—Permanence of Paper for Printed Library Materials. ANSI Z39.48–1992.

9 8 7 6 5 4 3 2 1

Contents

List of Illustrations — vi

Acknowledgments — vii

INTRODUCTION	Begging Context	1
CHAPTER 1	Godot behind Bars	12
CHAPTER 2	Waiting for Godot in Sarajevo and New Orleans	63
CHAPTER 3	*La Pensée Vagabonde:* Vagabond Thought	112
CHAPTER 4	Textual Indigence: The Reader in an Aesthetics of Poverty	143
AFTERWORD	Staging *Godot* in Zuccotti Park	178

Notes — 191

Bibliography — 223

Index — 231

Illustrations

FIGURE 1	Protest signs at Zuccotti Park during Occupy Wall Street, October 2011 (photo by Stacey Mickelbart)	180
FIGURE 2	Actors bear Beckett's tree into Zuccotti Park (photo by Alex Lukens)	184
FIGURE 3	Lucky (David Yashin) performs monologue near "Un-Repeal Glass-Steagall" (photo by Stacey Mickelbart)	185
FIGURE 4	Didi (Harold Dean James) and Gogo (Katie Schwarz) wait in front of signs reading "It's a Scandal"; "Think, Pig"; "AT LEAST LUCKY HAS A JOB"; and "Don't be a Gashole" (photo by Alex Lukens)	186
FIGURE 5	Didi (Harold Dean James) and Gogo (Katie Schwarz) huddle together (photo by Alex Lukens)	187

Acknowledgments

Abundant thanks are in order to the following people: Jonathan Bernstein, for his interest in this project and his help bringing *Godot* to Zuccotti Park, his colorful brilliance, his idiosyncrasy, and his radical love for life; Luc Kinsch, for his camaraderie and the incredible flint of his insight; Rosanne Altstatt, for her care in copyediting the manuscript and for her profound friendship; Ben Weaver, for his wit and endless evocation of maxims and apothegms; Alex Lukens, for pinning to my refrigerator an enlarged poster of Beckett that read, "Let us not waste time in idle discourse," and for documenting the production of *Godot* on Wall Street; Amy Pommerening, for marking up a copy of the manuscript as if it were a find-a-word; Rob Richardson, for proofreading a chapter and being a mensch; and my students Megha Anwer, Matt Varner, and Sean Purvines, for their support and kindness.

    I am particularly grateful to Rick Cluchey for sharing his incredible theatrical work and life story with me, by phone and in correspondence, and for reading my manuscript. A boxer who learned his craft in San Quentin, Rick signed all his letters to me, "Keep punching." Thanks go to Sidney Homan for sharing his unpublished memoir, *Embarrassment of Swans*, and for discussing with me his production of *Waiting for Godot* in the Florida State Penitentiary system. Alan Mandell kindly endured several phone conversations and my umpteen questions about his experience bringing *Godot* to San Quentin in 1957.

I thank my advisors at Yale University, Shoshana Felman and Susan Blood, who mentored me on an early version of this work, and my colleagues in the English Department at Purdue University. My particular gratitude goes out to Arkady Plotnitsky, Geri Friedman, Dino Felluga, Dan Morris, Nancy Peterson, Aparajita Sagar, and Bill Mullen for their creative and supportive responses to my text. Thanks go to my colleague Scott Schroeder for making the images from the Zuccotti Park *Godot* so much crisper. A travel grant from Purdue University allowed me to conduct research at the Beckett Archives in Reading, England.

I could not have completed this project without the expertise and brilliant navigation provided by Senior Editor Sandy Crooms, the meticulous attention to the manuscript from Copyediting Coordinator Maggie Diehl, and the support of Director Malcolm Litchfield at The Ohio State University Press.

This book is dedicated to my mother, Janet Duerfahrd, my brother, Kurt Duerfahrd, and to the memory of my father, Clement Duerfahrd, and to the memory of my aunt, Bernice Rossi. They were agents in easing me out of my dumbfounded state when I first took Beckett on as the subject of my dissertation at Yale University. My aunt proceeded to check out all of Beckett's books from her local library. She made herself fluent in absurdity and then read my dissertation. My father and mother also encouraged my Beckett thinking. They drove one night to a one-man Beckett monologue performed at a small theater in Providence, Rhode Island, even though they had little interest in Beckett. The fact that my parents endured a Beckett performance on my behalf moves me to this day. Before the show they purchased a small tape recorder and secretly concealed it my dad's breast pocket. My dad became the first man to officially bootleg Beckett. When I received the tapes in the mail two days later, I was astonished to find that all they had recorded was the noise of my dad's restlessness during the performance, a brushing static sound made whenever he crossed his arms or nodded off. Beckett, who described art as a stain on silence, would have approved of the way his own words were scrubbed away, and how the voice of the performer murmured faintly beneath the vast aerial surf formed by the contact of coat on shirt. That nothing sensible was recorded did not stunt my curiosity. On the contrary, I had a greater hunger for what might have been said. My dad went like a spy into a Beckett monologue and emerged from a small theater in Providence having managed to record the sound of an ocean.

Introduction

Begging Context

This book is about Samuel Beckett's destitute art. Though his body of work seems to offer audiences very little by way of lesson or entertainment, it nevertheless has an unusual performance history within settings of real-world crisis. In landscapes of ruin, *Waiting for Godot* emerges unexpectedly and Beckett's impoverished aesthetic begins to resonate. A focus on poverty is in keeping with the primary trajectory in Beckett's career, eliminating all excess from his work and seeking what Beckett calls "ultimate penury" in art.[1] Beckett offers us not a rich but a poor—and ever poorer—prose, and subject matter likewise stricken by poverty. Entwined with creation, poverty is for Beckett a dynamic condition, a "worsening" rather than an achieved state.[2] In conversation with Lawrence Harvey, Beckett observes, "What complicates it all is the need to make. Like a child in mud but no mud. And no child. Only need."[3] Beckett's work undertakes an endless subtractive movement, removing first mud, then child, leaving only need and then perhaps something less than need. His texts explore an aesthetic of worsening suitable to the inherent dispossession of his itinerant subjects, figures in a perpetual state of emergency. This enterprise to deplete representation places Beckett firmly in the camp of the avant-garde. Performances of *Waiting for Godot* in prisons, in Sarajevo during a civil war, and in post-Katrina New Orleans, however, reveal an alternative potential for his work. Abstruse to many critics, Beckett's postdramatic minimalism makes under these circumstances an immediate and unexpectedly emotive appeal, as the survivors of flood, siege, and carceral institutions become literate in Beckett through their predicament. This study explores the illuminating encounter between Beckett's theater and these environments.

The Work of Poverty is a discussion of "poor Beckett," but it also aspires to add to existing discourses about poverty and worklessness. I isolate four key Beckettian tropes: need, exposure/abandonment, enough, and begging the question.[4] Beckett uses the terms "exposure" and "abandonment" to describe the unsheltered condition of his evicted vagabond figure, for whom privation has supplanted privacy, similar to Walter Benjamin's "new poverty."[5] Beckett's term "enough," his measure for the barely adequate, resonates with Giorgio Agamben's concept of "bare" or "naked life," the biopolitical status to which the individual is reduced in the modern state. The way Beckett's work begs questioning provides us with the antithesis of Franz Kafka's literature of petition. *The Trial* and stories such as "The Building of the Chinese Wall" honor *petitio principii* to the letter: they situate their narratives around the investigation of a missing premise, for example, the basis of Joseph K's guilt and cause of his arrest.[6] Whereas Kafka actively raises questions within the text, thereby encouraging a hermeneutical response from the reader, Beckett begs questions and invites an interrogative relation to his work. Beckett's defense of the remainder and his pursuit of the barely adequate are key to the recurrent but critically underappreciated place of poverty in modern thought. Beckettian poverty differs sharply from depictions of the struggling poor in novels of Charles Dickens and Victor Hugo, which trade on "mere misery where destitute virtuous mothers may steal bread for their starving brats."[7] *The Work of Poverty* explains why Hugo's *Les Misérables* lands on Broadway while Beckett's hobos turn up in Sarajevo. It shows how Beckett's thematic discussion of poverty and his legendary theatrical, textual, and formal sparseness act together to propel the emergence of his theater on "stages of history," landscapes mired in the aftermath of catastrophe.

Although it has not yet achieved this status, Beckett's destitute theater ultimately deserves a place next to fellow modernist playwright Bertolt Brecht's aesthetic of didacticism, his Epic theater. Brecht approaches theater as a pedagogical instrument rigged to expose the contradictions of capital, showing the audience that theater is illusion. Brecht's theater aspires to deny the viewer empathy by interrupting the theatrical illusion and drawing the spectator toward a state of critical awareness. The actors' estrangement from their roles, the unexpected appearance of a stranger in the doorway, the immobilization of a scene into a sudden tableau are devices that tear away the theatrical veil and remind the audience of the mechanism of its production. To this, Beckett's *Waiting for Godot* provides a pointed antithesis. Not only does the play go uninterrupted, but its crux depends on a stranger who never shows up at all. The endless waiting for something to happen in Beckett's plays inverts Brecht's message that conditions must be understood in order to be changed.[8] On Beckett's stage, nothing changes and little is understood.

If Brecht's Epic theater seeks to educate and to make critics of his audience, what purpose are we to ascribe to Beckett's theater of destitution? This purpose is glimpsed in what I call the crisis performances of *Waiting for Godot:* productions in the impoverished contexts of Lüttringhausen Prison (1953), San Quentin State Prison (1957), and Raiford Prison (1974); McComb, Mississippi during the Civil Rights Movement (1964); Sarajevo in the midst of civil war and genocide (1993); post-Katrina New Orleans (2007); and in Zuccotti Park during Occupy Wall Street (2011). Beckett never stages crisis; rather, these crises stage Beckett. The reduction of the human subject in the prison, in the city under siege, and in the area devastated by flood meshes with the scant remains of persona and action witnessed on Beckett's stage. Though Beckett rarely commented on Brecht's work, Brecht was outspoken on what he took to be Beckett's apolitical stance. In 1953 Brecht made a stab at fashioning a *Gegenentwurf* (counterpoint drama) to *Waiting for Godot*, deleting some lines and adding others in order to make the play into a commentary on class. Estragon becomes *ein Prolet* (derogatory slang for a proletarian), Vladimir an "intellectual," Lucky a "donkey or policeman." Pozzo becomes *ein Gutsbesitzer* (landowner) and a noble, "Von Pozzo."[9] Yet Brecht cannot refunction the dysfunctional figures on Beckett's stage to his purpose and ultimately abandons the attempt to rewrite the play. Though it is the dramaturgical antithesis of Epic theater, *Godot* resists participation in dialogue with Brecht. The problem for Brecht is that Beckett's play advances very little. The play exposes a situation rather than posits a viewpoint. Because the play is the situation, Brecht has difficulty instrumentalizing it.[10] What can Brecht offer Beckett's outcasts? What counterstance can Brecht strike against their abandonment, against their postsocial condition? Outside systems of exchange of labor and capital, Beckett's vagabonds obstruct inscription into social context.

In fact, Brecht does resolve this impasse, and *The Work of Poverty* takes a cue from his resolution. Brecht opts to leave the text and performance of *Godot* intact. Instead, he contextualizes the play by projecting cinematic footage of social revolutions in Asia, China, the Soviet Union, and

Africa behind the actors. In the words of Clas Zilliacus, the tramps are not "dragged into society. Instead, they are shown as voluntary outsiders having chosen to part with a progressing world."[11] Brecht realizes, in other words, that he must put his eraser and pencil down and approach *Godot* through the situation of performance. Brecht's solution undoes the audience's fascination with Godot's absence as well as the religious and metaphysical speculations it has sustained. The audience is asked to critically divide its attention between the stage and the cinematic space adjacent to it. Instead of invading the play, Brecht chooses a display of force, massing the troops of historical revolutions at the border of Beckett's stage. The force exerted over Beckett's play by Sarajevo, San Quentin, and New Orleans exceeds that of a cinematic backdrop. These crisis settings permeate every aspect of the play: not just performance but rehearsal, production, and audience. Whereas Brecht's revolutionary filmstrips invite the spectator to dismiss Beckett's stage through dialectical contrast, these environments align themselves with the subadequate conditions of Beckett's stage. Crisis encircles Beckett's stage not to set it off (negate it) but to set off (like a bomb) the need and frailty of its images.

Brecht understands something crucial in his effort to elicit meaning from Beckett: though too poor to instantiate a reality, *Godot* demands juxtaposition to one. The condition of need on Beckett's stage exerts a radiant effect over contiguous spaces. Waiting consumes all the spaces adjoining the stage, including the seating, the lobby, and even the space of movement toward the theater. Drama theorist Elin Diamond remarks that *Godot* "paradoxically begs for meaningful context."[12] Brecht does not fabricate a context per se for *Godot*. His cinematic and archival images allow Beckett's play its autonomy while indicting it as a willful abandonment of history and political action. Beckett does not seek alienation for effect, and there is no redemption, no charity, no call to action that would alleviate it. For Beckett, alienation is tied neither to man's fate nor to labor. As we will see, need is not confined to the stage in San Quentin, Sarajevo, or New Orleans. Susan Sontag remarks that the separation of actor and role—the discipline demanded by both Brecht and Epic theater—is impossible in her Sarajevo production. The play calls for the character Pozzo to eat a piece of chicken and casually toss the bones aside in front of the hungry vagabonds. With no chicken available, Sontag resorts to a papier-mâché likeness. What need is there to expose the illusion, what opportunity is there for a lesson on class when the actor is himself hungry and where conspicuous consumption describes the actors' bodies rather than Pozzo's display of luxury on stage? In Sarajevo, chickens are for the pot, not the theater. Need is too urgent to allow the bird to become a prop. The actor does not have the freedom to alienate himself from his hunger. Beckett's work takes root in contexts that repudiate Brecht's strategy of alienation. The destitution of Beckett's characters is registered, even exacerbated, in the very process of producing the play.

Histories of Beckett performances tend to focus more on the directorial interpretation of his work than on an aesthetic of poverty. Critical emphasis on fidelity is partly a by-product of Beckett's meticulous attention to detail as a director, and of the playwright's absolute rejection of productions that "creatively" alter his text or stage directions.[13] The language of paternity and proper inheritance pervades the backlash by critics dismayed by Sontag's decision to cut *Godot* in half and turn Vladimir/Estragon into three distinct couples played by a total of six different actors. Everett Frost lines up with the Beckett estate when he makes a distinction between "Beckett's" *Godot* and the "bastard twin" that he names "*Godot*-as-metaphor," staged at the Youth Theater in Sarajevo.[14] Frost's emphasis on the purity of the textual *Godot*, which he calls the "full measure of the experience of the play written by Samuel Beckett," is made clear by this comparison of Sontag's production to a sibling abandoned at birth.[15] Yet this abject status befits Sontag's version of Beckett's vagabond drama staged amidst a siege. The challenge is in recognizing this poor bastard performance without trying to restore it to the lineage of sanctioned productions. The goal here is not to issue a critical imprimatur but to learn how the adversities of war, prison, and flood impose their marks and fractures on these performances. These alterations to the face of Beckett's play are not makeup added by the director (willful infidelity) but the look of suffering it assumes in response to its surroundings.

Literary critics who make no specific mention of these performances nevertheless evoke their possibility. In his 1967 essay "Beckett's Purgatory of the Individual," Darko Suvin writes that Beckett's work finds relevance in crisis: "The lack of a central and all-embracing relevance should not . . . make us forget what relevance can be found in Beckett's work: for where and when it is relevant, it is supremely so. I suggested earlier that it was relevant in random and closed situations of human experience: in war, camps, prisons, sickness, old age, grim helplessness of all kinds."[16] Some of the settings Suvin hypothesizes as settings for Beckett have in fact materialized in the performances I discuss: war (Sarajevo), camps (the Lower Ninth Ward, with the FEMA trailer camps nearby), and prisons (Lüttringhausen, San Quentin).[17] The other sites Suvin mentions provide us with food for thought, the possibility of *Godot* staged in retirement communities, hospices, and hospital waiting rooms. Suvin remarks upon the "random and closed" quality of experience under these circumstances. Such impoverished sites sustain experience without horizon and within an economy of the ever-same. The closed systems of these environments find their echo in the hermetic structure of Beckett's stage. In *Godot,* as in prison, "Nothing happens, nobody comes, nobody goes, it's awful!"[18] Though Suvin describes the experiences of the prison, the camp, and war as "random," we can observe that they are, in fact, just as structured and managed as the theater itself. *Godot* is summoned not before natural disasters but before unnatural ones: the wasteland by design of the carceral system, the combined engineering failure of the levee and inadequacy of governmental response following Katrina, the ethnic cleansing of Sarajevo.

Relevance is more personal than meaning for a play. Suvin underscores the "where" and "when" of the relevance of Beckett's work because it addresses people in particular situations—not just as theatergoers. *Godot* becomes relevant to audiences faced with "grim helplessness" through a mechanism other than representation (mimesis). In New York or Paris, *Waiting for Godot* is a highly mediated and avant-garde play. In the context of crisis, the play is self-evident, intuitive, even necessary. Vivian Mercier's observation that *Godot* is a play in which "nothing happens, twice" becomes jarringly real for the displaced residents of the Lower Ninth Ward.[19] Captive to forces deaf to their argument, prisoners understand the disjunction between the characters' declaration ("let's go")[20] and their subsequent immobility, but they see this predicament as familiar rather than absurd.

Marked by mass uprootings, illegitimately detained subjects, and manmade and natural disasters, our era finds its symptom in Beckett's literature of dereliction. Crisis productions of *Waiting for Godot* are neither an aestheticization of the world nor a mirror held to it. Sontag's production in Sarajevo and Paul Chan's production in New Orleans both appear on the front page of the *New York Times* and in other major news media. While the headlines treat the confluence of crisis and theater as a sensational novelty, I take it to be inherent in Beckett's design. The response of the flood evacuee, the inmate, and the siege victim help us engage the play's drastic address. As I will show, these audiences' reception illuminates waiting, structures of the waiting process, names for waiting, and the awaited. They help us read the play's first line, "nothing to be done," and the final stage direction, *"they do not move."*[21] Beckett's theater exists, in a sense, after the world is over: an impoverished theater of aftermath.

These audiences do not forget their situation in their encounter with the play. Martin Esslin remarks upon this as he introduces his classic study of avant-garde theater, *The Theatre of the Absurd*, with the image of 1,400 spellbound convicts watching Vladimir and Estragon on the stage. Esslin asks, "Why did a play of the supposedly esoteric avant-garde make so immediate and deep an impact on an audience of convicts?"[22] Prisoners, many of whom had never been to the theater before, were able to embrace a play that perplexed and angered theatergoers who were free to walk at intermission. In the early 1950s, Beckett's only unqualified success was with criminals. Yet as we will see, the inmates' responses are not entirely immediate, as if they were uneducated, nor do they construe Beckett's work as nothing more than a circus act. Their reactions are mediated by their experience of the institution. They have been schooled there in a way that the critic will do his utmost to avoid: in living with the situation depicted on Beckett's stage. After the performance in San Quentin, the convicts appropriate the names of Beckett's characters to designate functions within the prison hierarchy: "Lucky" is a man on death row, "Pozzo" is a guard.[23] *Godot* in these contexts takes these audiences where they happen to be. Catastrophe turns the prisoners into readers of Beckett.

Esslin overlooks the degree to which the setting is an active agent in this reception of Beckett's play. A 1954 production of *Waiting for Godot* in Belgrade, Yugoslavia, stands as perhaps the purest rendering of Beckett's absurd theater, as the play was performed for no audience at all. The performance occurs in the context of the Eastern Bloc's designation of modern theater as Western decadence. Prerag Dinulović, artistic director of the Belgrade Drama Theatre, agrees to begin rehearsals of *Godot* as a gesture of openness to Western culture. Concerned about the political repercussions of a Beckett performance, however, he eliminates the production in the announcement of the theater's official repertoire, continuing all the while to rehearse the play.[24] As the day of the premiere approaches, management grows increasingly wary of the plan to stage the play. Theater is important to Belgrade, and producing this play carries risks.[25] What will be the consequences of staging this most Western, most decadent piece? A compromise is found: the theater company will to go ahead with the production but allow no audience into the theater. Guards posted at the entrances allow only actors and stagehands to enter. The show goes on before an empty house, the spell interrupted only by a few intrepid theatergoers who manage to climb in unobserved through an open window and peek at the stage while crouched between the rows.

This performance is unwittingly Beckettian, and I read Soviet bureaucracy as a crisis environment. By letting the performance happen but only under the condition of sealing it off from all witnesses, the administration avoids the potential debate that shutting it down before opening night might have caused. Like a photo from which a suspect individual had to be erased, the *Godot* performance takes place, but without any aberrant subjectivity marring the historical record. The performance literalizes Beckett's idea of art as a "stain on the silence."[26] It also honors the suggestion Beckett made at the time of the play's first London production: "If they did it my way they would empty the theatre."[27] The evacuation of the audience does not represent an ironic "success" of the play but the fulfillment of its principle. When performed before an audience in a traditional theater setting, the proscenium arch issues an official limit, a property deed, to the no-man's-land on Beckett's stage. Performed before an "empty house," this emptiness does not end awkwardly with the front row. Likewise, the Belgrade production turns the prison performances of *Godot* inside out. At San Quentin, guards are stationed at the exits. In Belgrade, the guards are turned in the opposite direction. They are there to ensure that only theater workers enter. The guards do not interrupt the production, only the effects that the play might have produced. In Eastern Bloc absurdity, those effects are encountered by no one but the characters on stage, whose loneliness is actualized, whose abandonment is enforced by guards, and who really do just go through the motions as if opening night were indistinguishable from a rehearsal. Trees fall in theaters differently than in the proverbial woods. Beckett's skimpy tree falls and is permitted to make a sound, but only in official documentation and not in anyone's ear, not in anyone's memory.

Modern history provides more and more settings for Beckett's stage, conditions under which Beckett is to be rediscovered. Suvin concludes his discussion about Beckett's relevance by remarking, "As children of this century . . . we have seen that it is often very difficult to tell the centre from the periphery. The threat of grim helplessness hangs continually over all of us collectively."[28] Textual analysis of *Godot* might observe that Beckett's work precipitates the reversal of center and periphery by turning outcasts into dramatic personae. But Suvin here is looking off Beckett's stage rather than on it. He approaches Beckett's relevance by observing that the extreme conditions under which Beckett's theater finds its address are losing their exceptional status.

Situations beyond the stage, wherever there is shattering of the historical continuum, bring audiences into alignment with Beckett's world. This alignment does not happen with the solar regularity of the moon's rotation of the earth. It is episodic but frequent, the modern era's tendency toward recurring and ongoing catastrophe. Beckett's stage emerges in landscapes of dispossession, among people under threat. Beckett called this the "time-honored conception of humanity in ruins."[29] The crisis is not one of postmodernity (the structural loss of center) but of poverty, foretold by Beckett's impoverishing aesthetics, of an endlessly peripheral human subject. Beckett's aesthetics of poverty break the geometrical idea of periphery as a limit. His theater does not give us conceptual tools to think through our world. Instead, part of our world becomes visible in its déjà vu encounter with Beckett's stage.

Belgrade, New Orleans, San Quentin, and Sarajevo are not performances *in extremis*, spectacular and peripheral instances in which theater is called upon to resist the conditions that envelop it. In fact, the strange catharsis that prisoners and flood and siege survivors find in Beckett's postdramatic theater is part of a growing awareness about how history is unfortunately obliging Beckett's microcosm. Finding Beckett's relevance gives us an inkling of where we are headed as well as where we already are.

Chapter 1 explores the performances of *Waiting for Godot* within carceral institutions. What qualities of Beckett's play appeal to audiences "doing time"? How does the play read their situation? In the second half of the chapter, I reverse this question: how do the inmates illuminate *Godot*? What do they discover unacknowledged within Beckett criticism? Through the case studies of ex-convicts K. F. Lembke and Rick Cluchey, and inmates at Raiford Prison in the Florida State Penitentiary system, a different play emerges. The prisoners seize upon something only implicit within Beckett's impoverished theater. Former inmate Rick Cluchey, who later becomes friends with Beckett and Beckett's preferred actor and interpreter of the roles of Hamm and Krapp, told me in 2011 that prior to Herbert Blau's 1957 production of *Godot* at San Quentin, he "had never been in a theater, not even to rob one." Cluchey's transfigurative encounter with the play illuminates a possible response or outcome to Beckett's hermetic stage. Following the *Godot* performance, Cluchey forms an actor's workshop in San Quentin. He goes on to write plays (*The Cage* and *The Wall Is Mama*) that are critical rewritings of *Waiting for Godot*. Instead of breaching the "closed system" of Beckett's play, Cluchey works more deeply within it, first as an understudy reenacting Beckett's figures, and then as an author of theatrical prisons. Cluchey's career repeats and expands the range of the closed system of Beckett's work.

Waiting for Godot has also been summoned before a city under siege and a postdiluvian no-man's-land. Chapter 2 explores two performances that situate the play within disaster: Susan Sontag's 1993 production of *Godot* in Sarajevo and the Paul Chan/Classical Theater of Harlem production of *Godot* in New Orleans in 2007. How do these performances enlist *Wait-

ing for Godot to the cause of humanitarian intervention or political protest? Sontag's and Chan's productions force reconsideration of the traditional understanding of performance context. Directors have always refashioned the stage to localize or update the setting of a play, as in productions that resituate Richard III between the two world wars. The productions I discuss submit Beckett's play to conditions of need rather than just novel contexts. The play must meet these conditions like terms for a surrender: they affect the characters on stage as well as the actors and the production process.

Chapter 3 examines the intrusion of reality into Beckett's work at an interior and subjective level: the thought processes of his vagabond narrators. Though critics have referred to Beckett's characters as "learned" and even "philosophic," the vagabonds seem to disperse, rather than dispense, knowledge. Drawing from Beckett's prose works, I show how Enlightenment protocols of reason that shore up the autonomy of the individual cannot sustain defenseless and impoverished subjects. We encounter the impoverished condition of Beckett's narrators not mimetically but in the emergency state of thinking perforated by what the subject cannot possess. Beckett's trilogy gives us monologic vagabond thought: thought in rags and without shelter (condition) but also thought in a constant state of displacement (movement). I isolate several distinct modalities of vagabond thought.

In chapter 4, the role of the reader comes into view. What is an impoverished reading of Beckett? How can we maintain an unresentful disposition toward the indigence of Beckett's work and respond to its needfulness without substituting something of value in its place? I show how Beckett's work ultimately abandons the figure of the derelict and begins interrogating the worklike nature of the literary work per se. Decimated of both premise and possibility, late prose pieces such as *Worstward Ho* take begging to a new intrinsically literary level: they beg questioning. Our response to his literary work is structured primarily around the process of asking questions the work itself is unable to pose, as if his work were unable to afford question marks. Yet Beckett is not nihilistic. In *Worstward Ho*, a tract against nihilism, the work appears as its own writing manual in which the "less" and the "worse" are paradoxically "more" and "better." "Pox on void" is Beckett's pithy slogan against the zero.[30] It is counterbalanced by his striving for the "meremost minimum."[31] Beckett calls this process "perjorism," a worsening, in counterdistinction to "meliorism."[32] Beckett's destitute works culminate in the asymptotic nature of an escalating condition of need in which the figure for need, the hobo, is missing. I contrast Beckett's defense of the remainder, his injunction toward the less and the worse, with the more apocalyptic tone of his contemporaries, particularly Georges Bataille's imperative, following the devastation of Hiroshima, "to lift, in the instant, a form of life to the level of the worst."[33] I situate the final phase of Beckett's art of indigence as an infinite travail of reduction within his literary precedents, notably, the wisdom of Voltaire's Pangloss, who declares this to be the best of all possible worlds, and Edgar in *King Lear*, who observes, "The worst is not, / So long as we can say 'This is the worst.'"[34]

In the afterword I discuss my production of *Waiting for Godot* in Zuccotti Park during the Occupy Wall Street protests in New York City in October 2011. The Occupy movement sought to call attention to the iniquities of the global financial system that placed most of the wealth and political power in the hands of a privileged few (the 1 percent) while disenfranchising the many (the 99 percent). As with the other performances examined in the book, Zuccotti Park acquired the physiognomy of a Beckett stage before our group, the 99% Theater Company, performed the play. The Occupy movement, rather than march on the street in the manner of a more traditional protest, undertook vagabond existence, squatting on private land in a seemingly public space among the monoliths of capital that required constant policing. To throw light on conspicuous consumption, the protesters chose the route of conspicuous habitation. The production set the stage for a collision between Beckett's theater, a restless and downtrodden crowd of protesters, and hundreds of armed police that surrounded the encampment. Performances of *Godot* in Zuccotti Park resonate with San Quentin, Sarajevo, and the Lower Ninth Ward. A thread of Beckett's poverty links the dissimilar but similarly exposed and threatened communities of prison inmates, flood survivors, citizens living under siege, and occupiers next to America's most celebrated and yet possibly least hospitable street.

1

Godot behind Bars

You will be surprised to be receiving a letter about your play, "Waiting for Godot," from a prison where so many thieves, forgers, toughs, homos, crazy men and killers spend this bitch of a life waiting . . . and waiting . . . and waiting. Waiting for what? Godot? Perhaps. . . . We are all waiting for Godot and do not know that he is already here. Yes, here. Godot is my neighbor in the cell next to mine. Let us do something to help him then, change the shoes that are hurting him!

—Letter to Beckett from K. F. Lembke, inmate at Lüttringhausen Prison[1]

> I had never been in a theater. Not even to rob one.
> —Rick Cluchey[2]

Convicts Introduce the Absurd

Martin Esslin begins *The Theatre of the Absurd*, his landmark study of avant-garde drama, with the performance of *Waiting for Godot* at San Quentin State Prison in 1957. He asks, "Why did a play of the supposedly esoteric avant-garde make so immediate and deep an impact on an audience of convicts?"[3] Esslin never quite answers this question, but in asking it he exposes a crucial problem: how can an aesthetic whose chief offering is alienation, in a play that stages the consciousness of tramps and hobos, be so popular? Popularity implies familiarity. By whom, and under what conditions, is Beckett welcomed as familiar?

Prison inmates make a brief but stunning appearance in Esslin's study. They usher in the ostensible essence of the absurd in the book's introduction, titled "The Absurdity of the Absurd," and they endure as the audience that sticks in the reader's mind. Though Esslin does not pay them another visit until the conclusion of his book, the prison appears repeatedly in the periphery of his analysis, as if it were trying to force itself back into the picture and back into Esslin's consideration. About Genet, for example, Esslin writes, "It was prison that made him into a poet."[4] It returns again in his discussion of Beckett's visit to Paris's La Santé Prison, across from which Beckett would later live. Beckett goes there to see the pimp who had inexplicably stabbed the author one night on the streets of Paris. When Beckett inquires why he did it, his assailant replies, "Je ne sais pas, Monsieur." Of this response, Esslin notes, "It might well be the voice of this man that we hear in *Waiting for Godot* and *Molloy*."[5] The voice of Beckett's work, Esslin suggests, emerges through the prison's bars: this incapacity to reflect, a voice without motivation, memory, or knowledge, constitutes the poverty of self on view in Beckett's work. The prison seems finally to offer us an institutional framework for understanding the absurd. Even Esslin's operative definition of absurdity, borrowed from Camus, "the divorce between man and his life, the actor and his setting,"[6] resonates emphatically with life in prison. The fact that "living in prison" so easily merges with the phrase "life in prison"—the difficulty of separating one's existence in prison from one's sentence there—gives us a syntactical understanding of Camus's notion of the disharmony between who one is and how one lives.

Esslin describes the riddle of *Godot*'s popularity with criminals in this way: "What had bewildered the sophisticated audiences of Paris, London, and New York was immediately grasped by an audience of convicts."[7] How does a sequestered audience come to enjoy a play that metropolitan sophisticates regard as inaccessible? Esslin answers this question by developing a highly mediated approach to the absurd: he employs philosophy, the "criterion of psychological truth," and the historical contexts of Jean Genet, Eugène Ionesco, and Beckett in order to understand our encounter with their work.[8] His book is notably titled *The Theatre of the Absurd*, not *The Absurd Theatre*; indeed, Esslin's is a theater that is beholden to, and purveys, the concept of the absurd. It is hard to imagine such a tome on the shelf of a prison library, because it does not address what Esslin calls the "immediate grasp" of the criminal. He justifies his approach by observing that the theater of the absurd (and here he speaks of both the dramas and the critical text he is writing) "allows the audience to take home an intellectually formulated philosophical lesson."[9] Yet the question begged by his own introduction persists: *what do we take from Beckett if we have no home to take it home to?* People who have the ability to return home can convert their encounter with Beckett into a kind of philosophical souvenir. But what lesson is imparted by Beckett's play if this lesson cannot be consumed, like a novel or a philosophical treatise, in private?

Esslin remains spellbound by the immediacy of the convict's grasp and circles back to this audience to explain the goal of his study. "It is the purpose of this book," he writes, "to provide a framework of reference that will show the works of the Theatre of the Absurd within their own convention so that their relevance and force can emerge as clearly to the reader as *Waiting for Godot* did to the convicts of San Quentin."[10] According to Esslin, Beckett requires us, in one form or another, to do time. We must either break the law or read Esslin's book. But do these two paths get us to the same place? In aiming to reunite the audience of scholars with the audience of thugs and thieves, Esslin neglects to observe what the prisoners actually do when faced with Beckett. Where Esslin wants us to go through a framework of reference in order to see the relevance of the theater, the convicts do not distinguish reference from relevance at all. Instead, as I will show, they appear to respond to what speaks to their condition as prisoners. In collapsing reference and relevance, the prisoners create the address and elicit the force of the work. The pimp in jail is so intuitively familiar with Beckett's world that he is already the so-called voice of that work. What kind of encounter does his predicament, rather than his knowledge of philosophy, sustain with Beckett's work?

Mink Coats and Striped Suits

Beckett's play has been performed in numerous prison settings. These include performances done by and for prisoners (in Lüttringhausen, Germany, in 1953, which Beckett called "the true *Godot*"), by groups that brought the play to prison (San Quentin in 1957 and the Florida State Penitentiary system in 1974), and by outsiders who came to direct and train the convicts in the play (Jan Jönson in Kumla, Sweden, in 1985).[11] The prison is a strikingly unexpected place for theater not only to appear but also to thrive, much like Sarajevo and New Orleans were, as I discuss in chapter 2. The prison context offers a third kind of devastation area, one at only the slightest angle to both Sarajevo and New Orleans, as a ready-made backdrop for Beckett's play. The no-man's-land of prison is, ironically, inhabited only by men.[12] Yet as is suggested by its performance history, the appearance of Beckett's play is a recurring rather than a unique event. Sontag's and Chan's productions appear next to catastrophes that, according to the directors, have gone unaddressed. By contrast, performances of *Godot* in prison are almost as old as the play itself: opening night in Lüttringhausen Prison followed the premiere of *Godot* at the Babylon Theater by only eight months. The ongoing appeal of *Waiting for Godot* to prisoners is another indication that the institution of prison is an ongoing crisis. The performances I discuss call attention to how the play resonates with experience as it is structured by carceral institutions.

The failure of Beckett's play at its American premiere at the Coconut Grove Playhouse in Miami is well known. The headline of the June 4, 1954, edition of the *Miami Herald* announced the unintended alienation effect of the play: "Mink Clad Audience Disappointed in 'Waiting for Godot.'" What catches the eye is the way the distinctive evening wear of the spectators enters into the announcement of the play's failure, as if the critic were looking more closely at the audience than at the stage. It raises the question, does it matter what one wears to a Beckett performance? What is the correlation between one's place in the fashion system (here: the vacationing tourists in Miami) and the connection one might conjure with the shabby vagabonds on Beckett's stage? A comparable title for this chapter might be "Striped Audience with Numbers on Backs Wildly Fond of 'Godot.'" For one of the peculiar dimensions of Beckett's play is its continuing resonance with an audience forcibly deprived of all fashion statements, who are allotted a very standardized wardrobe, who are neither on vacation nor at work, and who dwell, as former inmate Rick Cluchey says, "in limbo, trapped in the greyness of your own uniform of flesh."[13]

The prison performances provide a substantial structure to the play. Unlike the Chan and Sontag productions, in which Godot is replaced by an expressly negligent public figure or agency (Clinton, FEMA), prison performances of *Godot* transpire in a sequestered and nonpublic space, without headlines and without clever proposals about who might terminate the waiting process. Staged in the recesses of the institution, the carceral *Godot*s exist in a kind of infamy, befitting the contraband status of a play that slips behind the walls. He who never appears (Godot) nevertheless keeps bringing his promise to arrive to Lüttringhausen, San Quentin, Kumla, and Raiford prisons. A population under siege or the survivors of a flood may seem to suffer differently than a prisoner suffers: what can the experience of war and evacuation, of historical time breaking open under the force of traumatic events, have in common with the experience of the meticulously measured time of the institutional setting? Yet Beckett's play links these dissimilar but equally exposed communities: Sarajevo, New Orleans, and the prison form a constellation around the uncanny solace they find in *Waiting for Godot*.

Exposure, Routine, Closed Space, Movement

When it is performed in jail, *Waiting for Godot* invites prisoners to relocate the performers and performance within their predicament, as the audiences in Sarajevo and New Orleans do. Four aspects of Beckett's play welcome this process: exposure, routine, closed space, and the movement on Beckett's stage. Vladimir and Estragon's unsheltered condition resonates unexpectedly with the inmate. Prisoners are exposed to a sea of forces, the cruelty of guards and inmates, in a manner similar to the vagabond's forced exposure to the elements. They are an exemplary instance of what Giorgio Agamben calls "bare life," *la nuda vita*, life in a permanent state of exception, shorn of qualities and traditional attributes.[14] The nakedness of Beckett's characters is not the one that they had at birth but one they acquired, what remains after an endless process of stripping down and exfoliation: "Under this coat I am naked. Far more than when I was born."[15] A mere residue to the implacable and barren stage, the characters display a placelessness that resonates with men shuffled around by an indifferent institution. The itinerant, like the prisoner, lives without assurance.

Waiting for Godot reduces drama to a set of routines. Critics have compared these routines to that of circus performers and clowns: "A music hall sketch of Pascal's *Pensées* as played by Fratellini's clowns," observes playwright Jean Anouilh in his review of *Godot*'s premiere.[16] These routines have also been compared to the movements of a prisoner. Underscoring first the weariness of these repetitions and then their futility, Adorno speaks of the "battered repetitions that Beckett's whole oeuvre irresistibly drags in. . . . The repetition compulsion is learned by watching the regressive behavior of the prisoner, who tries again and again."[17] Where Anouilh suggests that Beckett gives us philosophy (Pascal) articulated through the highly animated and effect-oriented pratfalls of circus performers, Adorno, by contrast, insists that the play gives us a lesson in regressive behavior, repetition, and ineffectuality. Adorno even proposes that Beckett's situation of impasse, in which every action hits against a wall, was *learned* from the prisoner.

Provisionality appears in the way Vladimir and Estragon kill time on stage. The tension here is between the improvisational quality that Anouilh and other critics attribute to Beckett's "clowns" and the provisional quality of actions performed against the backdrop of despair. *Provisional* is a key term in the Beckett lexicon and describes that which is temporary yet urgent, ephemeral yet necessary. Beckett applies the term in describing the provisional hospital of the Irish Red Cross, observing, "'Provisional' is not the term it was, in this universe become provisional."[18] Yet it accurately describes the way Beckett's hobo figures occupy the stage and the measures (i.e., the habits and routines) they take in order to cope there. If Beckett's figures evoke a music-hall sketch, as Anouilh claims, then they do so only through the most damaged kind of improvisation, one drained of the spontaneity and surprise usually associated with the term. Beckett's stage inverts Heidegger: rather than being "in time," Vladimir and Estragon live, eat, and speak "for the time being."

The aimless and habit-structured interaction on Beckett's stage speaks to prisoners who have every hour of their day organized from above. They grasp how habit, as Vladimir puts it, is the "great deadener."[19] In his essay on Proust, Beckett writes that "habit is the ballast that chains the dog to his vomit."[20] By showing only habit on stage, Beckett thereby implies the prisoner's chain. Even the sun seems to be going through the motions, as familiar and recycled as a summer-stock theater: "The day," says Vladimir, "is very near to the end of its repertory."

Martin Puchner notes the discrepancy that exists between the irrationality of Beckett's characters and the rationality, the methodical precision, of their movements. This rupture, Puchner observes, "must be seen as one of the strategies with which Beckett attacks the integrity of the actor. The association of verbal and corporeal expression and the expectation that they together represent a character are challenged by this dissociation of dialogue from gestural expressivity."[21] Vladimir's thorough investigation of the emptiness of his hat and Vladimir and Estragon's movements toward each other, one step at a time and only in between their moments of spoken dialogue, are actions that indicate a paradoxical deliberation apart from conscious awareness. The stage directions tell Vladimir and Estragon to step toward each other only when they do not speak. Implicitly, a different agency articulates their bodies. The directives come (literally) below the level of the script. These are the movements that the actor knows but which his body reads aloud.

Beckett's stage directions, more than those of any other dramatist, are rules for actors. Not coincidentally, he also does a great deal to confine his actors: in large urns (*Play*), mounds of dirt (*Happy Days*), and trash cans (*Endgame*).[22] Beckett's stage directions seep into the proceedings, under the principle that the less things happen, the more Beckett needs to keep watch over the things that do. The directions include complex readings of the tone and even motivation of dialogue: for example, when Pozzo tells Estragon, "Wait a little longer, you'll never regret it," Estragon's response, "We're in no hurry," is preceded by the stage direction "(*scenting charity*)." The actor is to deliver the line as if Estragon's nostrils could detect the prospect of a handout, and this hypothetical whiff of charity underlies his insistence that they will stay where they are. Beckett's objection to JoAnne Akalaitis's production of *Endgame,* printed on a program insert, shows how gravely Beckett regarded the breach of these parenthetical imperatives: "Any production of *Endgame* which ignores my stage directions is completely unacceptable to me."[23] From this we can see how much more invested Beckett was in the procedure of the play than in its vision or concept. What Beckett writes within parentheses—never heard by the audience but enacted by the performers—is the repository for his authority. Stage directions to Beckett are not mere suggestions for how actors might move or deliver their lines; they are directives to the stage itself, to the entirety of the dramatic space, which is crisscrossed by Beckett's invisible regulations.

Stage directions simulate a penal institution in their distribution of movement and stasis across the space of the stage. Beckett's directives include the arrest of the characters. The first and second acts conclude with Estragon declaring, "Well, shall we go?" to which Vladimir replies, "Yes, let's go." Only each time this resolution is followed with the parenthetical command *"They do not move."* The desire to leave, the proclamation to go, collides with the stagecraft of the play and provides this vow with a coda of futility. In that sense, the play might aptly be retitled *No Exit.* The characters in Sartre's play of that name cannot leave because they are beholden both to the judgments of others and to their own inauthenticity. But in Beckett's version, *No Exit* (or, more accurately, *Non Exeunt*) would receive its title from the play's stage directions, a force not encountered directly on the stage but rather one unconscious to the stage. A moment that Camus ("the divorce between the actor and his setting") and Esslin might term *absurdist* becomes jarringly real when performed in the context of prison.

Beckett's direction of *Waiting for Godot* in 1975 at the Schiller-Theater in Berlin suggests that he conceptualizes the rhythm of the play according to incarceration. In the theater notebooks, Beckett writes, "Thus establish at outset 2 caged dynamics, E[stragon] sluggish, V[ladimir] restless + perpetual separation and reunion of V[ladimir]/E[stragon]."[24] Beckett stages the simultaneous complementarity and opposition between the always restless and standing Vladmir and the sedentary and sluggish Estragon. Beckett reduces the four humors of medieval personality (melancholic, sanguine, choleric, phlegmatic) to the last two that are apparent in the bodies of the actors. During Lucky's monologue they leave and run back as if they were being driven mad or as if the cage of the stage could not accommodate their mutual separation. Stefan Wigger, who played Vladimir in Beckett's production, observes that Vladimir and Estragon come together time after time "like a rubber band." The elasticity of the collision suggests that something (like a wall) bounces them back together following their sudden departures and conflicts. This is the dynamic, and even the moral, noted by inmate C. Bandman in his review of *Godot* for the *San Quentin News:* "We continue to wait. When the scenery gets too drab and the action too slow, we'll call each other names and swear to part forever—but then, there's no place to go!"[25] The prisoner suggests that the rubber band described by Wigger is in fact closer to a chain. Bandman picks up on the caged dynamic between Beckett's characters, an involuntary rapport between opposites who can neither stand nor leave one another.

Beckett conceives of the stage space for *Godot* as hermetic. The closed space of the stage amplifies the feeling of imprisonment as well as the spectator's frustration. When director Alan Schneider proposed to do the play in the round, Beckett objected, saying, "I don't in my ignorance agree with the round and feel *Godot* needs a very closed box." He elaborated that the proscenium sustains a formal confrontation with the audience and heightens "the sense that the characters are 'all trapped.'"[26] Beckett desires the squareness of a cell over the circular stage that would allow the audience to saturate the stage with their stares. Instead of tiers of spectators behind the actors from every angle, Beckett prefers the retaining wall of the proscenium that emphatically separates the stage and guarantees the emptiness of the space around the actors. As discussed in the introduction, Beckett pushes this wish to the point of desiring an empty theater for his performances, that is, the ultimately closed box of an auditorium whose doors never allow an audience to enter. Erin Koshal explains Beckett's stipulation in this way: "In *Waiting for Godot* . . . solitude is never taken for granted. Didi and Gogo do not know what lies beyond the stage, but they continually wonder, listening for noises or making out forms in the darkness."[27]

Beckett's play stages the precarious and threatened solitude of the inmate. In prison, one is always next to others but never with others. The only real solitude in prison, solitary confinement, is involuntary. Beckett's Berlin production underscores the rapport between the characters and the empty space that surrounds them. He inserts four "inspection places" in which Vladimir and Estragon walk the perimeter of the stage and explore the three empty spaces confronting them, including the inaccessible "void" in the auditorium.[28] How are we to describe this walk in which Beckett's figures physically mark the periphery of the stage and take in the vast spaces that hem them in? Though they are "trapped," Beckett's characters move like guards on a night watch during an evening in which nothing's happening yet all is not well.

Limitation of movement is a condition with which the prisoner is intimately familiar. Two weeks before the arrival of *Godot,* adjacent to articles announcing the production, a column in the *San Quentin News* coincidentally makes note of how prison inmates ambulate within the yard. A prisoner by the name of "Etaoin Shrdlu" writes a weekly column titled "Bastille by the Bay." A week before the *Godot* performance he begins with this note: "THOUGHTS WHILE MILLING (Here one mills, doesn't stroll, wander, or pace.)" These "thoughts while milling" are the prisoner's retort to Schiller's *Spaziergang,* Wordsworth's strolls, and Nietzsche's climbs. The prisoner is peripatetic, but with deep restrictions; consequently, his philosophy—the thoughts generated by his movement in the yard—is different. The thinking generated by milling begins by finding a vocabulary for this movement, differentiating it, for example, from both leisurely *strolling* and professorial *pacing*. Over these Shrdlu chooses *milling,* a grinding in place, modeled on the repetitive movements of machines. Milling goes on in an enclosure: one mills *about* but never beyond. Two weeks later, Shrdlu will write one of the three reviews of the *Godot* performance. Perhaps without knowing it, Shrdlu was preparing himself to describe the movement of the actors he would see in Beckett's play. On the stage one doesn't stroll, wander, or pace. One mills. His choice pseudonym indicates how Shrdlu aligns even his writing process within a graphically confined space, something deader than a column. He takes his name from the lingo of newspaper typesetting. Linotype machine operators were unable to delete typing errors. When an error was made, the line could not be reused. The quickest way to get to the end of the line was for the operator to run his finger down the closest row of keys. The sequence of letters flagged the error for the newspaper compositor who would throw out the line. *Etaoinshrdlu* is therefore a nonsense phrase filling the dead space between the typing error and the end of the page, a codeword for *erase me.*

The characters in *Godot* encounter a stricture on their freedom through the expansiveness, rather than the limitation, of space. For Beckett, incarceration is not conveyed through a psychological condition such as claustrophobia. *Waiting for Godot* emphasizes both the formal limit of the stage and the vast emptiness beyond it. The fear he seems to cultivate in his characters is Pascalian: a fear of infinite spaces. This is apparent in Beckett's response to a 1961 television production of *Waiting for Godot:* "When the production was over, [Beckett] sat for awhile with his head in his hands. 'My play,' Beckett said, 'wasn't written for this box. My play was written for small men locked in a big space. Here you're all too big for the place.' And he went on, 'You see, you could write a very good play for television about a woman knitting. You'd go from the face to the knitting, from the knitting to the face.'"[29] It is the vast space of the theater auditorium, its atmospheric pressure, that encloses the vagabonds on his stage. The apparatus of television (its seeing and enlarging across great distances) reduces the incarcerating quality of empty space in the theater. Light operates in the theater to isolate the characters on stage and separate them from the darkened audience. Where the illumination of the stage emphasizes the recession of the vagabonds, the television projects their image toward the spectator and brightens the living room with them.

Beckett contrasts the locked space of the stage not only with the proportions of the television box but also with the type of labor dramatized on television. His example, not accidentally, is a drama of constructive labor: television could enlarge the slight and understated gestures of knitting, focusing first on the face of the knitter, then the craft, then back to the face of the knitter. *Waiting for Godot*, by contrast, is a labor of undoing, as there is "nothing to be done." In his "Notes Diverse Holo," Beckett calls this work of undoing "Penelopizing," after Penelope, wife of Odysseus, who took her knitting apart every night in order to postpone her promise to marry.[30] Television is the proper medium for Penelope by day. Penelope by night, however, is the province of theater. In *Godot*, as in the *Odyssey*, the unraveling of work, or Penelopizing, is tied to the activity of waiting.

Theme Not New to Cons

Waiting is the aspect of the play that resonates most emphatically with the prisoner's condition. Institutionalized time is empty time and *Godot*'s time. An adult education teacher at the performance in San Quentin states, "They know what is meant by waiting. And they know that if Godot finally came he would only be a disappointment."[31] This knowledge of waiting, and the implicit knowledge of its emptiness (for what is disappointment but yet another missed appointment), is consistently attributed to the prisoners by writers grappling with the success of *Godot* behind bars. The homology established between the play and prison life is not very different in an article about the return of *Waiting for Godot* to San Quentin in 1988: "There is a lot of waiting in San Quentin. Some 3028 inmates wait for meals; 777 guards wait for their shift to end; 225 inmates on death row wait for the gas chamber; and, on this sunny Thursday, seven men wait around a table in a cramped room. They are waiting for 'Waiting for Godot' rehearsals to begin."[32] The journalist lulls us with an enumeration of the instances of waiting in a prisoner's day, thereby implying the almost natural emergence of *Godot* within its walls. He claims, with a wink, that they are even waiting for the waiting in the play to begin.

The subheadline of the *San Francisco Chronicle* review of the 1957 San Quentin performance, "Theme Not New to Cons,"[33] throws light on one of the unique historical trajectories of high modernism. This is a moment in the early 1950s when *Waiting for Godot*, rejected by civilian audiences, required the audience of pimps, thieves, and murderers to keep its viability. The reviewer welds the event of the play, the nonarrival that constitutes its curious (in)action, to the life of the prisoner. The subheadline is testament to the way that performances before an audience of criminals transform *Waiting for Godot* from a perplexing novelty to something *not new*, from something challenging (to sophisticated theatergoers) to something popular (with inmates).

Yet these early reviews of *Godot* at San Quentin are the first instance of one of the myths of performing *Godot*, namely, that a rock-bottom community is forged between audience and actors in their wait. As Sidney Homan phrases it, "In the presence of such challenges to the meaning of our existence, we can only say—and say only—that on any given night of a performance of *Godot* we acted not alone but in concert. . . . Together, actors and audience, we waited for Godot."[34] Homan wants waiting to be beyond interrogation, sealing what we can say (and can only say) about it. Yet we lose our link to the play once we limit the ways we express waiting. The *Chronicle* author establishes waiting as something *known* to the prisoner (as if it were a skill) or, even more drably, as a *theme* (as if the inmates were watching an undergraduate essay on the play rather than the play itself). The journalists use the prisoner to block further inquiry into the temporal predicament both on stage and off. Can one know waiting? What does *Waiting for Godot* tell us about this experience of time, for example, that differentiates it from the suspense one would feel watching any other play? How does the theatrical waiting during Beckett's play address the institutional waiting of the prisoner?

The frequently proposed connection between the prisoner and the play resonates with the means that our culture employs to ingest Beckett. Prisoners initiate a way for audiences to access *Godot*; they provide a door into the very locked box of Beckett's stage. The wider public thoroughly domesticates (or thematizes) waiting because they have experienced waiting: for a taxi, unemployment benefits, a call, a spot, tomorrow, or opening night of *Waiting for Godot*. The last scenario, waiting for Beckett, is practically scripted by the frequent abbreviation of *Waiting for Godot* to simply *Godot*, so that *Waiting for Godot* seems already to designate what we are doing before the curtain rises.[35] André Gregory's production of *Endgame* in 1973 both evokes and implodes these idioms of waiting for a Beckett play to begin when, on the opening night of his production of *Endgame*, the audience was greeted with only locked doors and an empty theater.[36]

Before even seeing Beckett's play, audiences are formed, and formulate their response to the play, by taking up the implicit invitation to rewrite its title. *Waiting for Godot* has entered our culture primarily through this reinscription process (and secondarily through the syllabus). These endless reassignments of Godot's name extend utilitarian waiting (as for a bus or cab) to the central dimension of the play. Utilitarian waiting underscores the *for* in *waiting for*; it assigns a clear endpoint to the waiting process. Implicitly, the cause for waiting is also the terminal point of waiting. In the next chapter I discuss how Sontag and Chan repeatedly, and serially, inscribe various objects, authorities, and institutions in the blank space of "Godot," thus inscribing the play's waiting with an object and a terminus. These productions underscore the absence of the figure awaited by Beckett's vagabonds and rename that figure (as Clinton or as FEMA). They thereby highlight the absence of intervention, the undue negligence displayed by authorities toward the crises of Sarajevo and New Orleans. In sum, Sontag and Chan employ the most famous no-show in theater history to dramatize the need for intervention.

Prisoners also play this game of alternative baptisms, yet in a crucially different way. In the *San Quentin News,* Shrdlu's weekly column titled "Bastille by the Bay" serves as a kind of *New Yorker*–style "Talk of the Town" for convicts. The day after the *Godot* performance, we read the following comment: "WITS ABOUT THE YARD are belaboring the obvious as the result of the recent stage play and the recentest flick. Seems the picture was 'Doctor at Sea' with Dick [sic] Bogarde and Brigitte you-know-who. Which leaves the quipsters enough ammunition to chortle: 'You live your life and I'll live mine, I'm waiting for BARDOT!!!'"[37] To the prisoner, Godot's arrival seems as unlikely and as impossible as the arrival of a celebrity or the incarnation of Bardot out of her projected image. Bardot is at no less a remove from the prison yard than Godot, yet she enlists the prisoner in a different sort of waiting. Bardot gives the prisoner an image, whereas Godot gives merely the promise (through an intermediary, no less) to arrive. The image of Bardot is already in the prison, and its projection into the prison space allows the filmgoer to contour his desire to the screen. The theater, by contrast, gives something closer to a rumor, the rumor that someone cares, and hence is closer to the endless waiting that goes on in the carceral setting.

Strategies of renaming Godot gibe with the fact that people remember Godot's absence more than they remember the vagabonds' waiting. Yet it is this arduous process, rather than its purported and vaguely apprehended goal, that we see on stage. The headline of the *San Quentin News*, written by prisoners, provides useful contrast to the one already cited from the *Chronicle*: "Workshop Players Score Hit Here: San Francisco Group Leaves S. Q. Audience Waiting for Godot." The transaction that takes place in this headline leaves a bitter flavor in the mouth. *Godot* is not just a hit but, as a "hit scored," a robbery. The gang (the actors) got in and got out (they retained their freedom). In the process they leave an ambiguous gift at the crime scene. The gift of the play is not the play itself ("Waiting for Godot" is not italicized in the headline) but rather something meshing indistinguishably with the everyday condition of the prisoner. Beckett's lesson is neither moral nor conveyed by Brechtian slogans. The prisoners were aware of this. In his review titled "The Play's the Thing," inmate C. Bandman observes, "It asked nothing in point, it forced no dramatized moral on the viewer, it held out no specific hope."[38] While the hope the play offers may not be specific, Bandman does not say that there is no hope, much less that the play nihilistically embraces hopelessness. Kafka's observation that "there is hope, but not for us" leaves hope in the world but only as something unaddressed to us: we cannot take hope as one of our belongings. Bandman has something similar in mind here. He senses that the play offers no *specific* hope, but possibly an unspecific or generic hope. The hope that Godot offers the inmate is akin to the grasp of a new kind of drama: the absurd (and absurdly courageous) articulation of one's own powerlessness.

The lesson of the play brings to reflection what the prisoners were already doing, though perhaps without quite realizing it, and certainly without realizing it as a stageable drama.[39] This lesson includes, and even depends on, the recognition that the actors, unlike the inmate audience, are free to go home. When the actors are released, the abandoned condition of the characters on stage is transferred onto the inmate-spectators. There is no specific hope in Beckett's play, yet as the *San Quentin News* headline maintains, the visit of the actors and the nonvisit of Godot have already redefined the time spent behind bars. During the performance and in its aftermath, the prisoners formulate their relation to the empty time of the prison.

The prison does not trust the prisoner to wait. Waiting in prison, though a requirement for parole (at least among the nonlifers), is not a means to an end: it is not a waiting *for* something. Here, waiting is pure expenditure. It is not voluntary waiting, and it is not defined through desire or expectation for a thing or outcome. This waiting is society's punishment for the prisoner whose crime is one of emotion and control. Before serving his sentence, the prisoner effectively refuses perhaps the fundamental axiom of civilization: to defer gratification, to delay, to wait. So the institution takes waiting out of the hands of the prisoner. *Waiting for Godot* stages this conflicted relation to waiting, rather than the one that people assume in appropriating its title.

In Bandman's review of *Waiting for Godot* in the *San Quentin News*, he suggests that the vagabond's waiting on stage may be forcible detention. Bandman draws attention to the message relayed by the boy, and delivered twice in the play, that Godot will be coming—tomorrow. He calls the boy the "immemorial child-conscience which prods [Gogo and Didi] into waiting for something more, tomorrow night. Keep them waiting. Even though they cannot help it."[40] *Keep them waiting. Even though they cannot help it.* That they cannot help waiting implies that they do not choose to wait. The process cannot be begun, interrupted, or stopped. Waiting is not subject, claims Bandman, to deliverance or the idea of deliverance. The boy who delivers the promise of Godot's coming, standing in for Godot himself, provokes the painful illusion in the hobos that there will be an outcome, "something more" to the waiting than just waiting itself.

In the same edition of the prison newspaper, another reviewer writes that the boy "holds the slender thread of realism" of the play.[41] The boy holds a thread in the manner of Ariadne, as a means out of the labyrinthine prison, promising a possible end to waiting. The instigation to wait, not the illusion that one waits for, is real to the prisoners. Its realism is located in the physical quality of the promise that prods Vladimir and Estragon into imaging a purpose for their being on stage. In this moment they lose the chance to realize that they are just waiting, apart from any object, any outcome, or any Godot. The realization that the prisoner's life is consumed by a waiting done, somehow, by someone other than himself, by an agent other than the "I," comes across in an exchange in *Endgame* in a similar way. "Do you believe in the life to come?" Hamm asks Clov. Clov replies, "Mine was always that." In this format life is a living for a future that will not be part of life. Equated with life, waiting promises not more life but only more waiting.

Waiting versus Expectation

> I suppose he is Lucky to have no more expectations.
> —Samuel Beckett[42]

The successful reception of *Godot* in prison has much to do with this waiting beyond expectation. In *The Theatre of the Absurd*, Esslin claims that *Waiting for Godot* succeeded with the prisoners "not because it confronted them with a situation in some ways analogous to their own" but rather because "they were unsophisticated enough to come to the theatre without any preconceived notions and ready-made expectations, so that they avoided the mistake that trapped so many established critics who condemned the play for its lack of plot, development, characterization, suspense, or plain common sense."[43] The prisoner's wait is different from the critic's. Whereas the critic approaches the play knowingly and employs his familiarity with theater to process his encounter with the performance, the inmates are waiting but without anticipation: they are used to waiting for nothing. The critic employs his expectation to pass judgment and condemns the play. The prisoner, ironically, avoids the "mistake that trapped so many established critics." Esslin's observation testifies to the need to stage *Godot* not only in *unexpected* settings (in the prison, after the flood, during the siege) but in *unexpecting* ones. Jonathan Kalb notes that one of Beckett's legacies is the way "he actually changed many people's expectations of what can happen, what is supposed to happen, when they enter the theatre."[44]

Godot forces us to realign the relationship between our expecting and our waiting. Vladimir's question "Will night never come?" seems to counterbalance his refrain that they are waiting for the title character to come. There is no inevitability to the night sky of the stage. Vladimir's beseeching question about the arrival of night strikes the audience, particularly those seated in the prison cafeteria, as a fruitless expectation. Expecting Godot to arrive is no less uncertain. Pozzo links the two events: "If I had an appointment with a Godin . . . Godet . . . Godot . . . anyhow you see who I mean, I'd wait till it was black night before I gave up."[45] Esslin suggests that prison prepares inmates for this type of waiting within the play.

Why is expectation destructive of our experience of the play? No doubt because it seduces us into thinking we can envision the end of waiting and that we can see through to its other side. Where the performance of *Godot* begins unexpectedly—in Sarajevo, New Orleans, and prison—the waiting on stage continues the waiting inherent in the setting but, by staging the latter, transforms it. In other words, by showing that this waiting is stageable and dramatic, Beckett makes that real-world waiting (in the rubble of a besieged city, on the bayou, and in prison) worthy of fiction—and therefore life. In these settings Beckett's intention that the theater is to be re-expected becomes transparent.

Waiting on Beckett's stage and waiting in prison merge with one another. A letter to the editor of the *San Quentin News* gives us an opportunity to look at the dynamic of expectation and waiting in a particular convict by the name (or pseudonym) of "Ed Realart":

THE EDITOR—
I had to go to work before the play was over. Right between the first and second act. Will you please publish how it came out?
—Ed Realart

The editor responds: "It came out fine."[46] The inmate is forcibly removed from the audience because of work detail, and he is transferred from the cafeteria where the play is staged to another sector of the prison. Yet the interruption of his *Godot* experience does not make him stop waiting. Crucially, he does not employ his expectations at this instance ("it wasn't what I expected") to block further thinking about the play. He implicitly wants to submit to a further undoing of his expectations. He can neither guess "how things came out" nor believe the synopses volunteered by his fellow inmates (that the play really loops back on itself, the second act concluding in a fashion identical to the first). He thus becomes an author and writes a petition in order to become a reader of the play. He would like the newspaper to print the part of the play that he was not permitted to see. The editor replies laconically, Beckettianly: *it came out fine*. To one who has seen the play, his answer is simultaneously extreme understatement and hyperbole. Instead of delivering the kind of useful wisdom or opinion that one expects from such a column, the editor offers only a vague euphemism, but one that does justice to the difficulty of saying precisely how it comes out. His answer offers no satisfaction, no illusory wrap-up.[47]

Godot and Bariona

Waiting for Godot offers few concessions to prisoners, the audience that would presumably desire these most. It is illuminating in this regard to compare *Waiting for Godot* not to Sartre's *No Exit* but his first play, *Bariona, or the Son of Thunder*.[48] Sartre wrote *Bariona* while a prisoner of war in Stalag XII, and, on Christmas day in 1940, he performed it with and for his fellow prisoners. The play is set in Judea during the Roman occupation. Bariona, head of a small village, receives news that imperial Rome wishes to astronomically increase taxes. Bariona declares that his town will not pay the tax. After threats from the Roman army, he states that his town will pay the tax but "after us nobody will ever pay taxes again."[49] He proposes that the town no longer reproduce: he wants everyone's family tree to slowly resemble the one onstage in *Godot*. Sartre fabricates a landscape of growing destitution as the conditions for his carceral theater. Bariona adopts Beckett's asymptotic approach to poverty but in the form of his public policy, as an official order on resignation and dwindling. Beckett's work similarly dabbles in eugenics as a means of unreproducing the world, a critique of mimesis expressed by a draining of the gene pool. In Beckett's first play, *Eleuthéria*, Dr. Piouk articulates a sterility project a bit less sanctimoniously than Bariona.[50] Indeed, the nonreproductive policy of *Eleuthéria* may shed light on some features of *Waiting for Godot*, its all-male cast, and its literal superimposition of birth over the grave.

Yet Sartre, unlike Beckett, relinquishes what his title character calls the "religion of nothing."[51] Halfway through *Bariona*, there is a sudden dramatic turn. What arrives in Sartre's play is closer to God than even Godot: Bariona witnesses the birth of Christ. Birth is suddenly hailed as the hope for prisoners. Bariona proceeds into the street with his armed townsmen to fight the Romans. Sartre's play stages an allegory for the transformation of autonomous literature (one that, like Beckett's, withdraws from our grasp) into a literature of commitment. But this commitment is underpinned by the holiday of Christ's birth. The play concludes not with an aside from Bariona but with his direct address to the audience at Treves:

> BARIONA. *to the prisoners:* And you prisoners, this is the end of the Christmas play which was written for you. You are not happy, and maybe there is more than one of you who has tasted that taste of gall in his mouth, that bitter salty taste I'm talking about. But I think that for you, too, on this Christmas day—and every other day—there will be joy![52]

Beckett's *Waiting for Godot* is dedicated to that taste of gall in the mouth, the taste we cannot quite define. Just as Beckett avoids the dramatic downward turn, the *catastrophe,* his characters never turn directly to address the condition of the audience. That condition becomes apparent through the context of its performance. Sartre provides a play for prisoners, not a play about prison. Beckett generates a hermetic and microcosmal play that allows an alienated spectator to connect with it. Sartre's play, by contrast, uses the holiday on which the play is performed, the celebration of the birth of Christ, to bring its poverty to an end. Bariona seemed to be undertaking the long wait, a wait to which he would give his existence. What interrupts his wait is the very day of its performance, the sanctioned and measured time of the calendar.

A Prison Faces the Study

Waiting for Godot nowhere names the prison. Unlike Genet's *Haute Surveillance,* it does not take prison as its explicit setting. This quality is consistent with Adorno's observation about *Endgame* that "the name of the catastrophe is to be spoken only in silence."[53] Beckett described this quality as wariness toward "explicitation," that is, not only explanation but also anything that would upset the implicit and discreet quality of his work.[54] Beckett keeps mum about the motivating crisis, maintaining an anonymous core to his play. This sustains the challenge of Beckett's work: it is without ambiguity, at all moments as precise as an eye chart whose coherence at a formal level does not somehow add up at an abstract level, commit itself to our understanding, or reward us with digestible themes. Diverse strands of Beckett criticism unite around the effort to supply a name to these articulating silences. Joseph Roach reads the poverty of Beckett's work in connection to the Irish famine. Writing about the dead voices heard by Vladimir and Estragon but unheard by the audience, Roach observes, "To anyone who is prepared to listen, they speak of the consequences of the potato famine, or the Great Hunger, the effects which endured long after its deadliest years, 1845–51."[55] Noting that Lucky's dance is called "the net," James Knowlson deduces that "for Beckett man is, as Lucky's dance suggests, imprisoned in a net" and that we can see this dance "as expressing in a dramatically arresting way a much wider view of man as what might be termed a 'prisoner of life.'"[56]

What Esslin calls the "immediate grasp" of the play by the criminals suggests that the play does not necessitate the mediated grasp of the theorist. Though Roach claims we need to be "prepared" to listen and have our ears "sensitized" to the values he finds in Beckett, the desensitized prisoners with little interpretive training successfully connect with the play.[57] What theorists most urgently want to mediate about *Godot* are its breaks and silences, the qualities that make the play uniquely available to prisoners. *Godot* is "about" prison, but not because the institution is its content. The dimensions of the play I have highlighted—the exposure of the vagabonds, the routines of the actor, their management by an authority external to the actor, the closed space of the stage, and the separation of waiting from expectation—give only a *latent image* of the prison. These dimensions are "about" prison in the sense that they stake themselves near or around the institution, but without mirroring it. The danger of handling the silences of Beckett's work comes from confusing the activity of speaking about the play with speaking for it. It is tempting to ascribe a content to Beckett's silences and to move too quickly to metaphorize it. It seems unlikely that a prisoner serving a life sentence would speak of man as "prisoner of life"—or, for that matter, speak of prison at all within quotation marks.

The performance of *Waiting for Godot* before an audience of criminals helps us rethink the silences of Beckett's work. The prisoners' immediacy of reaction suggests that the latent image fulfills itself through their recognition. The imprisoned audience works to familiarize the play to themselves rather than trying to access the play through concepts that may help them interpret its meaning. The prisoners do not try to make sense of the nonsense of the play; instead, they recognize the nonsense as familiar.

Beckett's characters speak frequently of reasoning ("Stoutly reasoned!" shouts Pozzo) but almost never of reason per se. In like fashion, the prisoners adjust themselves to the reasoning of the play (which may resemble the reasoning of a joke, a bureaucracy, or a set of prison rules), but they make no amends for the absence of reason.[58] The fact that Beckett does not burden his characters and dialogue with context or explicit history makes these characters accessible to the audience at San Quentin. The director of the performance, Herbert Blau, writes that the play "had such an impact on the prison that the language of the play, the names of the characters—a Gogo, a Didi, a Pozzo—became part of the therapeutic vocabulary at San Quentin. It may be so to this day."[59] A "Lucky" becomes a man on death row, "Pozzo" a bull (a guard).[60] In the next chapter I discuss how Chan and Sontag took the name "Godot," already pointing toward the wings of the stage and toward an imminent arrival, and redirected it beyond the stage entirely, at authorities noticeably absent from the crisis at hand. Significantly, the prisoners show no interest in bestowing the title of Godot on anyone. Absorbed in the negative labor of waiting, they appropriate only the names of figures waiting on stage, relocating the names of Beckett's trapped characters into the prison hierarchy. In addition, they also transfer the gestures of power from the stage to their world. In Etaoin Shrdlu's column "Bastille by the Bay," we find not a review of *Godot* but evidence for the way it cut into the prison environment: "One clown dropping his headgear from the fifth tier caught a ground-floor eye. Eschewing the polite request, this one pointed the fateful finger: 'Haaat!!'"[61] The one who loses his hat from the fifth tier does not ask politely for it; instead, he becomes Pozzo, the character with the whip who condenses his orders to Lucky into single words: "Baassket," "Stool," "Think." The prisoner who dropped his hat reenacts Pozzo's shorthand, in which no elaboration, no address to the subject, is needed to get him to come running.

A biographical anecdote may help us specify how Beckett situates the theatrical institution in relation to the carceral institution. Beckett's apartment on the seventh floor at 38 Boulevard Saint Jacques has a view of three landmarks: Notre-Dame, the Panthéon, and the barred cell windows of the gray Santé Prison. In his biography of Beckett, James Knowlson notes that the prison faces Beckett's study.[62] In a direct sense, then, Beckett lives about the prison. He cannot help but note its proximity, for whereas the Panthéon never made a sound, he hears cries from the prison even at odd hours of the night. Beckett replies to the prison, using a mirror to communicate messages in Morse code to an inmate "housed in a cell clearly visible from Beckett's study window."[63] Beckett's German translator, Elmar Tophoven, reports that he came by the apartment to find "Beckett standing at the open window, clearly signaling to someone. Beckett promptly raised and lowered his arms to indicate to the prisoner across the way that the exchange would have to be interrupted because someone had just called to see him. He explained to Tophoven: 'They have so little to entertain them, you know.'"[64]

This anecdote offers a sense of the way that *Waiting for Godot*, which describes life as light that "gleams an instant" as off a mirror, speaks to prisoners. The method of communication that Beckett takes up is not very different from what prisoners use to communicate among themselves (e.g., tapping on a pipe). Without leaving his study, Beckett slips into the prison, communicating with the prisoner through unofficial channels. He foregoes the bureaucracy of visiting hours and phone calls made to someone visible through Plexiglas. This is not a choice, however, since Beckett, at least prior to communication by mirror, does not know anybody in the prison other than the pimp who stabbed him years earlier: whom would he say that he wants to see? Beckett begins by communicating with no one, until a gleam of light comes back at him and initiates a different flow, a new triangle formed by the sun, Beckett's window, and the cell.

In some ways this scenario fulfills a wish that Beckett expressed at a dinner party in 1937, when he was asked, "What would you most like to create?" Beckett's answer: "Light in the monad."[65] Yet the scenario also gives us something surprising, a light that comes from the monad.

Beckett's study faces the prison: Knowlson's description of the architectural layout of the Boulevard Saint Jacques is a model for the orientation of Beckett's work toward the prison. As a study of man, a dramatic anthropology of man's essence, *Godot* fulfills the humanist protocol. Prison never makes an appearance in Beckett's study, and yet it exerts pressure on it, countenances it, even shines a beam of information into it. Beckett says he was entertaining the prisoner from his study. He means that he entertains the prisoner as part of his study—something that enters his thought and temporarily retains in his thinking, but not as the subject of direct concentration, as he can only see Santé when he looks up from his work. Entertaining the prisoner from his study, his play became entertainment for the prisoner. Beckett's work, the condition it depicts, asks to be confronted by the prison, something that in fact happens when his plays are performed there.[66]

Beckett writes *Catastrophe* for a particular prisoner, Václav Havel.[67] The dedication "For Václav Havel" stands as the address "of" the play, paradoxically both where it is and where the play is going. As in *Godot,* there are no cells, chains, guards, or uniforms. It presents a director speaking to his assistant about an immobile, exposed, "ashen" figure standing on a plinth on a stage (looking like Didi or Gogo after the second blast). The director tells his assistant to make some alterations (whiten the subject's face, remove the gown). The assistant responds to the imperatives of the director ("I can't see the toes. I'm sitting in the front row and I can't see the toes") by saying, "I make a note."

The play's absence of explicit statements about prison seems to be at odds with the fact that the play was Beckett's contribution to a festival in which dramatists, including Ionesco, submitted one-act dramas as protest to Havel's incarceration. Enoch Brater describes two possibilities for theater, one aesthetic and the other political. "The energy of *Catastrophe*," he says, "cannot be contained by anything as neat as a swift denunciation of repressive regimes, however attractive such a statement from Beckett might be."[68] Brater concludes, "*Catastrophe* is far more a discourse on method, specifically theater method, than an argument about ethical imperatives from an agent provocateur. Theater tactics, not power politics, are implicated here."[69] *Catastrophe* is a study of a study: a rehearsal of a play in which the audience is to study this figure on stage. As the stage directions indicate: "D[irector] and A[ssistant] contemplate." Beckett in fact underbids the protest gesture by incorporating the assistant, who not only takes the requests of the Director to alter how the body is exposed on stage but also writes them down. She greets each request with the line "I make a note." What is the nature of this note-taking, this note-worthiness of the director's suggestions? He puts stenography (or narrow writing) on stage since it is the most neutral shorthand for expression. Beckett does not direct the audience to think in prescribed ways about power. Rather, he induces us to similarly make note and register the study of the play. The writing of the stenographer lives up to its name by narrowing the distance separating us from the effects of power.

Author as Warden

Before *Waiting for Godot* could appeal to prisoners, it first had to appeal to the prison warden who makes decisions about what kind of performances are allowed: it had to be compatible with the culture of prison. The warden permitted the performance of *Waiting for Godot* at San Quentin because of something missing from Beckett's stage, something that it filtered out of the picture, along with laughter and comfort: women. No women were allowed in the prison, and Beckett's play does not feature one. Entering the prison to perform requires the actors to go through another filtering for the prison: "We could take in nothing metallic."[70] At entry the actors were told that the prison would not negotiate for their release were they to be taken hostage by the prisoners during an escape attempt.[71]

Literary critic Mary Bryden makes an observation about *Godot* that we might conceivably find in a memo from Warden Duffy: "On the face of it, then, women (especially the fertile ones) are potential agents for disturbance, and are best excluded or (as in many Biblical genealogies) left in the wings."[72] Beckett objected to productions that featured women in the roles of Vladimir and Estragon. Thinking perhaps about the physiological basis for the incontinence suffered by the character Vladimir, Beckett justified his rationale by observing, "Women don't have prostates." Beckett's injunction has not prevented all-female productions of the play, such as Bruno Boussagol's at the Avignon Festival in 1991. These productions offer a reply to Beckett: the prostate is something performed, not given.

By agreeing to allow the play to be performed not because of what it contains but because of what it eliminates, the warden seems to enhance the alarm system already in place.[73] Likewise, the instruments of discipline employed on Beckett's stage were managed and shown to remain in the control of the guards. The troupe was permitted to use the rope and whip only under the condition that a guard hand the props to the actor who played Pozzo as he went on stage and take them back immediately upon his exit. The prison was evidently afraid of these items becoming useful objects to the prisoners, either for threatening others or for hanging themselves. Prisoners grasp the wistfulness of Estragon's line "If we only had a little more rope." The warden surveys the stage exclusively in terms of security, with the performance itself and the handling of props remaining under the constant monitoring of the guards.[74]

The work of the author who wants to remove ego from the stage gets along remarkably well with an institution that wants to do the same. Describing the tonal consistency of Beckett's work, Adorno picks up on this aspect of monitoring and control: "There is a constant monitoring to see that things are one way and not another; an alarm system with a sensitive bell indicates what fits in with the play's topography and what does not. Beckett keeps quiet about the delicate things as well as the brutal."[75] Adorno here compares Beckett's work to a securitized space, though he says it is done out of delicacy (*Zartheit*), not control. Beckett monitors everything that enters the stage and everything that transpires on it. It is as if Beckett were working during the tradition of actors being thieves, disrespectable reprobate types, and he needed to direct accordingly. The stage is fantastically sparse: the singular tree seems as if it were pulled through a barbed wire fence just to make its appearance. This stringency of Beckett is noted by Blau, who writes that *Waiting for Godot* and *Endgame* are plays "with magnitude, achieved through the most excruciating constraint. . . . Old endgame, lost of old, every move a crisis."[76] Blau emphasizes the constraint, Beckett's exterior exertions over the stage, rather than some hypothetical self-restraint by his characters. Beckett set a trip wire around his stage in order to produce, paradoxically, a shockingly *unalarmed* theatrical space. Nothing on Beckett's stage raises the characters' eyebrows or calls undue attention to itself, and nobody reacts or commits a wrong move. The stage requires us to take our shock up on our own time.

The Closed System

A recurring motif within Beckett criticism is the comparison of his work to a "closed system." Some background to this concept and its application to Beckett's work is needed before appreciating how the term might be relevant to Beckett's theater. Beckett invited the term into critical discussion of the work. His novel *Murphy* constitutes an anthology of theorems, generated by and applied to the world of the tavern. In the novel, the character Wylie says, "The syndrome known as life is too diffuse to admit of palliation. For every symptom that is eased, another is made worse. The horseleech's daughter is a closed system. Her quantum of wantum cannot vary."[77]

Picking up Beckett's cue in this passage, Hugh Kenner divides this moment of the closed system into the first and second laws of thermodynamics: "It is a world locally freakish but totally shaped by two laws, the law of conservation of energy and the second law of thermodynamics. The former law states that nothing is added to or subtracted from the system, but simply mutated, and the latter states that the degree of organization within this closed system grows constantly less and so constantly less improbable."[78] Kenner sees abundant examples for this hypothesis in Beckett's work. Wylie demonstrates the first law. To this we could also add the opening sentence of the novel, which heralds *Godot*'s description of the sun's repertory: "The sun shone, having no alternative, on the nothing new."[79] The second law of thermodynamics, according to Kenner, is the "real theme of Lucky's headlong oration," with its unfinished labors and its dissipation into "fading, fading, fading," "wastes and pines," "the great cold the great dark."[80] Darko Suvin's analysis of Beckett is deeply indebted to Kenner's discussion. *Terra Beckettiana*—Suvin's scientific term describing Beckett's world—"is an aimless island universe, not only desolate but constantly running down."[81] Yet for Suvin, Beckett's universe is not accurately described by the first two laws alone: "There remained unnoted [in Kenner's discussion] . . . the third law of thermodynamics (Nernst's theorem: absolute zero can only be approached asymptotically, i.e., getting ever closer to it without reaching it) which is just as characteristic of Beckett's rhythm and vision, and which should be accorded as important a place in any conclusion about him."[82] Suvin's inclusion of the third law addresses how Beckett's system tends toward an ever-reduced impoverished minimum, rather than the sheer zero of nihilism.

David Houston Jones's *Samuel Beckett and Testimony* offers the most recent and suggestive reading of the closed system. Like Suvin, he recalls a scientific figure left out of the critical discussion thus far: "Maxwell's demon," a thought experiment by James Clerk Maxwell, which hypothesizes an imaginary being able to prevent the loss of heat in a closed system, keeping entropy at bay, a scenario that would invalidate the second law of thermodynamics.[83] Jones claims that Maxwell's demon (a figure that enters into some of Beckett's aesthetic essays) sheds light on how Beckett's narrators "are neither (in *The Lost Ones*) part of the population of searchers nor human beings looking into the closed space from a distance [in *Long Observation*]. The details of Maxwell's scenario corroborate the immersion of the narrator in the closed space texts . . . while signaling his existence as *hypothetical*."[84] Jones therefore utilizes Maxwell's thought experiment to entertain the idea that Beckett's "closed space texts" are simulations, themselves experimental: "Rather than indicating a fully realized fictional world, they draw attention to the limited and unstable nature of that world, problematising the reader's imaginative investment in it."[85] Pushing toward the function of testimony in Beckett's work and the interface between technology and the human, Jones observes, "The extraordinary abdication of narrative authority in the closed system works also to produce a space which . . . must be understood as archival."[86]

The fourth contribution to the closed system theory of Beckett's text is less situated in scientific law. Former inmate Cluchey, whose case study I will discuss later in this chapter, uses the term while discussing the development of a drama workshop in San Quentin a few years after Herbert Blau brought *Waiting for Godot* to the inmates there. He writes, "All of the plays were acted and directed by convicts for convict audiences. And so every weekend in our little theatre in San Quentin, it was standing room only for imprisoned Americans; and rightly so, because if as Beckett has stated, his plays are all closed systems, then so too, are prisons. I personally can say that San Quentin is a closed system, a very tightly closed system!"[87] For Cluchey, his own experience is central to his contemplation of the closed system. He emphasizes its physicality, its tightness, rather than the law behind its operations.

In his analysis of the closed space of Beckett's *Lost Ones*, Jones explores the testimonial function of the narrative and what he calls the hypothetical status of the narrator. Cluchey basically says that the prisoner does not live in the world of thermodynamics or scientific principles. Only the first term of the phrase "closed system" catches the prisoner's attention, since the prison is not evidently closed but, as Cluchey says, tightening. It is paradoxically always closing. In his "believe-you-me" stance, Cluchey evokes not only his general understanding of the system but also his personal experience of the everyday pressure it exerts upon him. Only through the tightness of its collar does Cluchey become aware of how the system operates.

Staging *Godot* in prison gives Cluchey a heightened awareness of the closed system of the prison. He evokes the phrase while describing the physically crowded space of the San Quentin Workshop performance. Cluchey's use of the term "closed system" arises literally within that theater, rather than in application to it from the outside. How does "standing room only" for a Beckett play performed by and in front of convicts elicit Cluchey's citation of a "closed system"? First, the density of the group, the close proximity of convicts to one another, owes itself to the way the prison recycles old spaces: the San Quentin Workshop rehearsed and performed in the space previously occupied by the prison gallows.[88] In a closed system, the place for hangings is repurposed into a space for theater—and probably without much change. We can only wonder about the atmosphere this gave to the performances, and about how much room it provided for spectators. In his book on the sublime, Edmund Burke remarked that contemporary theater was so stultifyingly artificial that if ever an announcement were made of a hanging in the public square, audiences would rush out of the middle of a performance in order to attend it.[89] Divested of theatrical tinsel, Beckett's stage merges inconspicuously with the gallows on its day off. *Waiting for Godot* is the substitute sentence for execution: getting life.[90] The closed system of the prison allows these two spaces to overlap.

Cluchey employs the term "closed system" to describe the strange airless space that exists between convicts in the audience and their fellow inmates on stage. This must have had the same déjà vu quality as a masquerade ball on a cruise ship from which one is never allowed to disembark. What were these performances, free of outsiders, like? What desires did this strange monadological theater serve?[91] Do we not have here something different from theater (representation, action, drama), something closer to the transfer of heat? What becomes of what Suvin called Beckett's "aimless island universe" when it is performed within the aimless island universe of San Quentin? Cluchey says that at this moment, the inhabitants of the closed system packed the "theater" to look at Beckett's theatrical closed system. To Jones's question about Beckett's "cylinder" narratives, "How can a closed system be observed?" we must add "within a closed system."[92] Cluchey answers by making the closed system synonymous with jail: the prison mediates Beckett's play, rather than being a conception imposed from without. Through a sudden reversal, not only of Beckett and prison but also of reality and fiction, Cluchey claims that prison is packed with Beckett characters. His comment sounds vaguely like the one made by Esslin, who found the unknowing voice of Beckett's work coming through the bars of the pimp's cell. Writes Cluchey:

> If the critics are right when they proclaim that Beckett's characters are drawn from his early life in Dublin, the streets, bogs, ditches, dumps and madhouses, then I can only add that the most informed, knowledgeable and qualified people to portray Beckett's "characters" would be the inmates of any prison! For here more than any other place in the world, reside the true Beckett people. The cast-offs and loonies, the poets of the streets, and all of the "bleeding meat" of the entire system. The real folks of our modern wasteland.[93]

For a brief instant, the world outside the prison enters into the picture for Cluchey. The closed system is inhabited by the "bleeding meat" of the "entire system." Beckett's characters, Cluchey says, are best portrayed by people already in prison: prison has cultivated the Beckett character. This is another way of saying that prison produces only fictional or, to use Jones's term, *hypothetical* individuals. In prison, life is life in the same way that, as Beckett said about the stage of *Godot*, the sky is a sky: in name only. Adorno writes that Beckett's plays show us only "what is left of the subject," namely, "its most abstract characteristic: merely existing, and thereby already committing an outrage."[94]

Perplexed by the Prisoner's Response

About the impassioned response to *Godot* by his fellow inmates, Cluchey writes: "Our 'affinity' with the works of Beckett has perplexed many critics, but never our audiences."[95] In what follows, I will explore four examples of that affinity in prisoners, the way they express it, and how it pertains to the environment in which they dwell. I suggest that we can learn something particularly important about Beckett by learning how not to be perplexed by the prisoner's affinity with Beckett's plays.

What is our obstacle to understanding this affinity? Are we perplexed because we imagine prisoners to be less capable of empathy than ourselves? What is empathy to a convict, either within or outside a theater? Do we allot them only moral tears, those of regret? The empathetic convict contradicts the stereotype of callousness and brutality that seems to mark criminal life before, during, and after prison. If we stand within this bias, it becomes difficult to picture the criminal feeling something like an elective affinity for Beckett's work. Following a performance of *Godot* at the Florida State Penitentiary at Raiford, Sidney Homan remarks on how the prisoners rushed the stage, eager to talk about the play with Homan and the actors. He recollects "the discussions, those extraordinary discussions where these hardened, sullen men had opened up their hearts, had confronted a mystery in *Godot* that we can no more solve than avoid."[96] Even this description is fringed with Homan's surprise at the seeming paradox of the moved prisoner.

Our second obstacle to the prisoner's response pertains to an implicit understanding of Beckett's work. Do we honestly feel it is a play with which to empathize? *Waiting for Godot* persists in critical discourse as a marvel of theatrical experimentation. The obstructions it places before the capacity of our critical intelligence to identify what happens on its stage limit our capacity to identify with it. We note the difficulty of his text first, and then we assume that this difficulty pertains to (or even hinders) the feeling it may give us. Noting how the play fastidiously measures its breaks and the cadence of its silences, Blau writes: "*Godot*, indeed, gives the definitive turn to the idea of Alienation. A subterranean drama, appearing to care for nothing but its interior life, it searches the audience like a Geiger counter. No modern drama is more sensitively aware of the presence of an audience, or its absence. . . . *Empathy is controlled with diabolic precision.*"[97] In calling *Godot* the "definitive turn to the idea of Alienation," Blau suggests not only that Beckett's play subdues our experience of pathos (in the same way that Brecht's plays critique Aristotelian dramaturgy) but also that it benumbs the consciousness that is usually the windfall of distancation. Blau writes provocatively that the play sweeps the audience like a Geiger counter; that is, the play seemingly looks back at the audience for the afterlife (or, to go with the radioactivity of Blau's metaphor, the half-life) of our feeling for the play. What could this possibly mean other than that the play exposes us to feeling (our own as well as the characters'), and that our encounter with the exposed figures on stage leaves an emotional deposit within us, belatedly and almost subcutaneously? The radical challenge of Beckett's posttheatrical drama in fact rests in how we empathize with his vagabonds, how we orient ourselves toward what they expose (rather than simply give) to us. Is the way we encounter the vagabonds we see on stage any different from the way we encounter them in the street, where we might be able to *recognize* something (a gesture, a look, a walk) in the hobo's condition and yet pause before we call him *familiar*? Cluchey takes this a step further. He notes: "While all over the world audiences were puzzled and fascinated, the critics astounded by the plays of Beckett, we, the inmates of San Quentin, in fact found the situation normal."[98] What is normal for individuals who turned their backs on normal? How do the disjunctions of Beckett's theater become a mechanism by which the alienated recognize something about their place in the prison system? Blau says that our empathy is *controlled with diabolical precision.* Watching Beckett, prisoners identify with figures who cope under that diabolical control.

The prisoners help us unlearn certain habits of thinking about Beckett's play. A case in point: Cluchey notes that prisoners view the figures on stage as *couples.* Upon seeing Vladmir and Gogo, followed by a man whipping another, named Lucky, with a rope around his neck, "Prisoners knew the score."[99] Critics refer to these as "pseudocouples," a designation coined by the narrator of Beckett's *The Unnamable* to describe the characters Mercier and Camier.[100] The term has migrated from Beckett's fiction into critical discussion about that fiction. Discussing Vladimir and Estragon, for example, Jonathan Boulter remarks, "His plays and novels are filled with characters in painful relationships which seem to offer nothing positive. Beckett referred to the people in these relationships as 'pseudo-couples' because often there is nothing formal (like marriage or blood relations) binding them together."[101] In isolating the prisoner from the bonds of matrimony and family, prison activates new terms for recognizing the couple. Prisoners do not recognize Vladimir and Estragon as a "couple" in quotation marks. Prison inmates understand the couple as they who wait together. For them, the couple is formed nonconsensually, through their needs, their interaction, their inaction, their pathos. In *The Unnamable,* Beckett speaks of the "little murmur of unconsenting man, [murmuring] what it is their humanity stifles."[102] Vladimir and Estragon are a couple not formed by vow; they are tied through their endless murmur, a tie stifled by the officially sanctioned badge of "humanity." The stage, and not mutual fondness, desire, or even consent, bring Vladimir and Estragon together. They have nothing. Should we then disqualify them for having nothing in common? In 1955 the New Repertory Theater asked permission to stage *Waiting for Godot* with two actors whose temperaments, acting styles, and physicalities could not have been more antithetical: Buster Keaton (as Vladimir) and Marlon Brando (as Estragon).[103] If this production had gone forward, the end of the first act would have witnessed Brando/Estragon estimating that he and Keaton/Vladimir had spent "50 years maybe" together. Where would this statement uttered by Brando to Keaton acquire credibility? Where *but in a prison cell?*

Prisoners on *Godot:* Godot as Prisoner

The rest of this chapter will investigate four instances of prisoners who illuminate our understanding of Beckett. Each reads *Godot* in a different manner through the environment in which he sees the play performed: the prison context. K. F. Lembke, whose letter to Beckett provides this chapter with its epigraph, is not only the first prison reader of *Godot* but the most fanatical, breaking parole in order to meet its author. In 1953 in Lüttringhausen Prison, Lembke gets a copy of *En Attendant Godot* and proceeds to direct, cast, and stage his translation, titled *Man Wartet auf Godot.* (Lembke's rendering of the title emphasizes the anonymous "one" who waits, rather than subjectless waiting.) The actors and spectators are a UN delegation of scofflaws, the criminal castes whom he enumerates for Beckett in his letter dated November 29, 1953: "thieves, forgers, homos, crazy men and killers." Lembke's response to *Waiting for Godot* is symptomatic of the way that prisoners seize *Godot.* Lembke's letter makes clear that ownership of the play, performed in prison, has been transferred to the prisoners: "Your Godot was a triumph, something wild!—Your Godot was 'our' Godot, ours, our very own!" ("Votre Godot ce fut un triomphe, le délire—Votre Godot ce fut 'Notre' Godot, à nous! bien à nous!").[104] Repeating "ours" and "our own" several times, Lembke speaks of appropriation, not representation. His enthusiasm for the play befits its status as a piece of contraband. The delirium of someone enjoying Beckett behind locked doors (locked from without, not from within) is a curious rejoinder to the conventional wisdom about the tactical uselessness of modern art.[105]

Lembke's understanding of Beckett's play emerges within this affective connection to it. In his assertion that "your Godot is our Godot," we overhear the claim *Godot—he's one of ours.* Lembke's twist is not that we are waiting for Godot, where Godot designates some redeeming agency at a distance from us (like the warden). Instead he says, "We are all waiting for him and do not know that he is already here. Yes, here. Godot is my neighbor in the cell next to mine. Let us do something to help him, change the shoes that are hurting him!"[106] Lembke suggests that Godot (the figure, not just the play) is being held in Lüttringhausen. In the sea of prisoners, however, Godot's number does not stand out. We are waiting, but he is here: "Yes, here," Lembke repeats himself, as if having anticipated Beckett's (or his own) disbelief at the thought. Incarcerated, Godot is transformed into Gogo: "Let us help him then, change the shoes that are hurting him!" Lembke's analysis recasts the unseen Godot as one of the figures we see on stage. Godot ceases to be the promise both endlessly deferred and endlessly broken and becomes the adjacent and sluggishly corporeal figure who overdoes it on his carrots.

Lembke reads the play as an imperative to help one's neighbor. He inverts the dynamic of need in the play. We do not need Godot; our neighbor needs us. He turns the play from a destitute state of "nothing to be done" into an urgent call to assistance. Since this crucial first line follows Gogo's struggle to get his boot off, Lembke responds in Brechtian fashion to the situation: if we change Gogo's boot, we change the philosophy of the play. At the same time, the pragmatic moral that Lembke finds in the play cannot thoroughly withstand its transfer into the prison without modification. In trying to deflate the transcendence of Godot by assigning him a spot contiguous to ours, Lembke runs into a problem with the staging of his remake (his interpretation) of *Godot* inside the prison. This staging issue is apparent in the aftertaste of iron (rather than the taste of irony) left in our mouths by Lembke's phrase, "the neighbor in the cell next to mine." Proximity and distance are not antonyms in jail. Contiguous cells are impossibly removed from one another, and prisoners in adjacent cells communicate to one another in Morse code, the language of passing ships. Coming to one's neighbor for anything in prison is as difficult as finding a new pair of shoes for him. It raises the question: where precisely is Lembke pointing when he asserts that Godot is *here*, "Yes, here"? The here of the prisoner is always usurped by the "there" of the guard, and the way the carceral institution manages the movement of convicts through its space. This "here" is neither public nor private, only a perpetually scrutinized and unfree space: precisely the quality of prison that makes it resonant with Beckett's theatrical vision. Though he set out to attune our ears to the call of our neighbor, Lembke ends by envisioning a new play based on the infinite separation of neighbors: *Waiting for Gogo* (or maybe *Gogo Waits*).

Lembke's desire to make Godot less ghostly to us applies equally to his relation with Beckett. He invites Beckett to see the performance, and though Beckett declines, he casually suggests that Lembke call whenever he is in town. Lembke probably feels baffled by this impossible invitation of hospitality to him, an incarcerated man, as he is by Godot's absence. Lembke proceeds to go to work on Beckett's absence. He does this by breaking parole and journeying all the way from Wuppertal to Paris, showing up at Beckett's door unannounced. Lembke ceases writing letters to Beckett in favor of sending himself and accepts Beckett's invitation not formally but in person. Knowlson reports: "A frozen figure, dressed in lightweight summer clothing, turned up at the theater in a freezing cold Paris. . . . The penniless, half-starved prisoner had broken parole to come to see him. Blin offered temporary shelter and provided him with warmer clothing."[107] Since the prisoner has no identity papers, he cannot be checked into a hotel. Beckett, wary of meeting the prisoner on the lam (possibly because of his earlier run-in with the knife-wielding pimp), never goes to his door but gives Blin money to pass on to the prisoner, along with the information that Beckett supposedly will not be back in town for a long time. Lembke, having broken the law and turned himself into one of Beckett's vagabonds in his pilgrimage to the author, proceeds to reenact on Beckett's doorstep what he learned from Beckett's play and Lüttringhausen alike: he waits.

Prisoners on *Godot:* Waiting to Empathize

One of the most intriguing essays on *Waiting for Godot* is the review written by Bandman in the *San Quentin News.* The front page article of the November 14, 1957, edition of the paper offers straight reportage on the play and interviews with the actors (noting, for example, managing director Jules Irving's admission that "frankly, we were scared to death.") Bandman's column, by contrast, is an astonishingly creative response to *Godot,* unruly in its effort to devise a language for what took place on the stage in the "barn-like space of the North Dining Hall." Though Bandman structures the review as a summary of the play, he addresses the reader through a series of imperatives ("now look closely," "but wait," "see master Pozzo as the compelling spirit"). Bandman thereby directs our attention at what he is critically imagining for us. The essay is literally a re-view from the prisoner's standpoint, at once a description and a hallucination. The essay moves erratically across the registers of interpretation, imperative, hypothesis, objective description. About Vladimir and Estragon in act 2, for example, Bandman directs us to "watch them finalize into precursors of doubt, depression, and death." "Finalizing into precursors" is the prisoner's personal articulation of the mixed temporality of the waiting process. Vladimir and Estragon simultaneously terminate and herald as they metamorphose into the sign of their waiting. Bandman's sentences are tightly compressed, with dense terms crammed at odd angles to one another.[108] Each sentence constitutes both a holding pen and the effort to see over its wall.

Bandman's review is also a landmark in Beckett criticism for the way in which it speaks of *Godot,* years before its canonization, as a "world play." The phrase departs, however, from contemporary uses of the term: for Bandman, the term designates an object from *beyond the walls* of the prison. The term "world" recurs throughout Bandman's essay: he calls Pozzo the "drive that makes the world go round," a figure who "occasionally turns the shaft straight in our collective backs." Both worlds—the world on stage and the world outside the prison—turn at the expense, the exclusion, of the prisoner. Of each world, the prisoner is a pivot rather than one of its denizens. (Bandman writes the essay in the collective "we" of the yard.) Our notion of Beckett's play as a world play and as microcosm begins here, in the response of one deprived of world. The paradox of these two worlds is institutional rather than logical for Bandman: both worlds exclude the prisoner. So he brings in the term once more in a strong effort to appeal to his audience, to put it in their terms: "If you will allow an explanation, see this play with us as the *vast world* housed right inside your own mind." The prisoner in his cell may already suspect his cell, in its mixture of familiarity and unreality, to be his mind, and the walls of the prison his cranium. This staple interpretation of Beckett's theater has its origin in the nagging suspicion of the inmate.[109] The world shuts itself up in the mind when the prisoner loses the world.

More importantly, Bandman's essay bears witness to the ways in which the prisoner is conflictual in his empathetic response to Beckett. This hesitation is overlooked in Esslin's claims about the immediate response of the inmates. The title of Bandman's review, "The Play's the Thing . . . ," is a partial citation from *Hamlet*. Hamlet's mental anguish and self-divided monologuing provide an interesting antecedent to the harassed thinking of Beckett's homeless figures. Yet the title withholds the remainder of Hamlet's line: "wherein I shall catch the conscience of the king." Hamlet stages *The Mousetrap*, which "plays something like the murder of my [Hamlet's] father," in order to see if his uncle will evince signs of a guilty conscience while watching the play.[110] The reference touches a sore spot for Bandman, as it proposes theater as an instrument of institutional memory: *The Mousetrap* is designed to catch the involved spectator, whose emotional responses are turned into his rap sheet. *The Mousetrap* is supposed to *con* the *King*. Bandman voids the rest of Hamlet's quote because he argues that Beckett's play mobilizes catharsis but does so with a purpose other than pricking conscience or making guilt manifest.[111] Featuring two waiting vagabonds forgetful of where they were yesterday, *Waiting for Godot* elicits, for Bandman, a complex dynamic of emotion and reflection in the prisoner. His essay ends by returning to the quote: "The play's the thing. This one was effective." The essay shows us how prisoners discover new effects in Beckett's play, in percussion with their imprisoned state.

The dramatic structure of catharsis implicating both prisoner and prison gets particular attention in Bandman's discussion. Empathy for another's suffering begins on stage in act 1, when Pozzo arrives with his servant Lucky, who is tied with a rope and carrying his master's stool and lunch basket. In a gesture seldom seen in Beckett characters, Vladimir actually *objects* to Lucky's treatment: the stage directions indicate he is "exploding" as he exclaims, "It's a scandal!" Pozzo replies, "Are you referring to anything in a particular?" This reply is particularly cutting: Pozzo wants a citation for Vladimir's shock and disbelief. Vladimir tries to put his finger on the scandal, but is ultimately only able to repeat the phrase: "(*stutteringly resolute*) to treat a man . . . (*gesture toward Lucky*) . . . like that . . . I think that . . . no . . . a human being . . . no . . . it's a scandal!"[112] Estragon chips in with "It's a disgrace!" but the stage directions indicate that he is more interested in "gnawing on his carrot." Act 1 therefore calls for empathy and then defeats it. Lucky's state remains unaltered, and Pozzo remains uncriminalized. The play seems here to weld itself shut as a situation bearing no intervention.

Bandman's essay focuses on the improbable reemergence of empathy in act 2, when Pozzo reappears with Lucky. Pozzo is now blinded, a condition as inexplicable as Lucky's servitude, and cries for help. Bandman comments:

> Hear Pozzo's cries for help, for mercy. Feel pity for a beaten Fury, and hold out your hand—but wait! Should we forget what we've learned in waiting and watching? What's it worth? If we help him, then what? Let us ponder and discuss: weigh the pros and cons. And then, overcome with "spiritual" effulgence, help this flailing vital force in its sightless death throes. Yet in our selfless charity we overlook the obvious. Even blind, he is stronger than we! We fall. But resiliently. We are pulled down by the dying only to become renewed, and in turn set death on its feet again.[113]

Hear Pozzo's cries, feel pity, hold out your hand . . . *but wait*. At the very moment the spectator's hand is figuratively extended over the proscenium to the character, Bandman says to hold it right there. He thereby usurps the play's imperative to wait and lodges it within the immediate impulse to feel something for Pozzo. Bandman does not ask his spectator to be detached (Brechtian) or immersed, but rather to review his emotional allegiances. Recalling the undertow of futility in the play, he suggests that nothing is to be done either by the characters or for them: "Should we forget what we've learned in waiting and watching? What's it worth?"

Vladimir and Estragon bicker about empathy's worth on stage. Regarding their assistance to Pozzo as a promising employment opportunity, they debate how much they should charge him for their services (one hundred francs? two hundred francs?). Whereas the characters on stage debate the price for helping Pozzo, Bandman urges the inmate spectator to assess its cost: "If we help him, then what? Weigh the pros and cons."[114] Exactly what kind of advice is this to convicts, whose very name is given to the negative side of the ledger? Emotional catharsis is a losing wager for the criminal, and Bandman proceeds to lay out the reason why. "Do not overlook the obvious. Even blind, he is stronger than we!" The spectator remains curiously watched, not only by a blind man but by a blind man on stage. Feeling sorry for this blinded tyrant makes the inmate forget where he is in the auditorium. Bandman says, "Wait!" Look away from the stage not to cry into your sleeve but to remember the guards posted at every exit.

Bandman asserts that emotional release ultimately works to sustain something (a theatrical but clearly recognizable figure of power) that leaves the inmate spectator unfree. He says, "We fall. But resiliently. We are pulled down by the dying only to become renewed, and in turn set death on its feet again." What Bandman calls our "spiritual effulgence" toward the stage is something akin to a rendezvous, not unlike the one that is supposed to take place in the play: the spectator's emotional investment in Beckett's play, but this renewal is a meager concession from a process that destroys him. Fallen power merely cons the inmate's feelings and reasserts his place within the structure of authority. Bandman concedes that it makes the prisoner feel better and "renewed," yet he observes that this emotional transaction only allows a greater negativity to reassert itself. Theatrical catharsis originally serves a civic function: to purge distortion and emotion from the spectator and thereby clarify the citizen's judgment.[115] Its contrary theatrical model, Brecht's alienation, shared the same goal: "The point is not to leave the spectator purged by a cathartic but to leave him a changed man, or rather, to sow within him the changes which must be *completed outside the theater.*"[116] Catharsis loses its therapeutic function and retains only a negative one when access to civic space is denied. For the prisoner seeing *Godot* in San Quentin, unlike Brecht's or Aristotle's spectator, there is no "outside the theater." The emotional release is choked up by the cognizance of guards standing at the exits of the cafeteria. Using a Beckettian turn of phrase, Bandman says that the prisoner's catharsis merely helps readjust death's posture, as if it had simply been taking a breather: we "set death on its feet again." Bandman describes the dynamic between audience and stage as an exchange of postures: death stands up, and we fall as if we were standing, "resiliently."

A resilient fall, a more wakeful version of what Beckett would call in his late work a "slumberous collapse," is Bandman's way of charting positivity ("spiritual effulgence") within an exchange that only ends up on the bad side. The counter-Hegelian dialectic he detects between audience and stage never synthesizes, never resolves. It is Bandman's way of saying that the negative moment goes unredeemed. Or, in the language of the prison context, the con goes unrehabilitated. This aspect of Beckett's work has been widely noted by critics.[117] In his notes to Beckett, Adorno observes: "Very enigmatic remark about a kind of positivity contained in pure negativity. In view of such absolute negativity, one could be said to *quasi* live."[118] Bandman's observation differs from Adorno's insofar as Bandman discovers this *"quasi"* life within the prisoner's emotional investment during the play, rather than within philosophy per se. For Bandman, the spectator's immediate reaction to Pozzo sheds light on a curious kind of darkness: his own. Instead of "positivity contained in pure negativity" (Adorno), Bandman speaks of *Godot* as "the most provocatively negative synthesis of the mechanics of human culture that it has been our pleasure to enjoy for a long time."[119] The situation of the prisoner-spectator who "weighs the pros and cons" realizes the abject math of Beckett's play.

Bandman calls out to the spectator to employ a balance, the kind that Justice might use, yet he urges this metaphor upon an audience of thieves. His audience, Beckett's audience, knows the weight of that scale upon them; they cannot use it disinterestedly to monitor their own experience. So as he urges deliberation in the middle of their emotional surge, Bandman notes a very contrary effect of *Godot*. He calls it "an expression, symbolic in order to avoid all personal error, by an author who expected each member of his audience to draw his own conclusions, make his own errors." The resolute and methodical proceedings on Beckett's stage impress Bandman as an invitation to err. Beckett's work encourages the spectator to put the scales of justice aside. To make one's own errors, to undergo unguarded emotional investments and mental experiments, must have been appealing to the rule-bound audience.[120]

Prisoners on Beckett: Theatrical Recidivism

Cluchey says that before *Godot* came to San Quentin in 1957, he "had never even been in a theater, not even to rob one." The joke tells us something about what we expect a prisoner to take away from culture: nothing but the cash box. The theater is too bereft to heist. The aspect of the stage that turns away Cluchey the criminal ensnares him as a protégé of Beckett by issuing him a dare: what does one take from Beckett's destitute work? How does one undo its lock? Cluchey's work as a performer of Beckett's drama, as the playwright of *The Cage* and *The Wall Is Mama,* and as one of Beckett's preferred actors, indicates his debt to Beckett's theater. To understand the shadow that Beckett and *Waiting for Godot* cast over Cluchey, we have to reverse the agency in the joke: Cluchey did not break into the theater. The theater broke into him.

The circumstances under which Cluchey encounters the *Godot* performance tell us something about the trajectory to come. While 1,500 inmates packed the north hall cafeteria to watch the play, Cluchey, in prison for life and considered an escape risk, is forced to remain in his cell. Yet Cluchey has no choice but to listen to the performance, as it is piped over the prison's radio system into his cell. How strange it must have been to hear such lines as "The English say cawm" and "How's the carrot?" through the apparatus that habitually barked out the daily routine of the prison. It may have been the distance enforced between Cluchey and the play, rather than his proximity to it, that left its mark on him: *Godot* greets him not as a captivated audience but as a confined one, behind bars. The layout of Cluchey's first encounter with *Godot* inscribes him already as a Beckett character. Beckett's *Company* begins: "A voice comes to one in the dark. Imagine." The situation forces Cluchey, and us, to imagine that voice, that solitary one, that dark. Even though he commits no crime in a theater, Cluchey keeps returning to the scene. His life constitutes an incredible itinerary toward Beckett, toward that encounter he missed but which nevertheless came to him in his cell.

Where Lembke's pilgrimage to Beckett takes spatial expression, walking from Lüttringhausen to Paris, Cluchey's path is through acting Beckett. A telling memento is the slippers (Beckett's own) that Cluchey wears in his performance as Krapp in *Krapp's Last Tape,* under Beckett's direction in Berlin in 1977, and which Cluchey donated along with his papers to the Depaul University Library. Beckett is unhappy with the sound generated by other slippers against the floor of the stage. Only Beckett's own make the sought-after shuffling noise. Cluchey wears these slippers through several performances of Krapp over the next decade, performing the Krapp out of them and eventually donating the tattered slippers, held together by tape, to an archive. Cluchey therefore makes a pilgrimage, but only in character: he follows the path cut by the back-and-forth of his character across umpteen stages, and does so only in Beckett's slippers, which make the precise sound desired by the director.[121]

Cluchey's time in prison prepares him to be a Beckett actor. He founds an acting workshop in San Quentin, and between 1961 and 1963 he stages thirty-five performances of Beckett's cycle (*Waiting for Godot, Endgame,* and *Krapp's Last Tape*).[122] If prison, as Lenin claims, is a university for revolutionaries, then it might also be an acting school for performers of Beckett.[123] Cluchey methodically contours himself so closely to the everyday discipline of prison life that he does not break a single rule in his twelve years there. The warden announces this at Cluchey's release through a governor's pardon. "That's something," the warden adds, "when you think of all the rules we have here."[124] Cluchey strikes no revolutionary or transgressive stance while in jail and internalizes the irrational rules of the institution. This constitutes preparation for acting within Beckett's sensitively alarm-wired stage. Beckett's stage directions issue a restraining order on improvisation.[125] Cluchey himself notes how Beckett requires the actor to stop acting, to learn inaction, and to acquire "a commitment to listening."[126] Looking for greater colorlessness to the voice, Beckett would tell Cluchey, "Don't say it like that—they won't hear you." Beckett sees Krapp as "trapped in himself" and "full of a dangerous, concentrated violence."[127] His advice to Cluchey in performing this role is "Make the thing your own in terms of incarceration."[128] Beckett summons the prisoner to reappear on stage as Krapp. To make the character his own, Beckett suggests he use the terms of his incarceration. This is curious advice, since the thing that Cluchey was while in prison, "driven mad by my own calendar maker, the Warden and State of California," was not his own.[129] This self forcibly disowned of self inhabits Beckett's stage.

Cluchey's play *The Cage* revises *Waiting for Godot* from the standpoint of prison. The one-act play unfolds within the contained space of a stage bounded by prison bars, with occasional interruptions by the guards. It shows us the relations improvised between four prisoners in the cell: Al ("a deformed petty thief"), Doc (a black convict), Hatchet (criminally insane), and a new prisoner, Jive, who may or may not have just murdered his girlfriend. The play culminates in a mock trial of Jive, over which Hatchet presides as "judge." At the play's conclusion Hatchet gathers the verdict and strangles Jive before washing his hands in the water from the toilet at center stage. Unlike Lucky's monologue (to which his rants bear some resemblance), Hatchet's insanity comes with consequences.

The Cage resembles a transcription of *Godot* from memory: what Cluchey cannot recollect he fills in with his experience as a prisoner. This recidivism, in which Cluchey repeatedly returns to prison through the stage, is literally part of the play's conception.[130] Cluchey wrote *The Cage* while in San Quentin, using a typewriter he accessed in spare time while working in the chaplain's office. After parole, Cluchey substantially rewrote it in the process of bringing the play to prisons throughout the United States, employing only ex-convicts in the roles. *The Cage* materializes the no-man's-land of *Godot* within a prison cell. The curious immobility of Beckett's characters at the end of each act is no longer an overdetermined and half-internalized condition. Cluchey's play renders Beckett's "They do not move" more tangibly as "They cannot be moved . . . without authorization." *The Cage* articulates this immobility not as a stage direction but through the décor (the bars surrounding three sides of the stage). Cluchey's play does not imitate Beckett's play but acts as a developing agent upon it. Earlier I described how prison forms a latent image within Beckett's work and how it confronts his study rather than being ingested by it. Cluchey makes more patent the institutional force of prison felt in Beckett's theater. His play makes space on its stage for the guards who handled the props of Beckett's play offstage during the San Quentin performance of *Waiting for Godot*.

These guards in *The Cage* show how Cluchey gives a coercive turn to the inconsistency and discontinuity of Beckett's dialogues. When the play opens, two guards bring in a new prisoner. They rattle off instructions to the prisoner, speaking in alternation, before the prisoner who never speaks. Here are just a few of the lines that cover two pages of the script:

> Keep yourself clean at all times. Wash regularly—avoid disease. Never waste time, be productive. Stay busy, use the time well. Report everything to us. Remember gambling is forbidden. Never accept favors from other prisoners. Because they expect favors in return. It only leads to trouble. Cooperate with us, we'll help you. Do your time and let us run the prison. If you don't receive your mail don't worry. If you see trouble brewing, we're helping you. We want you to learn new ways.[131]

Separately, the lines all stand on their own, as insular as axioms. The statements are hard to remember because they perform different functions: they threaten, they cajole, they place ultimatums, they invite, they describe, they warn. The discontinuity is exacerbated because some of the lines continue the preceding thought ("Because they expect favors in return"). The total effect of this list is not unlike the abstract incoherence that plagues much of Beckett's dialogue, only in Cluchey the dialogue and effect is addressed to a particular subject: the prisoner, who must sit in witness to the dialogue and use it, hypothetically, as a way to survive in prison. The list of imperatives does not add up, and yet the prisoner must not make any mistake about them. Like Kafka, Cluchey makes us do a double take at the concern shown to us by officials and subsequently has us wonder about his intent: "If you don't receive your mail, don't worry" could be a message from Kafka's Castle.

Cluchey's play gives a more discernible shape to Beckettian futility. In *Godot* this futility is existentialist in nature and goes on and on. In Cluchey it goes on and on before a power. Beckett's waiting has frozen into detainment. Moments from Cluchey's play match up with others in *Godot* so that their gestures ghost one another. These afterimages in *The Cage* materialize the prison-ghost on Beckett's stage. In *The Cage* the new prisoner, insisting on his innocence, shouts to the exiting guards, "Does the Warden know I'm here?" and "Tell the Warden I'm here. I have to see him right away, it's important."[132] This resembles Vladimir's answer to the boy who asks what message he should deliver to Godot: "Tell him . . . (*he hesitates*) . . . tell him you saw us. (*Pause.*) You did see us, didn't you?"[133] Vladimir articulates the uncertainty of being seen either by the boy or implicitly by us, the spectators. By contrast, we detect the futility of the prisoner's question through its urgent repetition rather than through ellipses or hesitation. The plea to make an appearance before the warden takes the place of Vladimir's doubt about whether his existence on stage has been witnessed. The power structure of the prison in Cluchey's scenario resets the phenomenological doubt of Beckett's stage. Whereas Vladimir's question concludes each act of *Godot*, the prisoner's hopeless petition of the warden begins Cluchey's play. We are introduced to Cluchey's character by being introduced to his plea falling on deaf ears. The statement accompanies the arrival of the prisoner in the no-man's-land. Cluchey's cell telepathically channels and remixes lines from Beckett in accordance with the new stage reality of the cell. The nothing-to-be-done intoned within Beckett's absence of environment is reconfigured by Cluchey's character, who says simply, "I don't belong here. I didn't do anything."[134] In neither *Godot* nor *The Cage* is the stage a place where one belongs. On Cluchey's stage, the apprehended prisoner must endlessly revise Estragon's proclamation to himself: *nothing was done; I didn't do anything.*

Cluchey takes the dispossessed state of Beckett's vagabonds and shows it to be a thoroughly managed condition. Maybe it always was a managed condition, Cluchey suggests, only one managed in our world by the institution of prison, rather than for the stage by the institution of theater. Cluchey turns the vague and fruitless landscape of *Godot* into a structural wasteland. Beyond the stage lies not a void, à la Beckett, but merely more of the same, more cells. Offstage space acquires its unknown quality only by the prohibition placed on the prisoners' access to it.[135] The sound of "a steel door, the rustle of heavy keys, voices, pans" send the convict, Al, leaping to the bars, yelling, "Hey, it's garbage time. Hey Jesus, hurry up with the turnips will ya. I'm starving."[136] It is not accidental that Beckett's prop, the turnip, makes a reappearance here (or rather fails to). The meagerness of the tramp's life on Beckett's stage is pondered through a turnip that Vladimir has scavenged, kept in his pocket, and shares with Estragon as a poor substitute for a carrot. The inadequate quantities of carrots and turnips on stage enable Beckett's tramps to debate their comparative taste and produce an immediate nostalgia for carrots ("I'll never forget this carrot"). Yet in Cluchey's prison, the turnip is Godot. Food is rationed by an agency beyond the stage, that is, *outside the bars of the cage*, instead of from within, from the folds of Vladimir's pocket. Al's starvation is a transitive condition, performed on him by the prison that starves him, as opposed to Estragon's description of his condition: "I'm hungry!" In this way the rationality of the prison system exacerbates the absurdity of Beckett's stage.

Beckett's Silences in the Prison

The audiences of prison performances of *Waiting for Godot* are famously raucous, something unimaginable to the critic or theatergoer accustomed to decorum. Records of prison performances describe inmates' reactions almost as if the actors were in the yard with them, not before them on a stage. They interrupt the performance by shouting questions, making fun of events on stage, and thinking aloud loudly. Unlike critics or traditional theatergoers, the prisoners are not willing to trust that the postponement of their understanding of what happens on stage will eventually pay off. The performance of the play, rather than reflection on the performance, provides the prisoner with an opportunity for its interpretation. The comments and questions the inmates shout are in a sense the instant verbalization of the inchoate critical reception. The shouted comments indicate impatience with the stage action and with some of Beckett's more enigmatic formulations. In fact, as Sidney Homan notes, the audience of his production of *Godot* in Raiford Prison did not even allow Vladimir to complete his second sentence. Replying to Estragon's "Nothing to be done," Vladimir says, "I'm beginning to come around to that opinion. All my life I've tried to put it from me." As Homan describes: "At this point an inmate leaped to his feet and cried out, 'What the hell do you mean by *put it from me?*'"[137] The inmate immediately poses the question again once it becomes clear that the actors, refusing to fall out of their roles, will not answer: "I said, what the hell do you mean by *put it from me?*" The prisoner's confusion is not a question of vocabulary. The line, the third in the play, also seems to cut close to the intimate exchange the prisoner has with the power exercised over him. Vladimir uses physical terms to describe his attempt to forget or shrug off a conviction, as if this opinion ("nothing to be done") were something he had to literally relocate far from himself. The prisoner in the audience would be the first to wonder: where is it to go? What means are available to erase a conviction, in a place where every gesture is scrutinized and where every convict is synonymous with his crime and his sentence?

Photographs of the 1988 production of *Waiting for Godot* in San Quentin inspire Beckett to observe that he "saw the roots of my play" there.[138] Yet the mute images compel Beckett to raise a question about what he cannot hear in them. He asks Jan Jönson "about 'the sound' of his play in the prison environment. He wanted to know what 'the silence' of the play was like behind prison walls."[139] Are we to hear a bit of concern in Beckett's question? What chance does a silence have between the infinite clamor, the literal *mur-mur* that happens between prison walls? Alternatively, the prison would seem to give an opportunity for silence to happen. Sontag remarked that the silences of *Godot* permitted the sounds of sniper fire and armored vehicles to filter in to the stage and make an acoustic imprint upon the play. This sonic breach of the stage is not an option within the prison, where nothing enters without first being frisked. So the silences within the prison are inordinately connected to the silences that greet them from the outside world. Similarly, the silences of Beckett's stage in the play are not just the absence of noise from the characters but the sound of Godot's failure to respond. "The air is full of our cries," says Vladimir. Yet in the airtight system of San Quentin these cries are out of earshot of the outside world. No sounds from the streets can accidentally fill the silences of the play. In the stagnant recycled air of San Quentin, even these cries mesh with the silence. The cries fill the air, yet they form a kind of white noise.

Beckett's question goes to the heart of his play, noted in the earliest critical responses. Jacques Audiberti's review of the premiere of *Godot* at the Babylon Theater notes that the characters "speak like Charlie Chaplin. As he would have spoken, not as the Count of Limelight, but when he had nothing to say."[140] Speech and silence are deeply indebted to one another in *Godot*. Nowhere is this more evident than in Beckett's own production in Berlin. Beckett punctuates the play with sixteen moments of silence and stillness called *Wartestellen*, or points of waiting.[141] Walter Asmus notes Beckett's remarks about these tableaux: "There are fixed moments of stillness, where everything stands completely still and silence threatens to swallow everything up. Then the action starts again."[142] The stage directions give numerous indications of silence, as if it were something that could not adequately be conveyed merely by having no words on the page, or having come to the end of a sentence. So Gogo, quoting Pozzo, commands Didi, "Think, pig! (*silence*)." Or when Gogo asks Didi, "Do you see anything coming?" Didi responds "No," and Gogo replies "Nor I," followed by the stage direction "(*They resume their watch. Silence.*)." Beckett's production notebook underscores the text as a Cagean production of silences.

Yet the silences broken by the prisoners' replies are not the same silences prescribed by Beckett's stage directions. Again, this illuminates how the prison performances are helpful to understanding the play. The prisoners call attention to new and unforeseen silences. The prisoners ask for clarification from the characters about what their words imply. The inmates' questions try to drag into the open what remains unsaid within characters' articulations. During performances where theater etiquette imposes silence over the spectators, these moments of nonsense habitually go unresolved and hover in the air between stage and audience.[143] By contrast, the prisoners are quick to speak when things do not add up: they do not wait silently for meaning. Homan reports that Lucky's speech, a conspicuous anthology of incomplete meanings and a hymn to unfinished labors, was interrupted fifteen times. When Lucky proclaims, "God quaquaquaqua with white beard," for example, a prisoner shouted, "You taking His name in vain or something?"[144] Rightly, a prisoner knew to voice his suspicion of this speech that takes all names in vain, in a play in which things can only be done in vain. The interjection, which is both question and threat, sounds like the last words before throwing punches. The prisoner has added "or something" because he wants to allot Lucky a space of ambiguity, possibly to permit Lucky (if he could engage in dialogue!) a way out. He wants Lucky to back down or at least to clarify the matter and take accountability for his own monologue. At another moment in Lucky's speech, a prisoner shouts, "You know something those assholes behind you don't?" Once more, these are fighting words. This prisoner responds to the paradox presented by Lucky's fragmented and turbulent monologue, which begins at Pozzo's injunction to "think, pig!" yet offers only debris of knowledge (formulas, snippets of legalese and logical proofs, the taxonomies of sport). You think, the prisoner asks, but do you know something different from the assholes behind you? The disposition of the prisoner's question brings the ambiguity of Lucky's performance to a different level: it is both an invitation and an ultimatum.

In the closed universe of the prison, knowing something different from the others may be remarked upon with greater surprise and urgency. The prisoner greets Lucky's avalanche of speech with a coercive reply: you know something? Then let's have it! The prisoner adopts a practical and muscular stance toward dramatic ambiguity: he interrupts the torrent of Lucky's monologue to ask, "What's to know?" and "How is this performance any different from what we've heard already?"

In these instances, the prisoners raise some of the fundamental questions about the play, not in an essay or review but by hurling the questions at the play itself and at the character on stage: What is a performance of thinking? What knowledge (useful or otherwise) is rendered by the characters? How do we separate blather and thinking? When does the thinking on stage become our own thought? There is a vast difference between the prisoner's speaking at the character and rubbing his chin over these questions.

The play takes great measures to keep the characters' thinking from coagulating into knowledge, something for either us or them to know. We know that Vladimir and Estragon hate interrupted thought. They agree that "the worst is to *have* thought," where thinking stops, acquires a past tense, and becomes something to be assessed in retrospect. They renounce the Hegelian perspective in which the owl of Minerva only takes flight at dusk. As the play transpires in a trapped twilight ("Will night never come?" asks Vladimir), the owl of knowledge seems neither to leave nor to land. The prisoner breaks the hermetic seal on Lucky's monologue. Only by interrupting speech does thought come forth. Yet the prisoner does this not because he is interested in knowledge per se. The inmate wants to know if Lucky is just another asshole: who he is and how he figures, rather than what he knows.

Homan notes that the actors were frequently forced to explain and further define their roles to the audience. For example, after Vladimir says, "All my life I've tried to put it from me, saying you haven't tried everything yet. And I resume the struggle. So there you are again!" and Gogo answers, "Am I?" one of the spectators at Raiford Prison shouted, "Doesn't he know whether he's here or not?" Here, the convict heckler doubts Gogo's doubt and suggests that Cartesian doubt will never do away with existence in prison, that prison (and possibly the stage) condemns you to appear and offers no hiding places. Prison never gives you the chance to forget you are in prison. The prisoner asks, "Doesn't he know whether he's *here* or not?" rather than "there" (as Vladimir specifies). What seems to be a misquotation by the prisoner is in fact testament to the ineluctable and indivisible reality of prison. The slippage from *there* to *here* demonstrates how the prisoner is not in the same place as the critic. Novelist Alain Robbe-Grillet observes that the situation of the hobos on Beckett's stage "is summed up on this simple observation, beyond which it does not seem possible to advance: they are *there*, they are on the stage."[145] Further on, he notes: "They *are there*; they must explain themselves. But they do not seem to have a text prepared for beforehand and scrupulously learned by heart. They must invent. They are free."[146] To the critic, *there* designates the yonder of the stage. The proscenium allows the critic to divide the existence on stage from his own. The prisoner shrugs his shoulders at this claim: the point "beyond which he cannot advance" is not an irreducible existence on stage but existence (including the existence of the theater) in prison, in *here*. The critic points to the stage. The reality of the closed system (*here*) is one to which one need not point: the prisoners sit with crossed arms. Instead of being sanctioned by theatrical custom (a text that would place their characters in a recognizable world), Vladimir and Estragon have the opportunity, or rather the obligation, to explain themselves. The prisoners implicitly agree with Robbe-Grillet, yet their response demonstrates the inadequacy of the vagabonds' self-explanation. This inadequacy is not a matter of clarity but of address: the prisoners want the characters to align themselves to the prison context. The comments and questions shouted to the stage suggest a keen awareness of the unfreedom of the characters, rather than their ability to constitute their world at each moment. The contextlessness of existence is painful, rather than inviting, to the prisoner.

Literary critics describe these interruptions as tearing down the "fourth wall" of the stage. As Erin Koshal notes:

> The fourth wall of theatre enables spectators to become absorbed in the spectacle onstage in a way that ignores the physical and spatial contiguity between audience and actors, reality and fiction. It also helps construct a unilateral relation between dramatic performance and spectator in which the former reflects, educates, or in some way serves the reality outside it. These inmates, however, in offering their own advice to the figures, treated Didi and Gogo not simply as characters occupying a fixed dramatic register but as two figures occupying a theatrical space adjacent to their own.[147]

Koshal implies that the prisoners' responses have an unintended Brechtian effect, shattering the hermetic world of Beckett's stage. Fragmenting gesture, even forcing characters to repeat their lines, the audience distributes fractures into the play according to their needs. Koshal argues that this process tears down the fourth wall of the theater: the illusion of separateness "between audience and actors, reality and fiction" is undermined. Koshal here insists on the peaceful coexistence between stage and prison: the characters on stage "occupy a theatrical space adjacent to the [prisoners'] own." Koshal's analysis overlooks the ways in which the prisoners' responses are both more conventional and more alarming. The convicts engage the characters conventionally, through empathy. At the same time, however, this empathy is strangely coercive. Koshal's summary of these responses as prisoners "offering their own advice" to the characters misses the simultaneously empathetic, brutal, and above all analytic (on equal footing with critics) nature of these intrusions. In addition to experiencing a kind of *transference* (of a psychoanalytic nature) onto Beckett's characters, the prisoners undertake their *transfer* as well. Here we can reverse the directionality of Homan's comment that "it's as if they want to get into the play." It seems rather that the responses of the convicts constitute an attempt to transfer Beckett's characters from the stage to a world more familiar to the inmate: the prisoners want to authorize the movement of the characters from the institution of the stage to the institution of the prison. The hermetic state of Beckett's stage becomes surprisingly communicative to the inmates, whose responses merge the nowhere of the play into the *now here* of the prison. The convicts subject the proceedings to review, not of the traditionally critical sort (a critical review in which they evaluate or analyze), but rather a review that one might give to troops (actors form troupes, after all), something closer to a frisking, a pat down, a calling to order, an asking to declare. Vladimir, Estragon, Lucky, and Pozzo are called to explain themselves to the inmates and fall into line with the everyday power relations that structure the lives of the audience. Where critics deem Beckett's world unfamiliar, the prisoners set about to familiarize the characters to themselves, beginning with the gesture of hailing the character on stage as if he were just another person in the prison yard. The voice of the inmate is expected to turn someone, even someone on stage. Cluchey comments that he "felt secure with [Beckett's] characters . . . because they were so like the people in San Quentin: *extensions* of disconnection, decay and uncertainty."[148] This term "extensions" suggests that the literary and theatrical space appears as an add-on to the closed world of the prison, a space quickly annexed by the prisoners. Shouting at Gogo not to "take all that crap" and asking Lucky why he submits so silently and uncomplainingly, the prisoners request that the characters on stage reckon with the invisible forces that subject them. The prisoners' responses thereby call attention to (and thereby make more palpable) the coercion that pervades Beckett's play in a latent state, like the directives submerged within the stage directions (whatever keeps them from moving, or the fact that Lucky enters with a rope around his neck). The prisoners actively force the characters to take stock of the subtle dynamics of subjection and domination in which they are trapped but to which they seem blind. Through their interjections, the inmates drag out into the open what otherwise goes unsaid. Lines such as Pozzo's "The road is free to all" produce a kind of hollow echo, as if the assertion were waiting for someone to counterbalance its laissez-faire outlook with the state of unfreedom palpable on Beckett's stage. The convict assumes this articulatory agency.

Contrary to Koshal's assertion, these interruptions do not dispel the fictional status of the stage. As Homan observes, "Audiences don't speak to you in character."[149] The inmates' identification with the characters is so intense that it withstands, or is even articulated through, their shouting. These shouts do not address the actors, nor do they call attention to the artifice or judge the quality of the performance. The actor here is just a useful tool to the character, a conduit through which the character explains himself further, rather than the agency behind the character.[150] The inmates are not critical spectators, in Brecht's sense of the term. The distance the inmates take from Brecht is as vast as the one they take from the thing Brecht criticized, namely, empathy in order to forget oneself (we cannot accuse the prisoners of seeking "escapism"). This distance between the inmate audience and Brecht's alienated spectator can be measured through their smoking habits. Brecht advises the audience members to sit, removed from the action, behind their cigars. The prisoners, meanwhile, throw their lit matches in the air behind them after lighting their cigarettes, producing a "flickering luster."[151] En masse, the prisoners illuminate the stage with a cosmos of matches, investing the stage with the world familiar to them. They do not need a play to become alienated; they are already that. Instead of tearing down the fourth wall of the theater, they persistently remind the characters on stage that they are enclosed within the fourth wall of the prison—the one behind the audience's back.

Audiences attending *Godot* premieres in London, Dublin, and Brussels are equally incited to shout, but for reasons entirely different from those of the prisoners. These theatergoers react vociferously to what the play represents rather than to the intricacies of how it unfolds on stage. In Brussels, for example, a scandalized old lady stands up in the middle of the performance and shouts "to her astonished companions in the stalls, 'Why won't they work?'"[152] This irate patron wants the characters to do something useful, to produce the meaning, conflict, and action expected from actors on stage. Implicit in her objection is a criticism that Beckett's play does not perform its theatrical duty and that it does not "work" for her. A theatergoer at the London premiere yells, "This is why we lost the colonies!"[153] Civilian theater patrons feel free to assault theater etiquette under the affidavit of official culture. These comments bear the ethic of compulsory labor or melancholy for the dissolution of the British Empire. Breaking decorum becomes an opportunity to vent a greater outrage, as if the decision to interrupt the audience's silence during a performance revealed a symptomatic wound and not just an isolated instance of boredom pushed to the boiling point. These patrons address their complaints to their fellow audience members rather than to the stage. At the *Godot* premiere in Paris, disgruntled audience members take their seats after intermission, only to depart loudly at the beginning of the second act. These theatergoers take advantage of the fact that there are no armed guards stationed at the exits of the Babylon Theater, as there are at San Quentin. The critical gesture of disaffection depends entirely on the conjunction of these cries of outrage with the movement of the group out of the theater. The demonstration of these patrons, in other words, signifies only that they are spectators, not prisoners.

At the end of one of the performances, Homan notes that one of the prisoners yelled, "You guys—you oughta live here. That'd show you!"[154] Such an invitation can only be issued to a group that somehow already strikes the criminal as *familiar,* a group that has become recognizable ("you guys") to the cons through their interruptions. ("OK! I know this guy! Now, you can get back to the play," says one inmate after being answered.) As with the prisoner Lembke, who claimed that "Godot is among us," this vociferous prisoner offers not a reading but a *sentencing:* the audience member foregoes the activity of judgment on the play (the Brechtian response), the trial, and immediately offers them life in prison. What, exactly, would prison show them? That convicts know more about the total futility of waiting, starting with the fact that it lasts longer than two acts? That waiting may enlist our most miserable solitude, one whose non-sense exceeds the banter of the vagabonds on stage? That you live in prison as a character, and not as an actor? That your agency, your actor, is felt at every moment to have been locked out of the prison? That prison is a dangerous space in which one may be addressed as "pig" but commanded to do more than think? What does it mean to show the theater something? Is it not that this particular prisoner senses that Beckett's world is somehow attentive to the prison (studies the prison) but does not somehow yet incarnate the prison? That Beckett's stage is the prison's antechamber, or even its rehearsal? The shout reverses the priority of subject and predicate within Knowlson's description of the view from Beckett's apartment. The prisoner says, "Let your study face our prison. You should see your study from where we stand."

The Etiquette of the Theater

Koshal writes that "[it] is precisely their experience as the exceptions to [universal discourses of a shared humanity] that allowed prisoners to empathize with Didi and Gogo."[155] The supposition that prisoners do not have the status of humanity seems as cruel as giving a watch to someone with a life sentence. Prisoners exist not outside humanity but outside the discourse of etiquette and the pieties of bourgeois theatergoers. The inmates defy the idiom of "captive audience" that scholars winkingly apply to them.[156] In this regard they take their cue from the play itself: Vladimir and Estragon compare what they are doing onstage to vaudeville and the circus. Critics have noted these affinities between the antics of Beckett's characters and less refined forms of popular entertainment. Kenner notes, for example, how the "antecedents of Beckett's plays are not in literature but—to take a rare American example—in Emmett Kelly's solemn determination to sweep a circle of light into a dustpan: a haunted man whose fidelity to an impossible task . . . illuminates the dynamics of a tragic sense of duty."[157] Yet the comparison remains abstract for cultured audiences: Pascal as played by Fratellini's clowns. Only the inmates respond *as* a vaudeville audience.

Though Esslin claims that the prisoners are a "hypnotized audience," they are not hypnotized out of speech like well-to-do audiences, whose only assault on theater decorum is the sound of a nagging cough. In *Eleuthéria*, Beckett inscribes the spectator onto the stage. A character named Audience Member climbs over the proscenium and engages the actors in dialogue: tellingly, the first thing he does is to emphatically clear his throat: "This farce—(*He again clears his throat, but this time instead of swallowing the result, he expels it into his handkerchief*)—this farce has gone on long enough."[158] The "audience member" claims that he is a kind of collective subject: "I am not one audience member, but a thousand, all slightly different from each other. I've always been like that, like an old blotter, of extremely variable porosity."[159] Unlike *Eleuthéria*, *Waiting for Godot* does not inscribe the audience within its text. Yet the performances of *Godot* at the Florida State Penitentiary allow us to see how convicts assume, with great passion, this blotter function. A blotter is "written upon" only accidentally, as a surface underneath the paper to which one applies ink. The purpose of the blotter is to get the ink flowing from the pen onto the page: although a secondary surface, it enables the writing to begin. Using the figure from *Eleuthéria*, we might describe the criminal audience as being a blotter of such dense porosity that it absorbs *Godot* into carceral space. For the reasons I discuss, some lines of Beckett's bleed through more noticeably than others. This transfer of ink, like the prisoner's attempt to transfer the characters into the yard, describes a movement between institutions: from theater to prison. So much ink transfers to the blotter that this process produces a new script, the script of prison, composed of its gestures, its rituals, its relations under surveillance, and the immediacy of shouting at someone to get their attention. The blotter digests and bleeds back across the theatrical fiction of *Godot*. *Eleuthéria* depicts the audience-blotter as a passive surface that merely registers the excess ink. In prison, this blotter becomes the means by which Beckett's characters *are registered* with the audience and admitted into prison. The performance becomes intimately entwined with its effect on the audience, the mark that it leaves on the criminal blotter.

This absorptive porosity of the criminal audience becomes an agency during the performance. The inmates transfer their porosity over to the text itself, as if the ink absorbed by the blotter began to show through the page. Their interaction strangely fulfills what Beckett describes as his goal toward language. In a letter to Axel Kaun, Beckett states his desire "to bore one hole after another in it, until what lurks behind it—be it something or nothing—begins to seep through."[160] Refusing to be bored, the audience of criminals opens unforeseen holes in Beckett's text in order to let the content of the play seep into the something/nothing of prison. In the process, their responses open holes in our thinking about *Godot*.

Performances of *Waiting for Godot* in the Florida State Penitentiary system force us to consider how indebted our understanding of Beckett's play is to the conventions of the theatrical institution. Theater decorum ensures the riddle of Beckett's work as well as its canonization. One can speak only at the intermission or at the conclusion of the play. Our piety toward etiquette in turn requires that we internalize our questions and postpone our impulse to respond to Beckett's play. We must bite our tongue so often throughout the performance that this organ of articulation is in sorry shape by the time we are called upon to actually say something. We may never stop postponing our response to, and hence our encounter with, *Godot*. Indifferent to etiquette, the prisoners abandon their silence and thereby force the characters to abandon theirs (the unspoken rule that an actor speak only what is written in the script). Perhaps more than any other play,

Godot benefits from the decorum of the theater to sanctify a particular type of silence, to endorse those gaps authored by Beckett himself. *Godot* meshes with the simplest rules of bourgeois theater etiquette, the "Shhhhhh!" that provides Beckett's *Film* with its only sound. Concerned more about forcing the characters to explain what is inaccessible to them than postponing their own misunderstandings, the prisoners reject the wait-and-see attitude. In the process, the inmates refuse to have their silence hijacked as the meaning of Beckett's play, to have mere decorum be mistaken for the grandiose silence of an unresponsive Godot.

2

Waiting for Godot in Sarajevo and New Orleans

> Whatever is said is so far from the experience . . . If you really get down to the disaster, the slightest eloquence becomes unbearable.
> —Samuel Beckett

> Why not Bouvard and Pécuchet in Somalia or Afghanistan?
> —Jean Baudrillard[1]

Godot Summoned by Crisis

Shakespeare's observation that "all the world's a stage" turns unremarkable and everyday reality into space of dramatic potential. The stage gives the world its shape, its value, and its possibility. Yet in what moments does the world begin to resemble Beckett's stage? When does the world perform *Waiting for Godot*? Beckett's work emerges in areas already designated as theaters: theaters of war, of covert operations, of surgery, of crisis. In these contexts the term "theater" designates something other than a building with lobbies, balconies, and curtains. These theaters are formed by circumscribing action and shutting it off from Shakespeare's world stage.[2] Enclosed, sparse, needful, and populated by two vagabond survivors, *Godot* provides the stage for these theaters.

The catastrophe of civil war summons *Godot*. In 1993, at the height of the Bosnian crisis and amidst the violence of ethnic cleansing, Susan Sontag rehearses *Godot* in a partially destroyed theater in Sarajevo. Having "come to care intensely about the battered city and what it stands for," Sontag stages the play as a gesture of solidarity with those living under siege, calling attention to the city's state of crisis.³ Once a multiethnic, tolerant metropolis of "serious culture," which Sontag defines as an "expression of human dignity,"⁴ Sarajevo becomes a city scarred by genocide, shelling, and sniper fire. A play about waiting vagabonds casts light upon the political world order's failure to intervene in Sarajevo's abrupt turn from civilization to barbarism.

Godot is staged again in New Orleans by New York–based artist Paul Chan in the aftermath of the combined natural and man-made disaster of Hurricane Katrina. With assistance from the Classical Theatre of Harlem, which had just closed a Katrina-inspired production of *Godot* featuring a flooded stage, Chan stages Beckett's play in the Lower Ninth Ward and Gentilly, poor sections of New Orleans where the disaster is brutally apparent. The homeless state of Beckett's vagabonds in Chan's production resonates with the unremitting sense of displacement for the population of New Orleans caused by the official evacuation of many of its people to other states (without their subsequent return), the loss of habitable structures, the insufficiency of trailers provided by FEMA, the conversion of the city's inhabitants into refugees, and the memory of its unrecovered dead. Chan's play explores waiting in the continued chaos of disaster along class and race lines.

Godot seems ill suited to bear an agenda. Its reticence about the availability of its meaning to historical, political, or aesthetic interpretation is matched only by the reticence of its author. Existentialism provides the foundation for much of Beckett criticism: it seized the paucity staged by this writer's work to talk about man without faith or god, about ontology and existence. The existentialist, humanist, and new critical angles on Beckett inevitably shear off, one by one, the possible relevancies that can be derived from Beckett's text. Martin Esslin's claim that "no universal lessons, no meanings, no philosophical truths could possibly be derived from the work of a writer like Beckett" is typical.⁵ The ironic byproduct of Beckett's theater of insufficiency is that critics make Beckett's work a self-sufficient experience for the viewer. According to David Bradby, *Godot*'s disturbance to referential functioning makes rethematization or transformation of the play impossible: "[*Godot*] does not imitate an action (in Aristotle's term); it does not even tell a complete story. There is thus little or no scope for relocating the story or setting the characters in a different environment, as, for example, Richard III may be relocated to the period between the two world wars."⁶ Bradby claims that recoding Shakespeare's historical drama is possible because his play strives for likeness. By contrast, Beckett's nonmimetic art furnishes no representation to either warp or recontextualize. As proof, Bradby cites Beckett's remark about the work of James Joyce: "His writing is not *about* something, *it is that something itself.*"[7] Bradby isolates Beckett's work by equating it with an ontological state rather than the representation of one. This tendency culminates in critical works that suggest the audience should relate to *Godot* intuitively, as if to that which bears no message: music. Jonathan Kalb, for one, concedes that historical readings are possible, though he claims they interrupt our aesthetic experience of Beckett's work. "Searching for social and political allegories," he writes, "lead[s] viewers away from present-time experience, away from perceiving the play as music, and toward the refuge of older and more distanced viewing patterns."[8]

But even music is not necessarily a pure aesthetic object. Sontag's protest production was conceived, rehearsed, and performed in the harsh climate of the Siege of Sarajevo. It calls to mind Karl Eliasburg's astonishing performance of Shostakovich's Seventh Symphony performed in the summer of 1942 by a ragtag group of musicians before a starving audience in the midst of the Siege of Leningrad. Broadcast over the lines to the German forces, this performance shows how music can have a rapport with crisis and may in fact help decide the outcome of that crisis. In his essay on *Endgame*, Theodor Adorno reworks the musical model by which critics have strictly underscored Beckett's aesthetic autonomy: "In the act of omission, what is left out survives as something that is avoided, the way consonance survives in atonal harmony."[9] Therefore, Beckett becomes a witness to postwar experience by means of its explicit negation in his work.[10] Adorno claims, "It would be ridiculous to put Beckett on the stand as a star political witness."[11] Yet this is followed by a curious addendum about Beckett's work: "The name of the catastrophe is to be spoken only in silence."[12] Adorno first undercuts Beckett's suitability to stand as a witness: his name is not to be called. He then insists that if Beckett is called after all, he bears witness neither by speaking nor by remaining silent, but through a combination of both.

Critics aside, there is some evidence that Beckett himself discourages the engagement of history and politics with his work, and encourages a more hermetic critical and directorial approach. In Beckett's translation of *Godot* into English, for example, he removes the names Roussillon and Bonnelly, which provide context and situate the play historically.[13] Specifically these names bind the text to Beckett's own biography. They refer to the area in the south of France and the farmer with whom Beckett and his future wife, Suzanne, stayed while pursuing Resistance activities during World War II. Beckett eliminates the names Roussillon, Bonnelly, and Suzanne in a novel way. He replaces them with a snapping of fingers, making them vanish into Vladimir's amnesia: "But we were there together, I could swear to it! Picking grapes for a man called . . . (*he snaps his fingers*) . . . can't think of the name of the man, at a place called . . . (*snaps his fingers*) . . . can't think of the name of the place, do you not remember?"[14] The physical inertia on Beckett's stage becomes emblematic of a work where memory cannot be jogged.

How, then, in the face of this kind of evidence (or lack of it) can *Godot* be called to testify for historical crisis? Do Sarajevo and New Orleans offer conditions that are suitably absurd or "ridiculous," as Adorno claims, to call Beckett to the witness stand? As witness in these settings, does *Godot* offer only silence? The play clearly does not appeal through any therapeutic directive. Its only slogan is its first line: "nothing to be done." From there it advances only to break God's failure down into smaller degenerative disorders. Lucky hails "divine apathia, divine athambia, divine aphasia" (divine apathy, imperturbability, and muteness).[15] The abandonment of man by God is a theme that courses throughout philosophy. Martin Heidegger's essay "What Are Poets For?" describes a turning away not only from man by god, but from god by man.[16] Heidegger's essay even reads at times as a *Godot* explained to philosophers: "The era is defined by the god's failure to arrive."[17] Like Beckett, Heidegger discerns this abandonment as a condition of destitution and ever-growing need: "At this night's midnight, the destitution of the time is greatest. Then the destitute time is no longer able even to experience its condition. That inability, by which even the destitution of the destitute state is obscured, is the time's absolutely destitute character. The destitution is wholly obscured, in that it now appears as nothing more than the need that wants to be met."[18] *Godot* emerges within landscapes of crisis, however, because of its dissimilarity to these concepts. Ultimately, Heidegger is concerned with spiritual, philosophical, and aesthetic issues. Beckett's play conveys a curiously practical concern about the obstinacy of need: "curiously practical" because in conventional theater settings Beckett's reduced forms strike us as the apex of theatrical experimentation. Within the context of war-torn Sarajevo and post-Katrina New Orleans, these same reduced means strike survivors as the provisional terms of their existence. *Godot* renders poverty not as concept but as condition. Within the "Sottisier" notebook in the Beckett Archive, held at Reading University, we find what might be the closest thing to a Beckettian motto: "Penury is all."[19] The fact that this line remains in Beckett's notebook suggests it does not belong on his stage. Beckett's work appeals to people in situations of need because it refuses to generalize their condition or convert it into a moral (as "penury is all" does). Beckett furnishes no philosophy to the audience. Likewise, Lucky enumerates the symptoms of divine failure. Compared to the dramatic turn away by Heidegger's god, Lucky's etiology is at once more particular and more radiant. As Beckett describes it, "It concerns a God who turns himself in all directions at the same time."[20]

Replacing names and history with a snapping of fingers does not completely eliminate what is historical from the play. Taking Beckett's removal of Roussillon and Bonnelly less as an elimination of the historical than its odd displacement into the gestural helps us think about what role history and politics may have within the confines of the play itself. In other words, Vladimir's inability to remember the name of the historical place does not eliminate history from the play so much as personalize it. The audience is invited to supply the missing relationship, to remember where they might have been prior to the predicament that immerses them. For Vladimir, that memory is of picking grapes: for the survivor of the siege or flood, even the smallest memory of place might retain this utopic or Edenic flavor.

This personalization in the moments of silence in Beckett's text may help us account for the strange solace that besieged audiences take from Beckett's vagabonds. An affinity between Sarajevo and *Godot* can be heard faintly in the following description of the city by Juan Goytisolo:

> In this city where there is no wood to make coffins, you must get used to sleeping, moving, walking about fully aware of your defenseless, precarious existence. Nobody can guarantee that a crack marksman hasn't chanced to get your insignificant self in his sights or that a grenade or shell won't explode inside your room. The inhabitants of Sarajevo have withstood for more than a year this risk of extermination, their life as inmates of an open prison, with integrity, dignity, and sangfroid. But the combined effect of hunger, exhaustion, and a general feeling of betrayal and abandonment has finally overtaken them from the day the shameful Washington accord was signed, forcing their moral resistance to the limit of what is bearable.[21]

History conspires to turn the description of a city under siege into a synopsis of Beckett's play. Abandonment, hunger, the limit of the bearable, life without assurance: uncannily these are the fundamental terms for any analysis of *Godot*. It suggests that Sarajevo had become a living paraphrase for the play Sontag brings to the city. Most notably, Guytisolo mentions how inhabitants live "as inmates of an open prison." Sarajevo prepares its residents in the labor of useless waiting they see on Beckett's stage in the same way, as we have seen, San Quentin prepares Cluchey, Bandman, Lembke, and the other convicts. As with the inmates, it is not a question of what the Sarajevans see in the play but of how they experience a feeling of affirmation because the play sees (understands, anticipates) the audience. For Erika Munk, a theater critic who attends Sontag's production, the audience becomes an emotional viaduct connecting the play to the situation of its performance: "The *Waiting for Godot* directed by Susan Sontag in Sarajevo is impossible to think about, on some deep level doesn't exist, outside its immediate situation. The war's emotional consequences—fear, hopelessness, gallows wit, grief, defiance—permeated every moment and affected everyone involved, and the siege's practical effects dictated rehearsal conditions, lighting, sound, seating, performance times, and the physical space."[22] Under what conditions might Beckett's play provide not just an immediate reaction but only an immediate reaction? When might the *unmemorable* nature of a performance be a tribute to its power? While *Godot* dismays, perplexes, or invites appreciation from the audiences in the Old Vic, Lincoln Center, and the Babylon Theater, its performance in Sarajevo offers no residue for thought or memory. The experience of *Godot* expires in a transient emotive state, which afterward cannot rise into consciousness (let alone discourse). The catharsis is the work of a double performance: the war acts on the audience as much as Beckett's play. Munk's discussion does not make clear which way the audience is facing: toward the ruined city or toward the stage. The war's "emotional consequences—fear, hopelessness" are the themes of Beckett's play. In the Sarajevo performance, these "themes" lose their obstinate form, their articulation becomes frailer, and they become recognizable to the audience.

Beckett's stage exposes something to audiences who are already waiting, and the play emerges for them as a reading of their predicament. In the epigraph to this chapter, Beckett says that when you really get down to the catastrophe—the humble directionality of Beckett's approach is important here—the slightest eloquence becomes unbearable. Beckett may appeal to survivors by his very slightness (Beckett's signature minimum) of eloquence. Something like a stammer, rather than literary or political eloquence (speaking crafted for public effect), is needed in a catastrophe. This stammer is evident throughout the text of the play. Vladimir and Estragon frequently speak to one another as if locked in a game of hand over hand, having breath for no more than a few words at a time. This is how they diagnose the condition of Lucky, tethered with a rope:

> VLADIMIR. A running sore!
> ESTRAGON. It's the rope.
> VLADIMIR. It's the rubbing.
> ESTRAGON. It's inevitable.
> VLADIMIR. It's the knot.
> ESTRAGON. It's the chafing. [. . .] Look at the slobber.
> VLADIMIR. It's inevitable.
> ESTRAGON. Look at the slaver.
> VLADIMIR. Perhaps he's a halfwit.
> ESTRAGON. A cretin.
> VLADIMIR. (*looking closer*). Looks like goiter.
> ESTRAGON. (*ditto*). It's not certain.[23]

There is no steady progress through diagnosis here, just the heaping of statements that slightly mutate from one to the next. Instead of the conclusive authority of a second opinion, doctors Vladimir and Estragon offer only the slightly different, slightly redundant superaddition of an nth opinion. They set the tone for a play in which language doesn't entirely *take*. The twilit sky of *Godot* both inspires Pozzo's exaggerated monologue ("What is there so extraordinary about it? Qua sky?") and obstructs Vladimir's effort to describe it to his blind interlocutor:

> POZZO. (*anguished*) Is it evening?
> VLADIMIR. Anyway it hasn't moved.[24]

Beckett's play embodies waiting and a future that never arrives rather than a prescience. It thereby taps into a survivor mentality of weariness and futility mixed with inexplicable, unjustified persistence. The badges of despair and futility have been pinned firmly to Beckett's work, as they have been to Kafka's. The crucial difference between the two, and the reason why nobody volunteered to read *Das Schloß* aloud to the people of Sarajevo, is that Beckett's work does not try to foresee our despair. *Godot* forecasts nothing because it never hints that things can change. In *Godot*, even the weather is stuck.

Precursor to Sarajevo and New Orleans: *Godot* in McComb, Mississippi

Waiting for Godot appears in environments of need before Chan and Sontag. As part of the civil rights movement, the Free Southern Theater takes the play through thirty towns in the rural South. They perform for predominantly African American audiences in Mississippi, Louisiana, and Georgia before completing their tour in New York.[25] *Godot* is adapted to the agrarian clock: performances are scheduled for late afternoon so the audience can get home. Many of the spectators apparently have never seen a play before. Reports of the performances indicate that their fascination with the theater begins with the fact that "it wasn't a 'meeting,' and it wasn't a movie; it was something else. Someone opened the window."[26] Beckett's play opens the window to a different type of gathering combining the personal urgency of the town meeting with the distraction of cinema.

Critics doubted the relevance of *Godot* to rural audiences. Part of this is an assumed incapacity of rural audiences to "understand" a play that remains opaque to people thoroughly familiar with theater as spectacle. Actor and director John O'Neal writes that the *Godot* productions in Mississippi "irritated the hell out of people. Time and time again, the question was raised, 'What possible relevance do you imagine *Godot* to have to the lives of Black people in the South?'"[27] The irritated people are not in the audience, but are those who estimate the audience and have already arrived at a verdict on *Godot*. Their irritation implies Beckett's play is a refined work of culture beyond the grasp of country bumpkins: What is a line like "there's no lack of void" to these spectators, and they to it?[28] Is *Godot* accessible only through one's education, through research, or through criticism?[29] Should one audience of *Godot* presume to claim ownership over the play's relevance?[30] A spectator to the performances of the Free Southern Theater offers a rejoinder to these skeptics: "If theater means anything anywhere, it certainly ought to mean something here!"[31] This urgent exclamation is closer to the heart of Beckett's play: meaning is hypothetical and yet necessary, rooted in the place. The meaning of theater is not guaranteed. Though it may not exist, it might just have a chance in McComb.

The varied and extreme circumstances of *Godot* performances provide an indication not of the capacity of an audience to appreciate the play, but of the necessity of an audience to create its relevance. Relevance is more intimate than meaning, as it pertains to the way a work addresses us and how we situate ourselves before it. Can the relevance of *Godot* or any play ever be calculated?[32] *Godot* poses the question of relevance to the audience by removing the stable psychological reference points, welcoming chance into the audience's confrontation with it. Without these reference points the spectator (in the Babylon Theater in Paris as in McComb's town hall) must work with and against the play to discern how it happens. "Finding" the play relevant only signals the discovery of this process—something the audience makes rather than something foreordained by the play. This is the reason why Beckett's play persistently is interesting to people who have never seen theater, audiences unimpeded by either a preimagining of its relevance or an overexpectation of its uses for them. Richard Schechner observes, "The New York audience looked for meanings; they saw the play in the context of a hundred critics. In New Orleans and McComb they looked at Beckett's play—right in the face—and they laughed at the characters."[33]

The Free Southern Theater, part of the Black Arts Movement, enlists *Godot* not for the purpose of educating its audience, not to impart a lesson, but rather simply as an encounter. Noting how one man in the audience mumbled something toward the actors after the show, "slave . . . whupped him. . . . no! . . . ," O'Neal observes, "He felt something, but he couldn't get the words to say it. That's our job: to help this man find the vocabulary to say what he wants to say."[34]

The tour of Free Southern Theater's *Godot* sheds light on the way in which the play deceptively invites audiences to relate to it through their circumstances, who they are and where they happen to be. The performers suggest how audiences in New York engage the play differently from those in the rural South. Richard Schechner notes that "New York is a rich enough city for despair to become an occupation."[35] Despair is not a hobby for the New York spectator: it is a calling. By contrast, he notes, "The McComb audience doesn't have the kind of despair which depends upon the separation of thought and act. *Godot* was really a comedy in New Orleans and Mississippi. They laughed at Lucky; in New York they were embarrassed by a Negro at the end of a white man's rope."[36]

What happens to Beckett's play when its existentialism goes unnoticed by the audience? The despair of rural audiences pertains to other aspects of their lives, perhaps to the limitations imposed on the life of a sharecropper. But they do not invest in the despair emerging from the "separation of thought and act." Existentialism does not intercept their understanding of the play. Consequently, they magnify the actors' incapacity to move as a clownish game, not as the demonstration of a concept. Ironically, this audience's refusal of this type of despair allows *Godot* to become a play for the activist cause. Schechner reports, "'We're *not* waiting!' they said, during and after the play."³⁷ This connects the despair of the audience to something other than a philosophy of despair (despair as occupation or as hobby). The spectators in Mississippi therefore react to *Godot* in a highly relevant but critically unconventional way: they see it as an injunction to act.

Sontag and the Usefulness of Theater

Sontag's performance of *Waiting for Godot* is born of a desire to make herself useful to the cause of a battered city. In April 1993, when Sontag visits her journalist son covering the genocidal war in Sarajevo, then in Yugoslavia, she arrives in a city under persistent attack from artillery and snipers positioned in the surrounding hills. "Without water, gas, electricity, public transport, or telephones," observes Goytisolo, "Sarajevo looks at first sight like a phantom city, a dislocated skeleton or a lifeless corpse. But the intermittent crackle of machine-gun fire, the occasional blast of mortars, the whistle of snipers' bullets opportunely remind the visitor that its torture continues."³⁸ Sontag explains a need to take action: "I don't want to be a tourist—it's not, for me, enough to make a symbolic visit."³⁹ She expresses an idea to direct a play to Haris Pašović, a director who oversees wartime productions of Euripides's *Alcestis* and Sophocles's *Ajax*. When he replies, "What play?" Sontag notes, "Bravado suggested to me in an instant what I might not have seen had I taken longer to reflect: there was one obvious play for me to direct. Beckett's play, written over forty years ago, seems written for, and about, Sarajevo."⁴⁰ As Sontag admits, this is a radical, even if unthinking, proposal.

What makes *Godot* the "obvious" choice for Sontag? For her the play is not esoteric but illustrative, "so apt an illustration of the feelings of Sarajevans now—bereft, hungry, dejected, waiting for an arbitrary, alien power to save them or take them under its protection."⁴¹ It may also be obvious because of the monologue in the second act that pierces the haze of inaction on stage. Vladimir's speech is about the call to conscience, about responding to another's need: "To all mankind they were addressed, those cries for help still ringing in our ears! But at this place, at this moment of time, all mankind is us, whether we like it or not. Let us make the most of it, before it is too late."⁴² Vladimir defines mankind as those who hear the appeal for help. The cries ring in everyone's ears like a general alert, but "mankind" discerns how these address us, according to the place and time in which we happen to be. "Nobody can plead ignorance," writes Sontag, "of the atrocities that have taken place in Bosnia since the war started in April 1992."⁴³ Sontag claims the failure is not of knowledge but of response, the very topic of Vladimir's speech. "Why so little response to what happened in Bosnia?"⁴⁴ In her mission in Sarajevo, Sontag may have been emboldened by the powerful contraction in Vladimir's monologue: "all mankind is us, whether we like it or not." Only responding makes us human and it may not be our choice.

From Vladimir's speech Sontag borrows the notion of an address that marks its audience. She applies this in her claim that *Godot* was written "for and about Sarajevo." This transposition ignores the way *Godot* is not "for" audiences at all, let alone about particular audiences. Rather than being addressed to audiences, Beckett's work is abandoned to them. Beckett develops an aesthetic suitable to the indigence of the figures that populate his world. Though a few of Beckett's stories begin with a literal eviction notice, his whole oeuvre bears the stamp of one. One of his characters brings the vagabond moment back even further: "I gave up before birth."⁴⁵ If Kafka's work embraces primordial guilt, Beckett's embraces prenatal dispossession. Giving up predates having something to give up, or something on which to give up. Abandonment happens without prior ownership. His work does not welcome the model of reciprocity, of giving and taking, between a work and its audience. The last lines of Beckett's late play *What Where* indicate that it intends no transfer of sense to the reader. They instead issue a conflicting mixture of specific demand and open invitation: "Time passes. That is all. *Make sense who may.* I switch off."⁴⁶

What is the public utility of theater? Sontag claims that the play is "about and for Sarajevo" because she envisions it as useful to the Sarajevans in their plight. She discusses directing in relationship to plumbing: "I was not under the illusion that going to Sarajevo to direct a play would make me useful in the way I could be if I were a doctor or a water systems engineer. It would be a small contribution."⁴⁷ Brushing aside suggestions made by journalists that the Sarajevans would rather have escapist entertainment for their suffering, Sontag writes, "In Sarajevo, as anywhere else, there are more than a few people who feel strengthened and consoled by having their sense of reality affirmed and transfigured by art."⁴⁸

Ultimately, Sontag's argument for the utility of staging *Godot* is that the threatened condition of the vagabonds on Beckett's stage will evoke reflection upon the reality of the Sarajevans facing comparable threats. The utility of the play is also practical in nature: she gives a maximum number of unemployed actors in Sarajevo a chance to perform by turning Vladimir and Estragon into three couples. On this count she says the play becomes a microcosm of prewar life. The production "means so much to the local theatre professionals in Sarajevo because it allows them to be normal, that is, to do what they did before the war; to be not just haulers of water or passive recipients of humanitarian aid."[49]

Sontag defends the usefulness of performing Beckett in Sarajevo against the journalists who doubt her project. Much as the Free Southern Theater's staging of *Godot* in McComb, Mississippi, had been questioned, so too is the performance in Sarajevo: "Why theater, in the middle of a war and a genocide?"[50] "Isn't putting on a play like fiddling while Rome burns?"[51] and "Why not *Bouvard and Pécuchet* in Somalia or Afghanistan?"[52] By implying that war and genocide should go on uninterrupted by even the slightest impertinence, such questions implicitly cast their vote for the aggressor.[53] The query "Why theater?" never arises when Beckett's play is performed at Carnegie Hall. Where it is sanctioned by wealth and protected by convention, culture's uselessness elicits no questioning. Emerging in the midst of crisis, however, theater is suddenly called upon to account for its existence. *Godot* is an interesting artifact to put against this wall. The play offers neither an evident gesture of protest nor a wholesome lesson. It provides the opposite of an enriching experience. Performing *Godot* seems indeed very close to fiddling, but with a reservation. *Godot* does not accompany, like a soundtrack, the burning of Sarajevo. Closer to contrapuntal fiddling, this play breaks up the secondary meanings of music as war's accompaniment: to go with war, to vouchsafe for it, to supplement it, to befriend it. Jean Baudrillard attempts to rhetorically dramatize Beckett's uselessness by facetiously suggesting that Sontag bring Flaubert's novel (*Bouvard and Pécuchet*) to other settings of crisis. What if we were to honor Baudrillard's hyperbole? What *would* Flaubert's novel about two failures, engineers of countless futilities who clearly prefigure Vladimir and Estragon, sound like in a square in Mogadishu? By proposing for Sontag a work that is consumed in solitude, Baudrillard indicates that he misses the point of both performing a play and performing Beckett's play in particular. *Godot* begins by announcing that nothing is to be done. What it performs is all that must be undone, a diligently negative labor. It undoes the questions through which we coercively ferret out the practical value of the artwork. It requires us to rethink the use value of theater. *Godot* achieves this not by asserting its utility but by belaboring, even tiring out, all the variations on this question of "Why?"

Aquilex: Reading Beckett's (F)utility

One of the first casualties of the war in Sarajevo was the water and sewer system. Sontag locates Beckett's usefulness in relation to these public utilities. She says that as a director she does not have the same obvious usefulness to the city as a water systems engineer, yet she also says she produces something that treats the people of Sarajevo as "more than just haulers of water."[54] Comparing engineering, with its obvious necessity and applicability, to theater begs the question: What is the value of theater and how is that value measured? Furthermore, how is that value different in an impoverished landscape—or a landscape of poverty?

Beckett himself offers a way to think about the relationship between theater and water hauling. Specifically in an early essay on Joyce, he traces the author's debt to the work of Dante, Bruno, and Giambattista Vico. Beckett connects Joyce's fiction to the evolution of language described in the *Scienza Nuova*. Paraphrasing Vico, Beckett says the oldest poetry must be regarded "not as sophisticated confectionery" but as "evidence of a poverty-stricken vocabulary and of a disability to achieve abstraction."[55] The evolution of language into "a highly civilized vehicle, rich in abstract and technical terms, was as little fortuitous as the evolution of society itself."[56] Beckett says that Joyce's writing more closely resembles the materiality of the "poverty-stricken" vocabulary, in which content and form are entwined, than it does a "civilized vehicle," in which language functions as the neutral bearer of abstraction.[57]

Beckett's emphasis on the poverty and disability of language (over its "richness") anticipates *Godot*. It also tells us how to read Vladimir's gesture of snapping fingers as a substitute in the English translation of the play for specific places in France. As an example of the evolution of language out of its "dumb form" (gesture) Beckett discusses the etymology of the Latin word *lex*.

1. Lex = Crop of acorns.
2. Ilex = Tree that produces acorns.
3. Legere = To gather.
4. Aquilex = He that gathers the waters.
5. Lex = Gathering together of peoples, public assembly.
6. Lex = Law.
7. Legere = To gather together letters into a word, to read.[58]

I propose that *aquilex*, the fourth word in the etymology, provides us with a trope for understanding the utility of theater and offers a figure for reading Beckett. If Joyce's work rescues the hieroglyphic function of early sign systems, Beckett's oeuvre compels reading that activates the full declension of *legere*. Beckett's destitute work blocks reading defined as an abstract accumulation.

Grazing on the failure of anything to happen, the characters in *Godot* furnish little for us to inventory or synopsize. There is little by way of flora and fauna for us to glean. What we can gather is gathered like water. Like the figure of an aquilex, we sense how the term "gathering" already overstates our role. Reading Beckett, as the successful productions in Sarajevo, New Orleans, and prisons show, requires none of the expertise of the mushroom gatherer who must discern edible from poisonous. There is no expertise needed in the gathering of water. H. Porter Abbott uses the term "arbitrary winnowing" to describe the scattered and paratactic narration of Beckett's "From an Abandoned Work."[59] Winnowing, however, separates what is worth keeping from what should be discarded. It is a gesture of discrimination, whereas water gathering is a gesture of both need and futility. We know it to be impossible to capture a moving source. Water flows together but is not something that can be gathered like acorns. The impropriety of the term is relevant to the "gathering" that we try to do while reading Beckett.

The subadequate quantity of sense makes Beckett's work elusive. There is no rushing force, no dramatic dynamism. *Godot* abounds in moments we call negligible or impoverished only because they do not hang around long enough for us to take note. For example, Vladimir picks up the "thinking hat" that Lucky leaves on the stage and asks, "How does it fit me?" To this Estragon replies, "How would I know?"[60] The question of how he looks precipitates an epistemological crisis. Only after the conversation moves on do we belatedly register the difference between Vladimir's understanding of *fit* (Does it suit me?) and Estragon's (How tight is the hat?).[61] Such tears in the fabric of meaning—so small that they ask to go unaccounted for—propel the characters' dialogues. Sense, abandoned as soon as the vagabonds gather it, slips like water through our fingers.

That Beckett's work frustrates the reader's tight grasp over it is evidenced by an anecdote told by his friend, Romanian philosopher E. M. Cioran. Cioran meets with Beckett one evening and announces that he will not go to bed until he thinks up a French translation for the title of Beckett's short story "Lessness." Together they consider the gamut of forms suggested by *moins* and *moindre*, but "none of them seemed to us to come near the inexhaustible *lessness*, a blend of loss and infinitude, an emptiness synonymous with apotheosis."⁶² Trying to align Beckett's elusive term with a counterpart in French continues to gnaw at Cioran even after they part for the evening. He stays awake into the night, counting not sheep but derivations of the Latin *sine*, and goes to sleep only after settling on *sinéité*. Possibly because the term suggests a condition of being without, rather than being less, Cioran and Beckett decide to give up the search and settle on *Sans*. They conclude that "there was no noun in French capable of expressing absence in itself, pure unadulterated absence, and that we had to resign ourselves to the metaphysical poverty of a preposition."⁶³ Is this metaphysical poverty a resignation or an achievement? Beckett's poverty baffles the resources of language such that it requires the translator to mix the parts of speech. In clutching at a preposition in order to translate a noun, Cioran reveals some of the impropriety of speech contained in the term *aquilex*.

Whereas Sontag says *Godot* will address the audience as "more than just haulers of water or passive recipients of humanitarian aid," Beckett's work is careful not to have the reader exceed (either in value or cultural prestige) the water hauler. Beckett's work resituates the reader's activity around earlier gestural forms of gathering. In Sarajevo the audience is literally one of water haulers, despite Sontag's desire to have the play annul that status. The Sarajevans themselves speak of the difference between New York and Sarajevo as a difference in plumbing. This difference for them becomes the step toward reimagining the theater along Beckettian lines. As actor Izudin Bajrovic says, "Let me explain the difference between Sarajevo and New York theater. It's the same difference as the difference in significance between a four liter plastic water container here in Sarajevo and in New York. In New York you buy it full of water and you put it in the fridge and use it up and throw it away. No story. Here we can make a production about finding and filling this container which would last for 18 hours and a half."⁶⁴ Actor Emina Muftig quickly follows this up with "After that, with its contents, we could wash one human body."⁶⁵ Bajrovic pictures theater as a drama of the *aquilex*, beginning with the quest to find a container. The container is filled and emptied without stop, an infinite cycle resembling the punishment in ancient hell of the Danaïdes, forced to draw water using leaky buckets and hence guaranteeing their work would always be in vain. Bajrovic's hypothetical play is the Sarajevan street version of *Godot*, much longer, much emptier, and transposing the water gatherer from the audience onto the stage.

Theater without a Lobby

Sontag stages only the first act of *Waiting for Godot* and offers competing justifications for her decision to eliminate the second act from her performance. On the one hand, she grounds this decision in practical considerations: Sarajevo now lacks sufficient facilities for a full and proper production of the play, she says. On the other hand, Sontag invokes a humanitarian mission: the people of Sarajevo have been through enough already. They are hungry. They are injured. They have lost family members. A relentless shelling continues, and bombs threaten to destroy anything at any moment—including the space of the theater itself. It is too much to ask them to sit through a second act of *Godot*. Furthermore, Sontag seems to say, even if the theater were safe (which it is not), even if the people were not hungry (though they are), she would not stage the second act because it portrays a relentless hopelessness that runs counter to her mission and ambition for the play in Sarajevo.

Critics have mostly been unable to unravel the logic and complexity of Sontag's argument. They tend to emphasize either the infidelity of the production to Beckett's play or the supposed selfishness of Sontag's gesture. Everett Frost does both in observing, "Chopping the play in half for Sarajevo, as if it were the lady in the circus, makes at least as much sense as tearing it into digestible little bits, like Pentheus, for sticking into film documentaries on Beckett, on modern theatre, existentialism, etc."[66] In this highly colorful remark, Frost distances himself from Sontag's claim that abbreviating the play was a humanitarian gesture and blinds himself to Sontag's argument for its necessity. "Chopping" for Frost is a magician's stage spectacle performed on behalf of Sarajevo.[67] He compares Sontag's work to activities that go on ideally in isolation. Frost ignores how war is not a mere backdrop for Sontag's play but behind Sontag's decision. Cutting the play in two makes little sense, but not because it resembles a mysterious trick. It makes little sense because the break is precipitated by the senseless intrusion of the war into the theater. The war's arrival is as senseless as would be Godot's, were he to appear. Frost's comparison ignores the violence of the interruption. In the circus act, neither the box nor the woman is really sawed in half. The wooden box is imperceptibly cut before the performance so that its two halves can be separated on stage. Yet Sontag saws prior to this cut. The war induces a fissure in the play along an unprescribed line, short of the one set by Beckett through the division of the play into two acts. Like an audience member at the circus, Frost is spellbound by the removal of the second half, but what are we to make of the more preposterous removal: the amputation of the intermission?

What tangible and practical constraints are placed by the war, and how do they force the directorial hand? Although the theater itself where the piece was performed was apparently intact, shelling destroyed most of the auxiliary spaces, including the lobby. Sontag's performance deals with the loss of these spaces to the war. She describes how she had to take a path outside the range of sniper fire to get to the only usable entryway to the theater: a stage door in the back. She explains, "The theatre's façade, lobby, cloakroom, and bar had been wrecked by shelling more than a year earlier and the debris still had not been cleared away."[68] This is no mere architectural detail to Sontag's story. It shows the effect of shelling on the place of performance and seems in itself to make her point that war affects the theater (the building) before it affects the theater (the institution). Theater contoured itself and reimagined itself in accordance with the spaces available in the besieged city. Dubravko Bibanovic, director of the Sarajevo War Theater, takes this further: theater becomes a refuge, a strategy for survival. He performs his work *Bomb Shelter* in basements throughout the city, "not because they are appropriate environments for the theme but because they offer a safe haven from snipers and bombardments."[69]

But Sontag is not content just to assert that the physical space does not allow for the full performance. She also has a humanitarian mission: she says that the audience is itself bombed out. No more than the physical space of the theater is the audience capable of absorbing more Beckett. It is as if it, too, is shell-shocked and lacks, due to trauma brought on by the war, the capacity to experience the full play as Beckett wrote it. "How could I ask the audience, which would have no lobby, bathroom, or water, to sit so uncomfortably, without moving, for two and a half hours?"[70] Thus Sontag mediates the ruined performance space and the grimness of the play itself. The two seem to have an additive, even synergistic impact in that Beckett's drama and the impaired theater facility create an uncomfortable and immobilizing experience for the spectator. Sontag's practical impulse involves the physical world and physical and spatial limitations. Her humanitarian impulse is grounded in the psychological, the subjective condition of members of the audience.

The destroyed lobby of the Youth Theater of Saravejo changes the function of waiting for a play in which, like no other, waiting is essential. One way to tackle the question of the double emergence of the practical and humanitarian impulse in Sontag's writing on the production is to look closely at the role of the lobby in Sontag's directorial argument. In destroying the lobby, the war inflicted damage on the architecture of the *Godot* experience. The elimination of the paraperformance space exemplifies this lack of choice the war imposes. Stated differently, the war occasions only an uninterrupted *Godot*. In her introductory remarks to the audience before the play, Sontag suggests that it was the war that somehow cut the play in half. Only act 1 is performed because "Sarajevo itself seems to be in a historical first act."[71] The war forces Sontag to extract from *Waiting for Godot* that period of grace in which the spectator can ask whether she wants to go back, either for more or for less. The spectator returns either because her expectation (a type of hope) has not been adequately undone by act 1 or because she wants to affirm the futile waiting of the play and get away from the socialized waiting of the lobby space.

But because there is no place to go, no lobby for the audience to retire to and no space outside the space of performance, the audience in the Sarajevo production is quite literally pulled on stage. Illuminated only by the "uncontrollable chiaroscuro" of a few candles, Sontag has the audience huddle at the periphery of the stage.[72] War conditions bring the audience nearer to the waiting characters. In a separate context, Hugh Kenner remarks that "the stage is a place to wait. The place itself waits when no one is in it."[73] In *Endgame*, the curtain rises to reveal figures covered in sheets, like objects in storage protected from the gathering dust. Where *Endgame* confines waiting to the stage, the waiting process bleeds out of *Godot* into the spaces adjacent to the stage: the audience area and the lobby, a space less often noted as significant to Beckett's play. Soon after the curtain rises for act 2, Vladimir asks, "And where were we yesterday evening, according to you?" To this Estragon replies, "How would I know? In another compartment. There's no lack of void."[74] The structure of the theater consists of a series of waiting compartments: the lobby, the house, the empty prison cell, or the depopulated areas outside the Youth Theater. The stage is as empty and unremarkable as these other spaces. The Sarajevo performance of *Godot* without a lobby and before an audience—locked first in a theater of war and then in a theater during war—is in fact highly Beckettian. Sontag notes that the audience is as if paralyzed, "unable to move for two and a half hours." She does not clarify the source of the audience's paralysis, whether it is caused by Beckett's play (partially hypnotic, like a broken stopwatch swinging before the eyes) or the fact that this audience has nowhere to take a break, that is, *no recourse*.[75] The war triggers not only Sontag's decision to stage half the play (no lobby, no second act) but also an audience experience wholly locked inside the theater, in the manner of the prisoner in his cell.

The lobby is typically a theater's designated space for waiting. For every play, the intermission is when the audience waits for the second act to begin. The waiting during *Godot*'s intermission brings the waiting during the play to a different level of reflection. The spectators wait among each other and convert their waiting into opinion, chatter. The setting enforces a gregarious and more occupied form of waiting, yet the suspicions about what we are waiting for (during the play) do not abate. The war forces us to approach the question of directorial fidelity differently. How does one remain faithful to an intermission? What function is served by the pause between the acts of *Godot*? Focused on the production as she is, Sontag fails to ask these questions. She attributes the potential discomfort of her audience to two and a half hours of sedentary waiting. No play makes us more painfully aware of our seated posture as spectators: the characters' concluding vow to leave, freezing into an immobile tableau before the drop of the curtain, inspires an awkward uncertainty in us about getting up. While in the lobby we ponder whether we want to return to our seats. Without electricity the Youth Theater cannot even oblige the ceremony of dimming the lights to signal the end of intermission.

The lobby provides the space of a decision, where we either affirm or break our contract with the play. Only here can we curtail waiting without interrupting that of either the audience or the actors during the performance. Innumerable anonymous departures in the intermission counterbalance the one great no-show after which the play takes its name. We have, however, one departure on record.[76] Giacometti sculpts a tree and a single leaf for Beckett's stage in a 1961 production of *Godot*. Beckett writes, "Giacometti did a fine tree for *Godot*. . . . But at the Générale [he] left at the interval because he couldn't bear it any longer! His tree, he said, perhaps he meant something else."[77] Knowlson's comment that "both tree and leaf have disappeared" does not address the question: Why does Giacometti disappear?[78] Sitting at a forced remove from his own work, did the artist feel the waiting process eating into him? Was he dismayed at the way the vagabonds do everything but take an axe to it? Giacometti's luminous tree, resembling a subaquatic creature with long tentacles for branches, undergoes slow defoliation throughout act 1.[79] Did Giacometti depart out of pride? Vladimir and Estragon first want to instrumentalize Giacometti's artwork by hanging themselves from it, before it is made inadequate for that purpose. They undercut the singularity of the sculpture by suggesting Godot means them to wait by another tree—lone-standing, the tree is not unique and has a forest of likenesses. It might even be the wrong tree. They argue over its classification: willow or bush? The artist did not hang around long enough to hear Vladimir say, "[*looking round*] 'It's indescribable. It's like nothing. There's nothing. There's a tree.'"[80] The dialogue in the first act is a verbal handbook on how to disassemble not just Giacometti's tree but also the tree image Ferdinand de Saussure uses in his *Course on General Linguistics* to exemplify the imprint left in the mind by the signifier *arbor/ un arbre*.[81]

It is not clear whether or not Sontag needs or wants a lobby in Sarajevo, since there were humanitarian reasons not to perform the second act. The bombs ruin the lobby and make intermission impossible. The sedentary confinement of her audience offers only part of Sontag's reason to break the play off at intermission. She also says that their suffering outside the theater may be placated by her decision. She amputates their grief. About act 2, Sontag observes, "Not only has one more day gone by. Everything is worse. Lucky no longer can speak, Pozzo is now pathetic and blind, Vladimir has given in to despair. Perhaps I felt that the despair of Act I was enough for the Sarajevo audience, and I wanted to spare them a second time when Godot does not arrive."[82] Munk, in attendance at several performances of *Godot* in Sarajevo, echoes Sontag: "The unrelenting grimness of a second act in which things repeat themselves only to get worse was too cruel a gift for this audience."[83] An intermission in this context would only offer a pause in the steady escalation of misery in the play. Sontag's production ultimately replaces this worsening with a finality. She underscores the positive by-product of this decision. By seeing nothing happen only once, and not twice, hope would be spared for the audience: "Maybe I wanted to propose, subliminally, that Act II might be different."[84]

What Is Enough: Is Beckett's Intention Lost in Sarajevo?

Regardless of its context in Sarajevo, Sontag's reading directly counteracts the intended experience of destitution in Beckett's work. Beckett's play is an experiment in subtraction: not only are the characters' states worsened, but the waiting process gnaws deeply into the *now* of the performance, following the logic that the more things stay the same, the more things change (for the worse). The crucial interception and misunderstanding of Beckett's work is in Sontag's statement of how the despair of act 1 was enough for the Sarajevo audience. Is it the director's responsibility to decide what is enough despair for her audience? The intermission between acts in fact forces the spectator to ponder this ceiling of misery for herself.

Beckett's play offers a language with which to question Sontag's decision. She justifies her decision of a terminal limit with a word drawn from the play itself: "enough." Does her use of the term here indicate an understanding of Beckett's play, and what kind of reading of *Godot* does Sontag enact with her justification? Vladimir and Estragon push the term "enough" back and forth tirelessly. "Enough" seems to designate a provisional measure, wholly in keeping with the play's world of immeasurable destitution. The term makes meek adjustments each time it is uttered. As Estragon is trying on recently found boots, Vladimir inquires, "They don't hurt you?" to which Estragon replies, "Not yet." (That is the hurting in this world, by the way. You cannot say no to the pain of a shoe, only "not yet.") Vladimir's inquiries increase in their intensity:

> VLADIMIR. Then you can keep them.
> ESTRAGON. They're too big.
> VLADIMIR. Perhaps you'll have socks some day.
> ESTRAGON. True.
> VLADIMIR. Then you'll keep them.
> ESTRAGON. That's enough about these boots.
> VLADIMIR. Yes, but . . .
> ESTRAGON. (*violently*) Enough! (*Silence.*) I suppose I might as well sit down.[85]

In this "Enough!" we see the suddenly exposed skin of the conversation, suggesting an impatience we do not expect from those condemned to wait. How do the hungry get fed up? Estragon's "enough" signals a kind of irritated limit where need grinds against need. Screamed, the word actually induces silence from Vladimir. Yet the term registers neither a lasting limit nor a new topic for conversation (no new leafs are turned in this play). The beggars constantly scrutinize the adequacy designated by the term as well as the adequacy of the term. When Vladimir says, "DON'T TELL ME," emphatically indicating he has no interest in hearing his cohort talk aloud about his dreams, Estragon replies, "(*gesture towards the universe*) This one is enough for you?"[86] Sontag passes a verdict on the enough, decreeing one act to be adequate despair for the audience. In doing so, she tries to play the role of Vladimir, saying to Beckett's play, "Don't tell me!" Estragon's gesture therefore encompasses both Sontag and Sarajevo. Estragon suggests that Vladimir's desire not to hear him is his satiation, even complacency, with the world-as-nightmare. His gesture toward the universe echoes his earlier one over the rags he wears. It is a gesture sweeping over rubbish we plainly see and offered anew to our consideration. His question addresses Vladimir's censorship by pointing out the sorry state of the world. The world is a joke, so you don't want to hear mine? In this moment Estragon gruesomely mirrors the title of the James Bond film *The World Is Not Enough*. In the film, wanting more is the only option, and the world becomes just another object for desire to exceed. Estragon starts here, with the inadequacy of the world as dream. The world is not enough for Estragon, but from the standpoint of need, not desire. Estragon configures the world as dream because it is the model for a half-remembered and unpossessed experience, one that remains at odds with conscious life. During the performance of the Sarajevo production, Estragon waves his hand over the debris of the ruined Youth Theater. His question highlights the inadequacy of Sontag's limit of adequate despair.[87]

Measures for need are at best temporary and unstable. "Enough" has a troubled valence. It can suggest both a maximum and a minimum, too little (just barely enough) and too much (enough already!). The irritability with which Vladimir and Estragon employ the term suggests it can designate both at the same time. Sontag thinks she can use the term to issue a ceiling to the despair of Sarajevo, as if to say, "Enough with despair; act 1 is enough." She fails to hear how the play works to remove the illusory satiation (of both joy and despair) from the term. For Beckett, the most slender quantity designated by the enough, its minimum, is not enough: not because we need more but because we need less. Beckett creates *Godot* as a laboratory of the enough in which the vagabonds whittle this negligible quantity (of hope, of meaning, of carrots) down further, rather than whittling time away, as is often claimed. When we think meaning has hit a maximum state of depletion, Estragon pushes it further.

> VLADIMIR. This is becoming really insignificant.
> ESTRAGON. Not enough.
>   *Silence.*[88]

Sontag employs *enough* only as a limit, without taking into consideration the possibility that it is also an injunction: to reduce, to get worse, to mean and to become less.[89] Estragon's Beckettian poverty is a worsening condition and not a static one.

Chan's Inspiration: Terrible Symmetry and the Uncanny

The landscape of post-Katrina New Orleans has been described as many things—a moonscape, a postnuclear disaster, the fulfillment of a biblical prophecy. When Chan visited the city in 2007, he saw Beckett's stage. Chan ascribes this initial impression as the inspiration for staging *Godot* in the most devastated areas, which retained the appearance of a ghost town two years after the flood: "Friends said the city now looks like the backdrop for a bleak science fiction movie. Waiting for a ride to pick me up after visiting with some Common Ground volunteers who were gutting houses in the Lower Ninth, I realized it didn't look like a movie set, but the stage for a play I have seen many times. It was unmistakable. The empty road. The bare tree leaning precariously to one side with just enough leaves to make it respectable. The silence."[90] The impression this scene makes on Chan lies between what he sees and something he half remembers. Chan's friends respond cinematographically to the post-Katrina landscape. They push New Orleans into the future and into the background of the future. Grasped as a potential film image, the disaster is one that is both yet to happen and already will have happened.[91] This landscape does not exist for Chan in the future any more than the past. It has a different kind of implication for him—not as something unseen, not as something recorded in biblical mythology. Though it is devoid of signs, the landscape suggests a déjà vu moment. The destroyed city is familiar, writes Chan, but neither as imaginary wrath nor as film, and not from the other disaster areas to which he has been witness, such as Baghdad after the shelling by US troops and the "ghost town known as downtown Detroit."[92] New Orleans compels an involuntary memory of *Godot*, filling Chan with inner conviction: "It was unmistakable." In this vision, theater and disaster mutually articulate one another but do not synthesize into one thing: "What's more, there was a terrible symmetry between the reality of New Orleans post-Katrina and the essence of this play, which expresses in stark eloquence the cruel and funny things people do while they wait: for help, for food, for hope. It was uncanny."[93]

Chan's impression passes through the aesthetic experience of the uncanny. In fact, he repositions the notion of the uncanny through the rapport between Beckett's stage and the devastated landscape. Chan turns Freud's definition of the uncanny inside out. In his essay on the topic, Freud explores the uncanny (*das Unheimliche*) as a disturbance to the familiar, an interruption to our seamless intimacy with the well-known.[94] Freud's examples include Hoffman's *The Sand-Man*, a short story featuring a doll that takes on the appearance of an animated being, and the figure of the double in psychoanalysis.[95] Freud also cites from his own life in exploring his definition of the uncanny. Discussing his experience of "walking in the deserted streets of a provincial town in Italy which was unknown to me," he describes his repeated attempts to get out of a certain section of town, only to find himself once again back in the same place.[96] Freud remarks that this failure to navigate a foreign city, illuminated by the sudden familiarity of the spot one was trying to leave, "recalls the sense of helplessness experienced in some dream-states."[97]

Chan's use of the uncanny has a twin focus. In New Orleans, the stage becomes the unexpectedly animated double of the living environment, and Beckett's stage is the space to which Chan returns in trying to find his way through the unfamiliar city. Chan thereby merges Freud's two examples of the uncanny. Like Hoffman's doll, Beckett's stage loses its customary "theatrical" status and the stage disappears. Chan calls this "the realization of the play through the city."[98] Chan finds an exacerbation of the *Unheimlich* in this city where the citizens are renamed refugees and where for months after the flood innumerable stoops escalate into empty space leading up to a vanished home. As sections of the city are made foreign and uninhabitable, New Orleans becomes uncanny on a scale greater than Freud's experience in the provincial Italian town. The helplessness that Freud considers reminiscent of "dream-states" becomes an everyday waking-state reality for the survivors of Katrina. A landscape of people displaced from their homes or finding it impossible to feel at home in their trailers becomes the setting for a municipal uncanny.[99]

For Chan, *Godot* ultimately provides the means to understand and artistically process devastation. In particular, Chan envisions the performance of Beckett's work as a way to remark on losses suffered by the community in New Orleans. "Seeing *Godot* embedded in the very fabric of the landscape of New Orleans was my way of reimaging the empty roads, the debris, and above all, the bleak silence as more than the expression of a mere collapse."[100]

New Orleans attracts many artists with the same intention. Graffiti artist Banksy leaves his stenciled figures on buildings in Tremé, another impoverished and devastated quarter, and the flooded Lower Ninth Ward. One of Banksy's graffiti features the Morton Salt Girl. In this version, rain pours down on the girl from under the umbrella while she reaches out her hand to catch a single drop of oil sludge rolling off the umbrella's exterior. Painted years before the 2010 BP Deep Horizon gulf oil spill, Banksy's vision prophetically compresses that disaster with the Katrina catastrophe. He allegorically reworks an iconic brand figure. The umbrella is a longtime symbol of insurance agencies and works here like the failed levee. Though designed to keep the girl from getting wet, it is in fact the source of water falling upon her. Instead of reimagining the catastrophe à la Banksy's dense layering of meanings, Chan says he seeks to "reimage" it. This means using the stage as an echo chamber for the empty roads, the debris, and the silence after the flood. Chan's theater allows us to notice these elements of the landscape, to take stock of them through a stage meshing with the environment in which they appear. Reimaging means imaging them in order to make them more visible, to cultivate within the spectator that déjà vu between Beckett's stage and the Lower Ninth Ward that inspired Chan's project. Filming these elements within the post-Katrina landscape, as Chan's friends imagined, would only metamorphose them into a sensationally empty landscape. Film would transform the condition of mere collapse not into expression but into spectacle. Where cinema would extend our rubbernecking, Chan's theater elicits a double take in which we take stock of landscape, characters, and audience.

Theater of Aftermath: No-Man versus Anybody

Staging *Godot* in the Lower Ninth Ward and Gentilly raises questions about the specificity of performance in Beckett's work. Here, a tension arises between keeping the play generic and giving it a specific dimension, a specific meaning it may assume by placing it within the landscape of a historic disaster. Many critics argue that the play rejects this. Calling *Godot* "outside all temporal reality," Bert States, for example, describes how the dialogue uttered by the vagabonds "implies the same refusal to come to rest in a specific history as the refusal of the play's tree (a squandered space) to abide by the laws of botanical growth."[101] States emphasizes the timelessness within Beckett's play and argues that this accords the play its classic status. States regards Beckett's generic as purity easily contaminated by details involved in any specific performance:

> You can destroy the generic effect of Beckett's wasteland ("A country road. A tree. Evening.") or at least set it at odds with the action it is to contain, by simply littering it with the content of a history (refuse, ruins, billboards), things heavy with a definite past and consequently destined for future use. Chekhov's famous remark that if there is a pistol on stage in Act I it must be fired in Act IV is a condensation of this idea: objects in the dramatic universe are "waiting" objects; like traps, they exist only to exert their potential.[102]

For States, ruins are a directorial choice, placed on stage through littering. This refuse vitiates the utopic emptiness of the play as it would the grass in a brochure from the parks department. Cluttering Beckett's wasteland with proof of its wasteland status only counteracts the play's "refusal of history." In his reference to litter, States may have in mind such productions as the 1955 Broadway version, which "takes place in what appears to be the town dump, with a blasted tree rising out of a welter of rusting junk, including plumbing parts."[103]

Chan's production constitutes a reply to the claim that Beckett is intended as generic and that historical specificity is a betrayal of Beckett's intention. Chan stages *Godot* in an environment where ruin exceeds confinement to the stage or the delicate status of litter. The dump is not staged; it is real. Debris is not ornament, but inevitable and constitutive of the performance place: signless posts, an empty road without street signs, a storm-bent light pole, a sea of weeds where houses once stood, stoops ascending nowhere, a FEMA trailer, and (in Gentilly) an abandoned house. In the setting of desolated New Orleans, this is already the generic. To remove the litter would be to introduce a specificity that Beckett did not intend. These remnants of the flood are, as States claims, "things heavy with a definite past." Yet we cannot piece their sense together into a future the way States claims, for they do not "exist only to exert their potential." The Lower Ninth Ward setting reverses the temporality of Chekhov's example because the gun has already gone off.

Andrea Boll extends the metaphor of Chan's Lower Ninth Ward production in which the generic conditions for Beckett's play are achieved through the wearing down or stripping away of specificity. She notes that following the play the actors as well as the audience members disappear into the wasteland. For Boll, the lesson of the play arrives only as an afterthought and with the disappearance of both actors and audience. What we have witnessed is not a no-man's-land but "somebody's life." She observes, "The lights fade. The play ends. We applaud. The cast disappears into the black night as does the audience. And yet, the setting remains: a destroyed house in a sea of destroyed houses. Not a backdrop, but somebody's life they do not know what to do with."[104] The landscape is not there to merely provide our line of vision with an abstract point of disappearance. Not the disappearance of vision, but somebody's life they (the somebody? FEMA?) did "not know what to do with," life in a state of extreme obsolescence. This suggests another angle from which *Godot* in the Lower Ninth Ward forces us to rethink the status of the generic. No-man's-land and anybody's life are emphatically different types of anonymity. The no-man's-land is States's vision of Beckett's formal purity, a space born generic and without qualities.

Chan (and Boll) underscore the imperfect and acquired anonymity of Beckett's landscape, whose defining characteristics and contours have been forcibly wiped away. *Anybody* is a person dispossessed of the right to be somebody, or to be known, to have a name. Critics frequently discuss Beckett's vagabonds as the Everyman. Yet this term only underscores allegorical possibility and an inclusiveness that suggests the vagabond to be a leviathan figure.[105] *Anybody* suggests intrinsic vacancy, a slot no longer occupied by this anybody. Boll notes how this context affects how she overhears certain lines in the play:

> So when a blind Pozzo asks Didi what it looks like out here and Didi replies, "It's indescribable. It's like nothing. There's nothing," "nothing" takes on a different connotation than the setting Beckett had imagined as "A country road. A tree. Evening." This sort of nothing is worse—more terrifying because this sort of nothing has been created by loss, by the absence of what was once living and whole, filled with light and possibility rather than a nothing that is nothing because it never existed.[106]

Boll's stocktaking of this difference between nothing and loss is the effect of theater in the aftermath. The fracture between *no-man's* and *somebody's* is initiated in Chan's decision about the location of the play. Beckett's generic space has a name and can be found on the map of New Orleans after the flood.

Thus the Lower Ninth Ward and Gentilly designate places the disaster levels into noplaces. They have become shorthand for the way in which the city was destroyed along lines of class and race, as the poorer, lower-lying sections of the city are inhabited mostly by African Americans. Areas around Tulane University, by contrast, go unharmed. The failure of the levee system, not Hurricane Katrina, destroys New Orleans. The leveling of the city does not follow the indiscriminate swath of a tsunami. The disaster discriminates according to the class that can only afford to live in the low-lying areas. Vladimir and Estragon are played by J. Kyle Manzay and Wendell Pierce. Chan's *Godot* played before a predominantly white audience, and in this regard differed sharply from the prison and Sarajevo performances in which the line between actor and spectator was only faintly drawn. The waiting figures in the play are performed by African American actors. Chan confines the more evident hierarchy of master-slave (Pozzo and Lucky) to white actors.[107]

The tree created for this production signifies the hybrid nature of the disaster. The base of the tree is a light stand. Halfway up the stand is a metal arm that resembles a branch. A thin wooden trunk, from which a wooden branch extends, completes the vertical. Cardboard is haphazardly gathered at the base of the tree, seemingly to conceal the extended legs of the stand. In the context of the Lower Ninth Ward, this tree is no longer required to emblematize the barrenness of the stage. Instead it becomes a cue, a weather vane, to the hybrid of the man-made and the natural. Its construction points back to the conjunction of forces that crafted the disaster.

The spectator literally keeps this disaster in view. At the far end of Prieur Street the levee is clearly illuminated. Its distance from the stage endows its image with the quality of an afterthought or an insurgent memory. Productions of *Godot* in traditional theater settings labor to create an indistinct horizon on stage, a grey backdrop in which ground and sky merge indistinguishably. Yet the point of disappearance in the Lower Ninth was a spotlight shining on the levee as if it were something to be watched closely, even at a distance. Chan devises two spatial scenes for *Godot:* the play before us in which nothing happens (twice) and this other scene where something catastrophic (a failure of civil engineering) had already occurred. Instead of foreground versus background/backdrop, Chan's staging introduces a terrible symmetry between two events (the levee and the play, the disaster that transpired and the disaster of something not transpiring).

The aftermath quality to the performance reveals itself in the resonance words have in the setting. The disjunctive dialogue between the vagabonds generates tools for the displaced. In her review of the play, Boll envisions the conditions of the Lower Ninth Ward as the setting in which Beckett's play fulfills itself:

> "What is there to recognize?" asks Gogo. Yes, what is there to recognize anymore? One day you wake up in your formaldehyde FEMA trailer, and somebody has chopped down all the trees on your street because even though they appeared to be alive, they were actually dead. An entire block of houses has been demolished. Everybody has left except you.[108]
>
> You will confess like Gogo to your best friend, your neighbors, your contractor, yourself, to anybody who will listen, "I can't go on like this," and have them pat you on the back and say with amusement like Didi, "That's what you think."[109]

Boll suggests that context does not restrict the meaning of Beckett's play but releases it. The performance of Beckett's play in a disaster setting does not produce interpretations per se, but rather a deeper echo of the work within spaces and situations throughout the city. For Boll, Beckett lets us see the tragicomic gesture in the contractor's pat on your back. Beckett adds his aftermath to that of the disaster. In the process, it acquires an address, perched somewhere between anybody and somebody: the *you*. "Everybody has left except you." Boll does not hereby personalize the experience of Beckett, even as this "you" is not the collective you of her readership. She addresses the single you, the one deprived of context, neighbors, and what the law calls all personal effects. This you is the last you, the generic particular.

Beckett's Poverty in Sarajevo and New Orleans

Beckett's play resonates in environments where the destitution exceeds that of Beckett's stage. In these environments the very production of *Waiting for Godot* colludes with the stage deprived of its *deus ex machina*, leaving only the scantiest of theatrical machines. The memory of a couple living without shelter informs Sontag's vision for the play. She models one Vladimir and Estragon pair "on homeless people I'd seen in downtown Manhattan."[110] Yet Sontag experiences the force of the play, its central topic of futility and the inadequacy of means, most clearly in the effort of putting the play on: "Sometimes I thought we were not waiting for Godot, or Clinton. We were waiting for our props."[111] The candles that light the stage seem to arrive mysteriously. Like the boots Estragon finds on stage in act 2, the candles just appear: "When I asked for additional candles, I was told there weren't any. Later I was told that they were being saved for our performances. In fact, I never learned who doled out the candles; they were simply in place on the floor when I arrived each morning."[112] She cannot find any rope for Pozzo until a week before the opening, the bowler hats and boots materialize only in the last days of rehearsal, and the costumes arrive the day before the opening. Sontag notes how carrots are in such short supply that she substitutes rolls "scavenged" from the Holiday Inn where she is staying.[113] The rationing inflicted on Sarajevo by the war makes it impossible to find not only a chicken for Pozzo but an edible substitute for one. To paraphrase Hamm in *Endgame*: "There are no more chickens" in Sarajevo, "nor are there any counterparts." Sontag designs a fowl for Pozzo out of papier-mâché. The absence of electricity forces Sontag to rehearse and perform the play by flashlight and candlelight. Even Beckett's text has to be parceled between the three Didi/Gogo couples on stage. An interviewer's question, "How did you decide what to give to whom?" suggests a secondary motivation for tripling the pair: to distribute two roles among six unemployed Sarajevan actors and subsequently to ration their lines from an already skimpy text.[114]

The staging of poverty that Beckett's play demands is difficult outside of devastated areas, such as Sarajevo and New Orleans. Beckett's play does not illustrate sociological conditions of poverty. These conditions are not illuminated, as they are in Victor Hugo's work, by what people are forced to do on account of them. Beckett's poverty militates against self-evidence, and the recognizable markers of destitution are put in retreat in the process. Critics sometimes become accountants in trying to enforce a verisimilitude over Beckett's work that is only too apparent in the New Orleans productions. In his study *Beckett/Beckett*, for example, Vivian Mercier states his goal to "establish the extent to which [Beckett's] leading characters can be said to have 'come down in the world' in a social and economic sense as well as a psychological or even moral one."[115] Mercier quantifies the "formal education" of characters (and hence their "comfortable upbringing") by tallying the "unambiguously learned references" they make.[116] In discussing *All that Fall*, Mercier gets down to brass tacks: "If we are to take Mr. Rooney's calculations seriously, he earns only about £2 a week yet pays £12 a year for his season ticket alone. Clearly he is losing money by going to the city every day. But in all probability, since he owns a house in a desirable location, he has a private income."[117] Mercier here audits Beckett's characters rather than listens to them. Mercier wants to establish positive textual proof for the destitution of Beckett's characters, wants to close the condition by ascertaining its beginning and end. This method ignores Beckett's more thoroughgoing poverty, which pushes beyond the question of character income and includes our engagement with it. Here we might recall Beckett's remark in his essay on Joyce: "Literary criticism is not bookkeeping."[118] For Beckett, criticism should not convert the literary work into data. More importantly, the critical gesture cannot keep or retain possession of the book it addresses. The book is to recede from and baffle the critic, and the interpretation is not to interrupt (or arrest) the dereliction of the book. We witness this recession by the text of *Godot* in the moment Estragon calls attention to the visible index of his impoverishment: his rags. Vladimir says, "You should have been a poet." Estragon replies, "I was. (*Gesture towards rags.*) Isn't that obvious?"[119] Here the play inserts a new (and, to us, foreign) understanding of the obvious, the sign in its state of maximal exposure. Should it have already been obvious to Vladimir and to us that Estragon was a poet or that poetry is the only suitable preparation for dereliction? Beckett makes it difficult for us to separate the joke from the commentary, the gesture of *ecce homo!* from one that furnishes proof.

The landscape of New Orleans conjures the image of Beckett's destitute stage without the need for Mercier's calculations. Speaking of the devastated areas of the city, Chan notes, "It was truly a landscape of impoverishment."[120] Chan ultimately stages *Godot* in two areas from which people, road signs, and habitable structures have been notably uprooted by the flooding: an intersection in the Lower Ninth Ward and an abandoned house in Gentilly. Here Chan experiences something like an involuntary memory of Beckett's stage: "Standing there at the intersection of North Prieur and Reynes, I suddenly found myself in the middle of Samuel Beckett's *Waiting for Godot*."[121] The setting hallucinates Chan into *Godot*.

In a seeming answer to Chan's visual image of devastation, Lois Oppenheim notes in her analysis of Beckett's visuality, "In Beckett's theater the image outweighs the word: The two tramps of *Godot*, Winnie in her mound, heads peering from within trash cans and funerary urns in *Endgame* and *Play* have a force more enduring than the scripted text."[122] Oppenheim ascribes enduring force to Beckett's images of bodies trapped within monstrous enclosures, the mounds of dirt, urns, and trash cans that usurp our focus. The couple, Vladimir and Estragon, however, form a memorable image through an inverse condition: exposure. Exposure both to the elements—Estragon says he sleeps in a ditch—and to the spectators' view combine to make the stage a defenseless space, both temporary and restrictive, like an unauthorized encampment. This is the precise environment of both Sarajevo and New Orleans. As Goytisolo observes, every remaining inhabitant of Sarajevo "must get used to sleeping, moving, walking about fully aware of your defenseless, precarious existence."[123] The exposure of Beckett's characters is accented in Chan's production by the absence of a proper stage, which is signaled only by the sudden and impertinent grouping of the audience risers at an abandoned intersection.

In the light of the exposed condition of destitution, we must qualify Oppenheim's claim that Vladimir and Estragon form an image of enduring force. Their endurance comes from a place other than strength. Vladimir and Estragon weather their exposure with something closer to obduracy than to traditional courage. They endure as survivors who have fallen through the cracks; they endure by chance. They bring to mind what Kafka says about the wax Odysseus puts in his ears to save himself from the Siren's song: "Proof that inadequate, even childish measures, may serve to rescue one from peril."[124] In the dispossessed world of Beckett's characters, Odysseus's wax would strike us as sheer luxury. Vladimir and Estragon seem without means, even inadequate or childish ones. Unlike Odysseus, they consequently have no choice but to take in the silence that engulfs the stage. At the end of his study on Proust, Beckett writes that Proust's narrator is preoccupied with an "invisible reality" of art that "damns the life of the body on earth as a pensum [a routine burden] and reveals the meaning of the word 'defunctus.'"[125] Where Proust's narrator reveals the meaning of *defunctus*, *Godot* just reveals the state.[126] The exposure wrought by Beckett's play is not to be confused with "explicitness," with a conveyance of meanings. Nothing works, usefulness is a quaint idea, and life itself has become an anachronism, yet this does not come to us courtesy of a character's soliloquy. The poverty of Beckett's stage offers no terms or conditions for itself, just a condition.

The destitution wrought by the war in Sarajevo is visible in the very bodies of the actors on stage. Sontag notes how the actors evince physical exhaustion in excess of the script's talk about futility and hunger: "The actors were visibly underweight and tired easily. Beckett's Lucky must stand motionless through most of his long scene without ever setting down the heavy bag he carries. Atko . . . asked me to excuse him if he occasionally rested his empty suitcase on the floor. Whenever I halted the run-through for a few minutes to change a movement or a line reading, all the actors, with the exception of Ines, would instantly lie down on the stage."[127] *Godot* in Sarajevo illuminates how labor-intensive it is to be (or even just play) the vagabond—a character who seems to have nothing to do. Vladimir and Estragon conduct methodical ceremonies of movement on stage. The Sarajevan actors, by contrast, register more emphatically the physical exhaustion that accompanies futility. Where Beckett's hobos use the pauses in the script to think, to listen intently, or to survey the stage, the performers in Sontag's production seize upon these to lie down. Sontag's words give a glimpse into a historical situation that overlaps the truth of Beckett's stage where simply standing vertically or holding a suitcase throughout rehearsal of act 1 constitute labors that push the human figure to the brink. The war environment rations even the postures of the actor.

Both in New Orleans and Sarajevo the audience is already trained in waiting. At theaters with prestigious addresses, Beckett's wait is absorbed with the patience of understanding that one gives to a uniquely demanding piece of theater. In the Lower Ninth Ward and Sarajevo, waiting can be tempered neither by patience nor impatience. Whether it be waiting for FEMA, for NATO, for Clinton, or for the bombs to stop falling, waiting is endemic to life after a catastrophe. Waiting is the temporal dimension of poverty, and the vagabonds' wait is one that famously does not pay off. Audiences in New Orleans and Sarajevo, like the characters on stage, do not rightly know for what they are waiting, or stated otherwise, the waiting itself is so long and so inevitable that it usurps any reason for waiting.

Part of the frivolousness of the Beckettian waiting is the way its terminus abruptly changes. The characters are waiting for Godot, waiting for night, and also waiting for nothing—just waiting.[128] Waiting makes the *now* of Beckett's stage recede in this manner: waiting displaces the things Vladimir and Estragon do while waiting, and yet the things they do also seem to negate waiting. (We encounter this inability to see waiting and acting simultaneously any time a waiter at a New York restaurant assures us that he or she "really" is, in some other but distant reality, an actor.) In the context of postapocalyptic New Orleans, waiting undercuts any coherent message that the play might seem to offer. The occasional reminder of what the characters are waiting for seems only to interrupt their antics on stage. In the shadow of this afterthought of Godot, they resume their cycle of games. Action and waiting impoverish one another. The abstract inactivity of the waiting process makes it impossible to act on stage or give it a form (something we can "see happening" on stage). The form waiting assumes is the repetition of the play's title.

Titles usually stand outside or above the work, as an umbrella term for the work, providing the identity by which the work is formally recognized (by copyright offices, institutions, etc.). Beckett's is the only play whose title provides its own enigmatic purpose, what we might call the *irrationale* of the play: simultaneously description, justification, and (implicitly) question. The title is immersed within the locution of the play, surfacing whenever Vladimir and Estragon offer their reason for being on stage (phrased as an inability to leave): "We're waiting for Godot." The repetitions of the title within the dialogue merit the retitling of Beckett's play *Godot 26,* after Anouilh's *Amphitryon 38,* dramatizing the innumerable versions of its mythic tale. Recirculation within the dialogue wears the gleam off the title. It does not become more lucid, just more familiar. The play turns the title into a sentence (in all senses of this word). Vladimir and Estragon add a "we." Yet the intratextual movement only saps this announcement of its function. Instead of furnishing the vagabonds with a purpose, their declaration/citation only sounds like a confession that they are here for the play, that they constitute the acting troupe assigned to perform the impossible: to act waiting.

In the setting of the Lower Ninth Ward, waiting is inscribed within a landscape that is self-evident for the audience. Director Donald Harworth asks Beckett a question that Chan would never need to ask: "Why is there nothing on the road? Beckett replies, 'Because it's not a road, it's a track on wasteland.' Silence. Then, smiling as though seeing the two friends in that place, he leaned back and said, 'They play a series of games. When one has ended, they start another.' His smile lingered."[129] Beckett clearly wants to cut down or away from the associations Harworth gleans from the stage direction, "a country road": traffic, people, cars, business. Beckett here feels obliged to impoverish what seems on the face of it an already impoverished term—a road. The director's discussion is helpful. It follows the same course of impoverishment that Beckett's work takes, a progression from a road to a track on wasteland. "Track" suggests repetition, like an athletic track, where doing the same thing dominates (rather than a country road suitable for a stroll, as in Kerouac or John Denver). Beckett underscores his stage as closed system (the vagabonds' endless resumption of their games) rather than as a road that is either a destination or a means of traveling between two points. In its very existence, the Lower Ninth Ward incorporates Beckett's reductions. Its unnerving desolation is incarnated through *force majeure* rather than Beckett's stage directions. Dismissed by some critics as Chan's "overtly clumsy attempts to blend in" with local culture, the gumbo and second line/marching band served a vital function in helping the spectators find the stage.[130] The corner of Prieur and Reynes constitutes not a theatrical no-man's-land but a municipal one, as street signs were still absent and the roads remained undesignated. Chan's is the first *Godot* locatable only through GPS.[131]

Beckett's poverty exposes without explanation. This makes seemingly simple critical gestures rather difficult. What, for example, do we call Vladimir and Estragon? The play instills a hesitation in us before naming their status. This hesitation is overcome in Mercier's attempt to ascertain the class status of Beckett's characters, as it is lost in Oppenheim's list of Beckettian images: she names Winnie and names the body parts peeking out of the urns and trash cans. *Godot* ultimately bequeaths to us the image of the tramps rather than that of Vladimir and Estragon. Many critics note that the term "tramp," like the term "clown," is never mentioned in the text or stage directions.[132] Yet it displaces all others in critical discussion of the play. Its massive circulation turns Vladimir and Estragon into the play's emissaries and Beckett into a celebrity. Herbert Blau speaks of Vladimir and Estragon as refugees, long before they appear on the stage in New Orleans. Blau has it right. The term "refugees" as opposed to "tramps" suggests a more forcible displacement or eviction surrounding their condition.[133] And yet, though the term applies to the people of New Orleans en route to Houston or elsewhere, would *Godot* be as widely disseminated through culture were their figures designated as refugees? "Beggar" would underscore the demand made by the figure, rather than their movement of tramping. Akin to "bumpkin," "tramp" makes the state of need more digestible to the spectator. It implicitly forges an alliance with the cinematic tramp, Charlie Chaplin. Beckett's characters, however, share none of the pliancy with which Chaplin adapts to his environment (fed into a machine, Charlie emerges unscathed). Where Chaplin communicates across his silence, his eyebrows stamping the mood for us like emoticons, deep silence punctuates all the things Vladimir and Estragon say, but leave unaddressed, to each other.

Chan's production of *Godot* engages the scarcity of recognizable markers on Beckett's stage. Weeks before the opening, Chan posts the famously concise stage directions of Beckett's play at intersections and dilapidated areas throughout New Orleans: "A country road. A tree. Evening." Chan takes the stage directions out of hiding and posts them among the other makeshift signs—ads for contractors, homemade street signs—that multiply on telephone poles and park benches following the disaster. Made visible, the stage directions lose their informational function (to stage designers creating a world to be measured by its fidelity to the recipe) and gain a designatory one. The conditions for Beckett's stage play become an index to the existing condition of the city. Chan's production contests the traditional model of site-specific artworks, which are uniquely contoured to a particular landscape.[134] The dispersal of Beckett's directions to the stage calls our attention to New Orleans as a set for multiple productions of *Godot*. Chan uses the play to situate the city and its many forsaken areas rather than tailoring his work to it. Possible stages abound in New Orleans because this play requires the very opposite of a site-specific work. *Godot* needs a space without qualities, a no-man's-land, a generic site.

The impoverishing effect of waiting can be illuminated in contrast to Emmanuel Levinas's concept of vigilance. Levinas differentiates between attention, "which is turned towards objects," and vigilance, "absorbed in the rustling of the unavoidable being and which goes much further."[135] In this absorption into impersonal being "I still become aware of this anonymous vigilance, but I become aware of it in a movement in which the I is already detached from the anonymity."[136] He continues: "Our affirmation of an anonymous vigilance goes beyond the *phenomena*, which already presupposes an ego, and thus eludes descriptive phenomenology. Here description would make use of terms while striving to go beyond their constituency; it stages *personages*, while the *there is* the dissipation of personages."[137] Levinas makes a clear separation between the anonymous vigil and conscious attention to phenomena that "presuppose an ego." For Beckett, the ego is not so easily shed:

> ESTRAGON. We always find something, eh Didi, to give us the impression we exist.
> VLADIMIR. (*impatiently*) Yes, yes, we're magicians.[138]

In these lines Beckett, more than Levinas, expresses the futility of letting go of the ego. If Levinas wants to go beyond the ego, Beckett shows how its occasional reoccurrence (the trivial things it does to give us "the impression that we exist") only testifies to the dreadful norm—an impressionless existence. This stage coincides with the state of survivors of disaster, who are only reminded of being alive. The "I" in *Godot* is never fully detached from anonymity, and hence waiting never transforms into vigilance. Levinas suggests that philosophy can do without the theater (i.e., phenomenology, which "stages personages"). Beckett uses the stage to suggest the irrelevance of philosophy. The vagabonds, partially anonymous, slowly wither away. Levinas is helpful to people whose understanding of need is part of a conversation that includes its opposite: the rich and varied discourse of civilization. This is to say that nobody reads Levinas after a disaster. Levinas's figure faces the other, and this sets ethical obligation that precedes existence. Beckett stages something that is in danger of falling short of existence. Need occurs on the stage but outside a dialectical framework. Obligation is replaced by compulsion and inexplicable inertia. People in historical crises forcibly deprived of home, like Didi and Gogo, empathize with the state of anonymity on Beckett's stage, which offers no countenance.

Unlike Levinas's vigilance, Beckett's waiting demands a scarcity of objects rather than their erasure or dismissal. Adorno notes the careful monitoring of what appears on Beckett's stage. He notes, "The strict ration of reality and characters which the drama is allotted and with which it makes do, is identical to what remains of subject, spirit, and soul in view of the permanent catastrophe."[139] Western theater is bound up in the notion of mimesis, the adequation between stage and world. Adorno keys in on the *inadequacy* upon Beckett's stage to counteract this tradition. Whereas Aristotelian theater depends on reason (*ratio*), Beckett's reality depends on the ration. Artaud ascribes the birth of theater to a gesture of useless expenditure. During the plague, he writes, "[The] dregs of humanity, apparently immunized by their frenzied greed, enter the open houses and pillage riches they know will serve no purpose or profit. And at that moment the theater is born. The theater, i.e., an immediate gratuitousness provoking acts without use or profit."[140] According to Artaud, theater begins with an obscene disturbance to the property of the rich: the moment the "dregs" gratuitously pillage their coffers. Beckett's plays begin not in gratuity but in scarcity, one prior to any act or gesture. The dregs Artaud speaks of are on Beckett's stage but are fishing carrots out of their pockets:

> VLADIMIR. How's the carrot?
> ESTRAGON. It's a carrot.
> VLADIMIR. So much the better, so much the better. (*Pause.*) What was it you wanted to know?
> ESTRAGON. I've forgotten. (*Chews.*) That's what annoys me. (*He looks at the carrot appreciatively, dangles it between finger and thumb.*) I'll never forget this carrot. (*He sucks the end of it meditatively*).[141]

Every object seems somehow to have penetrated the fundamental vacancy of Beckett's stage. Beckett's world is no less administered than Kafka's. Yet the labyrinthine bureaucracy that crams Kafka's novels is felt but not seen in Beckett through the ration, through the logic of scarcity.[142] Beckett disposes of the idea that need has a natural basis (mere hunger). Every item, everything edible, appears on his stage with the precision of a bowl of soup pushed through the door to a prisoner in solitary confinement. Need is managed. Moments of excess are infrequent. "You overdo it with your carrots," Vladimir says to Estragon.[143] Vladimir's expression echoes like a verbal remnant from a distant world where people could intimately chastise one another for wanting something in excess of its necessity. The weakness before excess and the articulation of desire over need make little sense between two hobos who have nothing. Here nothing is to be done, let alone overdone. We blink at Vladimir's statement because there is only a single carrot on stage.

We connect this strict rationing behind the play to the privative condition of the beggar. The scantiness of what remains of "subject, spirit, and soul" and even carrots is incorporated into the survival of the characters. In the postapocalyptic scenario of *Endgame*, by contrast, the characters survive the objects. It surpasses the point reached in *Godot* in which objects seem marked for extinction. Characters openly proclaim, almost as a reminder to each other, that an array of objects has achieved extinction: "There are no more coffins!" and "There are no more bicycles." This "no more" is the idiom of Beckett's poverty. But whereas *Godot* suggests there "are no more carrots" for the beggars, *Endgame* suggests the catastrophic absence of these objects: bicycles are no more. Scarcity escalates into gone. If in *Godot* it seems that objects interrupt the void of the stage, *Endgame* declares the end of the world as to a customs agent: object by measly object. As befits a bomb shelter, there is mention of a "larder" in Clov's kitchen. This space of reserve crucially changes the economy of scarcity and allotment in *Endgame*. Even if locked (only Hamm knows the combination), it suggests a potential "more." The total exposure of the vagabonds' condition in *Godot* depends on the absence of any reserve off stage, any place for potential stockpiles. Their only larder is in their pockets.

Naming Godot

The Sontag and Chan productions of *Godot* share the common political ambition of publicizing the vulnerability of the cities of Sarajevo and New Orleans. This project becomes visible if we compare the titles of Sontag's essay ("Waiting for Godot in Sarajevo") and the book Chan edits (*Waiting for Godot in New Orleans: A Field Guide*). These titles lack an indication that a play is being staged. Instead, the titles emphasize the waiting and suggest that these cities are places in which Godot is awaited. Both Sontag and Chan underscore what I describe in chapter 1 as utilitarian waiting. This type of waiting focuses on the "for" in waiting for someone or something and thereby assigns a clear endpoint to the waiting process. The waiting inscribed in the play is different because, although Godot is putatively the objective, the characters in fact have little expectation or hope that he will ever arrive and waiting itself—and the character of waiting, rather than waiting for Godot—takes precedence. The waiting of Vladimir and Estragon only resembles waiting for a bus if that bus is being anticipated in Sarajevo or the Lower Ninth Ward.

The Sarajevo and New Orleans productions are political because they encourage a figuration for Godot and the waiting process in the play. Both productions serially inscribe objects, authorities, and institutions in the blank space of "Godot." Though Beckett's play wages war on this "for," both Sontag and Chan calibrate the need afflicting their cities by suggesting a number of possible Godots. Chan remarks, "In New Orleans in 2007, Godot is legion."[144] Sontag speaks of "waiting for Clinton" and waiting for props: "'You'll definitely have the cigarette holder tomorrow,' I was told every morning for three weeks."[145] True to his grassroots approach, Chan distributes a questionnaire to the residents of Gentilly, a Gallup poll of need asking, "WHAT ARE YOU WAITING FOR?" The answers enumerate familiar failures: "FEMA," "Waiting for the Tzar, Blakely, to do something," "Waiting for the Road Home people to give me my money. It's been a long wait."[146] Other responses reveal the surprising absences in post-Katrina

Gentilly: waiting for street signs; waiting for someone to get onto the people who are not back and make them clean up their properties; waiting for the shopping center to reopen; waiting for more police, not military police: we need community-oriented people patrolling our neighborhood; waiting for a plan; waiting on money.[147]

Chan's question furnishes the residents' answers with a structure: "I am waiting for . . ." This is a leading question: it leads to all of Godot's namesakes. For this reason, very few answers respond to the question's implicit interrogation of the worth of the waiting process (i.e., *what good is waiting?*). Sylvester Desponza, resident of the St. Roch neighborhood before the storm, describes waiting as "waiting for the utilities to stop going on and off." Yet his other answers impulsively protest the structure of the question. Desponza writes, "Everything that has not happened is disgusting." The "not happening" in the play itself, but without any reference to a Godot, is disgusting. "I am not waiting," Desponza says, "but puking."[148] He fashions a truly provisional response to Beckett's drama: he does not need a Godot, he needs a Dramamine.

Responses to the Chan survey draw our attention away from hypothetical cures to the visible dislocation of post-Katrina New Orleans.[149] Desponza's comments have an urgency not seen elsewhere in the questionnaire: "Go to the 2900 and 3000 block in St. Roch and see how empty it is—the conditions are still the same."[150] Instead of an answer, Desponza offers an injunction outside the political compass set by Chan's poll. Desponza is saying enough with this Christmas list; "go see St. Roch for yourself, without the actors and risers." He senses that the arrival of these objects, people, and policies, each a Godot we await, would only be the start, not the end, of what the flood survivor needs. Maurice Blanchot writes, "When [literature] names something, whatever it designates is abolished; but whatever is abolished is also sustained, and the thing has found a refuge (in the being which is the word) rather than a threat."[151] Desponza suggests that listing and naming what the residents of Gentilly want (awarding them the title of *Godot*) only destroys that thing as an option. The title of Godot is not a threat but a refuge, because these things only remain true to Beckett's play by staying absent. Desponza suggests that the panoply of existing options should not provide us with our only possibility.[152]

Sontag and Chan articulate the political message of their productions through the figure in absentia. Though they stage a play about vagabonds, Sontag and Chan are interested less in a state of abandonment per se than in the figures by whom the characters (and the audience) have been abandoned. This message is curative and optimistic and conforms to the existing political structure far more than does Desponza's despondent rage. Naming Godot allows Sontag and Chan to orchestrate vectors of need, desire, and absence around a more possible, more earthbound figure. They wrestle with the figure of Godot as with a weather vane they redirect so that it points no longer at the theater (to some figure waiting in the wings) but out to our world.

Since the no-man's-land has been removed from quotation marks, how will we do the same to "Godot"? This is the real question asked by both Sontag and Chan. Can Godot's prestigious stage absence be mobilized to coerce a political figure or agency from the shadows? The play itself instigates this sudden incarnation of its title, as Vladimir and Estragon repeatedly mistake Pozzo for Godot. It schools us in the ease, but also the error, with which Godot is recognized. Characters in the play are dubbed Godot, not officially as by the queen, but painfully as in a desynchronized kung fu film where sound (the name) poorly matches the image (the body). Absurdity and amusement abound in the effort to grapple with the potential of the name "Godot," to bestow the proper name for something that never arrives or that may have always been there. The audience tends to remember Godot's absence rather than the vagabonds' need for him. This allows them to maintain the comic value of this no-show rather than the arduous poverty it entails. The casting call for a Wall Street production of *Godot* I discuss in the conclusion receives many replies. One is from a wag claiming he wants to play Godot. I wrote back: "Sure, but only if you have the wardrobe." Our joking hides what we do not know about waiting.

This reconsignment of Godot's name allows Chan to integrate his production into the local political landscape. *Waiting for Guffman* is a popular reworking of *Godot*. In the film, an amateur theater group tries to get its shot at the big time by inviting an established drama critic, Guffman, to their performance. They are confident that Guffman's critical approval will change their summer-stock status. They reserve a seat for the esteemed critic in the front row. The seat remains empty throughout the play until an individual walks in and takes the seat midway through the performance. Figuring their Godot has arrived, the actors are palpably excited until they realize after the performance that this audience member is not Guffman. Instead, the spectator is merely a passerby who enters the theater to get a balloon for his child. The man is a kind of Mr. Godin or Godet—as Pozzo twice mistakenly names Godot. The film turns the topos of Beckett's play inside out, as it is the stage actors (rather than the characters) who are waiting, and they wait alone, unaccompanied by the audience. Throughout the performance, the players' eyes can only look askance at the empty seat.

The emptiness of the seat facing the stage goes unnoticed by the audience, which is unaware that this drama of waiting is the real drama beneath the one they see on stage.

The performances of *Godot* in the settings of New Orleans and Sarajevo allocate not only the actors and the characters in the play but also political powers that be. Their presence or absence from the city is exemplified by their presence or absence from the production itself. In Chan's performance, this is highlighted by the drama surrounding the invitation of Ray Nagin, the mayor of New Orleans, for whom a seat has been reserved. The densely packed audience in the Lower Ninth Ward calls attention to the emptiness of his seat, which remains starkly empty throughout the first half of the play. Here Chan taps into the Guffman scenario. Unlike *Godot*, *Guffman* suggests that intervention will not come from the stage but from the stands and the area around the stage. Nagin never does arrive, possibly because he was informed that he would not be allowed to make a speech.[153] Chan assigns Nagin a seat in the audience rather than a spotlight on the stage. Forced to be more a Guffman than a Godot, and unwilling to watch the play in solidarity with the audience, or to become a witness to the city, Nagin opts not to come. Chan sets up a seat for him as critical spectator whose response, like Guffman's, may have intervened to change the state of the actors at the corner of Prieur and Reynes.

Performance Context as Inscribed within *Godot*

Every performance of *Waiting for Godot* abuts its environment in a highly idiosyncratic way. *Godot* asks where an event that does not take place is supposed to take place. The play is not content with displaying a missed encounter for us. Instead, it pulls the audience in by actively subtracting from the stage. As they try to recall where Godot said to meet them, Vladimir and Estragon throw the time and place of the stage they occupy into an acid bath of doubt: Is this the tree? Is it today? Where were we yesterday? When Vladimir declares that Godot says to wait on Saturday ("I think"), Estragon replies, "But what Saturday? And is it Saturday?"[154] Vladimir can't remember whether he wrote it down somewhere and looks for it in his pants and coat, "bursting with miscellaneous rubbish."[155] For a brief instance the content of the play, and our encounter with it, rests upon the archival power of a hobo's pocket. The play does not give us a no-man's-land so much as the wrong no-man's-land. In this way Beckett scours away at our own appointment with the theater and dethrones the stage as a site of expected dramatic encounter. *Godot* offers a theater as rendezvous in the wrong place, kept at one end, by one party only.

Beckett's play delegitimizes its own space in that whatever happens goes on in default of the anticipated meeting with the title character, Godot. Emerging out of the happenstance gathering of vagabonds and spectators, and within a wholly provisional space, *Godot* assimilates itself to the conditions of theater under war or within a landscape of aftermath. After Vladimir is unable to locate Godot's card in his pocket, Beckett's stage directions inform us that Vladimir is to be *"looking wildly about him, as though the date was inscribed in the landscape."*[156] Sarajevo and New Orleans become landscapes into which the date for this appointment has been written, but illegibly, by the disasters of war and flood.

The rapport between stage and off stage is the very topic of Chan's and Sontag's plays. The dialogue envelops the surrounding space in its devastation. Vladimir and Estragon periodically name the horizon by pointing toward the audience and the wings. Discussing with Estragon whether the place looks familiar, Vladimir says, "All the same.... that tree ... (*turning towards the auditorium*) that bog...."[157] Later when Vladimir asks, "Do you not recognize the place?" Estragon replies, "(*suddenly furious*) Recognize! What is there to recognize? All my lousy life I've crawled about in the mud! And you talk to me about scenery! (*Looking wildly about him.*) Look at this muckheap! I've never stirred from it!"[158] Beckett gets rid of what Estragon calls scenery, settings designed for consumption, in favor of the muckheap. The theater projects a hypothetical disaster area. The characters' turns toward the audience are closer to surveying land than traditional asides. Instead of providing the characters' inner thoughts, these moments merge the spectators into the unrecognizable landscape. The characters absent us from their address, as if the "house," our space as designated in theater parlance, had been abandoned.

Localization and Performance Context

How do performances treat the desolation of Beckett's stage? How much concrete detail does a stage provide—or withhold—in rendering a work that aspires to be nondescript? *Localization* refers to the way directors use the stage to create a specific social or political context for a play. JoAnne Akalaitis's *Endgame* at the American Repertory Theater, for example, turns the stage into a blasted-out subway tunnel, replete with life-sized subway cars, a charred corpse, and Philip Glass's synthesized music. Akalaitis's stage establishes the aftermath setting of Beckett's play with sensational clarity.[159] By contrast, Beckett's scenario suggests the apocalypse that has transpired has taken all evidence of the event with it.[160] Likewise, the production history of *Waiting for Godot* is punctuated by efforts to bring its potential meanings into definite focus. Ilan Ronen, for example, situates the play within the Israel-Palestine conflict by casting Arab actors as Vladimir and Estragon (speaking Arabic) and Israeli actors as Pozzo and Lucky (speaking Hebrew).[161] Other directors supply greater historical definition to the gray backdrop of *Godot*. In his 1991 production in Nanterre, Joel Jouanneau populates the stage with the ruins of an abandoned electrical plant, morphing Vladimir and Estragon into urban street trash. Pozzo and Lucky are cast as a "cynical bourgeois exploiter" and immigrant laborer, a precursor to the *sans-papiers*.[162] Bradby remarks that the director "did not want to show a generalized picture of humanity, but to give his characters clearly localized, specific qualities: 'restituer l'image de la dérive d'êtres exclus dans la France des années 90.'"[163]

Localization is a powerful way for a director to develop meaning, but this comes at a cost. Fully mobilizing the décor to contextualize Beckett's play in a particular place and within a particular debate, these directors turn Beckett's exposed stage into *exposé*. The difference between these like-sounding terms becomes apparent in Jouanneau's statement about his intention to "restore the image of drifters, of people excluded from the France of the 1990s." Jouanneau seizes Vladimir and Estragon as an opportunity to both create and renew that image of excluded people and thereby recall them to political discussion. In exposing the vagabonds to the elements, to view, and to an unknown trajectory, Beckett's play impoverishes their image. Photographically speaking, Beckett simultaneously underdevelops and overexposes the image of the vagabonds.

Savaging the idea that theater is a place for types (the armature of literature as sociology), Beckett withdraws his couple from culture's repertoire of images (including that of "couple"). The play joins in with the termite activity that Vladimir and Estragon perform on the set itself, as their dialogue eats away at the sorry image of the tree before our eyes. Where Beckett wants to subtract fantasy, these directors want to add it. This fantasy invested into Beckett's work goes by the name of infidelity. Bradby makes infidelity a condition of making *Godot* politically resonant: "To give the play a specific political meaning, it is necessary to alter it, however subtly."[164] Akalaitis, Ronen, and Jouanneau must stray from their relation to Beckett's work in order to have it articulate the desired network of references.

Sontag's and Chan's productions break with the notion of context as enforced by the localization of a play. They submit *Godot* to a *condition* of war and flood rather than a fabricated context. This condition exerts pressure on the very process of the play's production, affecting the actors and not just the characters, the play's process and not just its effect. Representation, staging, and the whole parade of mimetic questions that a director considers are obviated by the setting given by the crisis itself and overwhelm them. The ground for performance is a space unresolved and in the lurch, like the audience itself. The disaster environment, spectacularly confined to the stage in Akalaitis's production of *Endgame,* spills in all directions from the stages in New Orleans and Sarajevo. War and flood produce the lifeless décor for a Beckett play exceeding the space of the stage. In light of a landscape fraught with suitably desolate stages, the choice of performance space in Sarajevo or New Orleans has a provisional and arbitrary quality. Where the proscenium arch conveniently contains Akalaitis's aftermath, Sontag's performance space cannot adequately withstand the siege of the context, cannot ensure that the theater will hold out if an adjacent building is struck with mortar fire. In this way the war provides conditions to the play, as for terms of surrender. Sontag notes how *Godot* involuntarily registers the situation outside the theater because the play's protracted silences are no longer silences: "The only sounds were those coming from outside the theatre: a UN armored personnel carrier thundering down the street and the crack of sniper fire."[165] Something similar takes place in the Lower Ninth Ward, as the locale becomes part of the performance by necessity rather than design. Anne Gisleson describes how the staged silence invites context: "The soundscape was just as integral: distant police sirens, tugboat and train horns, the sharply wailing birds, all pulsing quietly in the background, muted by the once-treacherous canal and the empty lots of former homes."[166] These performances absorb the environment beyond space of audience and stage, not like a sponge but like a concussion.

Alterations to the actors' roles and even to the text of the play itself function differently in crisis environments. Chan's production at Gentilly, for example, transpires in front of an abandoned house, a placeholder for the many others in the area. During the performance, Vladimir spray-paints "Godot" onto this house. It is unclear whether by this gesture he is vandalizing a set, tagging, or contributing to the rest of the graffiti in post-Katrina New Orleans. (This ambiguity would not characterize the identical gesture performed on a conventional stage.) The defacement channels broader questions: is he defacing a prop, and if so, has the whole of Gentilly become a collection of props? After the flood, many abandoned buildings become archives of acerbic commentary: "AS NOT SEEN ON TV," for example.[167] These painted barbs compete with the fluorescent orange markings of official search parties, which designate inspected buildings or those with bodies found inside. As writing on the wall, Godot is cosigned: within Beckett's play, the name functions as a protest for the endpoint of the waiting process, but also as shorthand for the futility and deathly absence at the heart of the waiting process.

Chan also contextualizes the waiting of Beckett's characters through popular culture. Vladimir and Estragon wile away their time through impersonations: a Louis Armstrong impression, Michael Jackson's moonwalk. These citations of African American performance markedly contrast with the countercelebrity status of the black homeless characters we are watching on stage. What is their poverty (and their performance) to the immediately recognizable figures they cite with their voices and bodies? Does pop culture distract the African American community from their aftermath condition? What dream or escape from the conditions of Beckett's poverty is enlisted by imitating a performer rather than performing the long wait?

Parable and Asymptote

Critical response frequently regards Sontag's and Chan's productions as variations on the theme of localization, as if the disaster areas of Sarajevo and New Orleans were no different from the one Akalaitis constructs on the stage of the American Repertory Theater. Though offering her guarded approval, Oppenheim, for example, faults Sontag for diminishing Beckett's vision: "While the primitive, brutal even, dimensions and the alienation, illusion, hope and despair that characterize the work are without a doubt relevant to the Bosnians' situation, the parabolic vision of the play is clearly diminished both by its localization within a highly charged political arena and the substitution of a collectivity for a single couple."[168] On the one hand, Oppenheim concedes how the Sarajevans respond to the "primitive" quality of Beckett's work. This brute uptake, however, contaminates the dimension of Beckett's work that holds itself in reserve and outside application to the world: its status as parable. Oppenheim constructs an opposition between the supposed immediacy of Beckett as depiction versus a more reflective and meditative mode of signification.[169]

Yet in what ways does *Godot* exhibit a "parabolic vision"? Parable gives us the fruit of learning without its painful acquisition process. *Godot* offers us no such leverage, no outcome of the learning experience. On Beckett's stage, bodies monstrate rather than demonstrate principles for the spectator. A character cannot be a mouthpiece when his mouth is crammed with his last carrot. These qualities make it difficult for us to take the first step in receiving *Godot* as parable: we do not *disembody* Vladimir and Estragon. Their stage presence evinces the dolor and sluggishness one imagines Aesop's animals might have when not talking or when not in the limelight of parable.

Oppenheim clearly mistakes the loss of qualities in the vagabonds for the advent of some general condition or concept. The parable remains a genre indebted to the humanist tradition, and existentialism has seized the nakedness of Beckett's characters as an opportunity to discuss "humanity" on his stage. Adorno succinctly warns against this move in his notes to Beckett's *Endgame:* "Subtraction, not abstraction."[170] That is, Beckett does not wear down action, ego, stage, and tree in order to filter out everything unnecessary, leaving only a concept in its wake.[171] Subtraction cannot be equated with a refinement into concepts. Beckett's technique does not follow the path of Husserl's phenomenological reduction or *epoché*, bracketing whatever does not contribute to a study of the essential.[172] The last words of *Endgame,* "You, old stancher, you remain," indicate the play's survivor to be the half-bloodied cloth with which Hamm cloaks his face. Beckett's work seems to retain only inessential and downtrodden elements, obtuse forms that cannot be subsumed under rational concepts. The inexplicable residues derail the parabolic function and should not be confused with exemplary monuments.

To recover the truth of Oppenheim's critique of Sontag, we need to turn her image of Beckett's "parabolic vision" by ninety degrees, that is, her parabola must be made into an asymptote. Instead of parabolic vision, Beckett's work enacts a parabolic function. Etymologically, "asymptotic" derives from the term meaning "not to meet" (a mathematical synopsis for Beckett's play) and designates a curve that approaches zero without ever attaining zero.[173] Oppenheim notes that the parabolic vision is not lost but merely "diminished" when contextualized in Sarajevo. This reduction of meaning, of potential, complies with the asymptotic process in and around Beckett's play. The scantiness of means, the doing with less, the barely enough: these describe what Vladimir and Estragon are enduring as well as the actors who are rehearsing to play them.

Oppenheim claims that theater has no chance in "the highly charged political arena." She seems to say theater (high culture, refinement) does not belong in the arena of either politics or vulgar sport. Beckett does not agree with this, as can be seen by the way he brings theater asymptotically to near zero, diminishing our expectations and subtracting from theater its pretensions, its ornamentation, its theatricality. In revising theater, Beckett's work emerges as a theatrical experiment that echoes the dismal political experiment going on in Sarajevo and New Orleans. This political experiment entails the revision of the institution of the arena: in New Orleans, the Superdome ceases to be the space where the Saints play and becomes a massive and enclosed holding center for citizens displaced by the storm. In Croatia, the stadium in Slavonski Brod functions as a holding area for civilian refugees and is a frequent target for Serb artillery. Beckett's revisionary theater emerges in settings where arenas are refunctioned as holding pens.

Absurdity

Contrary to the tradition within literary criticism, Paul Chan suggests that *Godot* is not an example of the theater of the absurd, but rather a theater that responds to the absurdity of the world. The irrationality of the levee failure outbids the nonsensical banter between Vladimir and Estragon:

> It didn't look like a play. . . . It looked more to me like the emphatic expression of a community trying to come to terms with the irreconcilability of it all. What happened, and what is still happening, makes no sense. This nonsense has its own reason. And this reason must not be the only one worth using to make sense of what is happening to us, around us, against us. *Waiting for Godot in New Orleans* wanted to create another reason, to make another kind of sense, because art, if it is in fact art, is the reason that makes reason ridiculous.[174]

Godot offers another reason, the reasoning of art. The sense of art is not subsumable under the instrumental reason that is operative everywhere in society, from its machines, to its bureaucracy, to its levees, to its management and facilitation of disaster.[175] Art's poverty and impotence, the fact that it cannot enter the world and remains useless to it, is its utility. In remaining only in terrible symmetry with the world rather than dissolving into it, Beckett's play becomes a gym—one in which non-sense is exerted, exercised, and sweated, where one undertakes preparation for the "irreconcilability of it all," which is the irreconcilability between sense and the world, between people, between people and their situation, between need and the measures taken to address it, between individuals and their own waiting.

The image made by *Godot* in Sarajevo and New Orleans differs starkly from images of the respective disasters disseminated through television and other media. Images from Sontag's and Chan's productions demand a new understanding of the situation on the ground in devastated cities and a new understanding of Beckett's play. Chan and Sontag are focused primarily on this first goal. They turn toward the seemingly anachronistic medium of the stage in order to offer an echo chamber for it rather than a reproduction of it. In the media-saturated landscape of Sarajevo, Sontag remarks, "Suffering is visibly present, and can be seen in close-up; and no doubt many people feel sympathy for the victims. What cannot be recorded is an absence—the absence of any political will to end the suffering."[176] Television saturates our vision with close-ups of the disaster, turning the absence of intervention into an image of interest.

Photographic documentary of the disaster equally falls under Sontag's indictment. Her observation supports Walter Benjamin's assertion that photography "makes poverty into an object of consumption."[177] Two well-known photographic studies of Katrina's aftermath, Robert Polidori's *After the Flood* and Chris Jordan's *In Katrina's Wake*, demonstrate Sontag's and Benjamin's points. The fascination of these images lies in the mixture of nausea and curiosity they inspire in their registration of landscapes dismayingly emptied of all people. The work of both photographers relishes the sheer mass (a better word might be *wealth*) of possessions disengorged from people's homes by the floodwaters. Polidori establishes the photographic idiom of this disaster in three phases: photos of homes' exteriors (watermarks near the roof; clear signs of abandonment); the mucked interiors of homes (furniture rearranged by the strong waters, lines indicating where the floodwaters rose up to a father's chin in the family portrait); and the survey of possessions strewn across the desolated landscape of New Orleans. Both Polidori and Jordan position us within the aftermath of the flood. Like Beckett, they even ask us to take stock of this disaster. Yet in these photographs this stocktaking is made literal while it becomes the mourning of lost property. Our eyes comb through the swath of possessions dispossessed of owners. Sadly, the name brand emerges here as a life raft for our perception. The "quirky" image of a refrigerator lodged up in a tree, a Hammond organ overturned in the water, the Barbie doll stuck in the mud, the purse and shoes forcibly wedged within the fence. The photographs hook our eye with these muddied and sullen commodities. The emotional effect of the photographs depends so forcibly on such merchandise that we slowly realize we are auditing the images (as if we were representatives for an insurance company) much more than we are replying to the disaster they signify. In contrast to this decisive instant of recognition in the photograph, Beckett's theater suggests temporality (the long wait without promise of its end) and protracted misrecognition to be crucial parts of the disaster experience.

But Sontag's and Chan's productions not only raise our awareness about the war or the flood; they also help us understand the play itself. *Godot* in Sarajevo does not try to record the absence of an intervention by Clinton; Godot in New Orleans does not merely record the failures of FEMA or an inability to "make it right." Instead, the play registers the effects of this absence. The play is already a tightly wound articulation of this condition. But Sontag's and Chan's performances enact a subtraction process directed at the remnants allotted to the stage. From the destruction of Sarajevo that transpires in default of intervention, the media make images sufficient unto themselves. By means of vagabonds speaking in rage and irritability about the "enough," Beckett produces images insufficient unto themselves, which echo (rather than merely indict) the absence of Godot.

Beckett's vagabonds exist on the periphery of culture, yet suffer its blows and imperatives most directly. To audiences enduring the war or the aftermath of the flood, the performance of *Godot* illuminates the condition of abandonment overlooked by public officials and the news media: George Bush's "I'LL FIX IT" headlining the front page of the *New York Post* on September 3, 2005, or the moral imperative that serves as the title for Brad Pitt's neighborhood rehabilitation project, Make It Right. *Godot* dramatizes the "nothing to be done," the inertia of life cut off from the transformative rendezvous. The play remains responsive to the unfixable, incurable, irresolvable nature of catastrophe. The dislocated inhabitants of Sarajevo and New Orleans encounter this incapacity as the daily condition of their lives. To them, *Waiting for Godot* comes like a State of the Union address.

3

La Pensée Vagabonde

VAGABOND THOUGHT

The first two chapters explored Beckett's aesthetic of poverty as public performance and how *Waiting for Godot* becomes an echo chamber for the powerlessness, need, and inconsolable waiting beyond the stage. This chapter turns inward to the private crisis of Beckett's characters. Beckett's figure of private crisis is the vagabond who speaks in interior monologue whose interiority crumbles in the face of unsheltered experience.

Early in *Waiting for Godot*, Estragon begins to relay a dream to Vladimir, and Vladimir violently interrupts:

> VLADAMIR. DON'T TELL ME!
> ESTRAGON. Who am I to tell my private nightmares to if I can't tell them to you?
> VLADIMIR. Let them remain private. You know I can't bear that.[1]

Vladimir does not permit Estragon to speak his subjective nightmare, the monologic and private crisis that constitutes the consciousness of the vagabond. Vladimir enforces strict decorum over what can or cannot be divulged in the course of a long wait. Estragon's dream cannot be shared and thereby brought into consciousness without paining others and does not belong on stage, though as we will see shortly, Lucky does stage vagabond thought before he is similarly silenced by Vladimir and the others. Beckett's prose lifts this interdiction on the utterance of the vagabond's private nightmare. What goes unseen (like Estragon's sleeping in a ditch, his nightly beatings) and unsaid in *Godot* become the topic of Beckett's prose. Beckett's trilogy gives utterance to the vagabond dream, the work of the unsheltered dreamer who sleeps in full view. In *Godot*, instead of wandering off the stage to be besieged by something other than dialogue, the silenced Estragon merely threatens to leave:

> ESTRAGON. (*coldly*) There are times when I wonder if it wouldn't be better for us to part.
> VLADIMIR. You wouldn't go far.[2]

Estragon cannot leave any more than he can speak his dream. These two prohibitions ultimately give *Waiting for Godot* its form. The dialogue rests on the ban of monologic consciousness and on the restriction on the vagabonds' erratic movement. The play sublimates derelict wandering into yoga, Vladimir and Estragon's exercise routine of levitations, elongations, and relaxations.[3] *Godot* then sacrifices these elements of vagabond experience so as to give us the couple on stage, dialogue, waiting: in short, Beckett's theater.

Vagabond Thought

Beckett's work is about characters decomposing and the consciousness of their decomposition. I call the decomposition of consciousness *la pensée vagabonde*, or vagabond thought. *La pensée vagabonde* means both "vagabond thought" and "thought wanders." It suggests both a kind of thought and the erratic movement by which it cuts a path for thinking. The two meanings are simultaneous and entwined: "But how can you think and speak at the same time, without a special gift, your thoughts wander [la pensée vagabonde], your words too, far apart, no that's an exaggeration, apart, between them would be the place to be, where you suffer, rejoice, at being bereft of speech, bereft of thought, and feel nothing, hear nothing, know nothing, say nothing, are nothing, that would be a blessed place to be, where you are."[4] Underlying the idea of vagabond thought in Beckett's characters is the separation of thinking from writing. These activities never occupy the same place and work on separate tracks. They are inherently apart: the one did not wander from the other. Hope for uniting the two is as improbable as being deprived of either one or occupying what the narrator calls that "bereft" space lacking both thought and speech. Beckett's impoverished characters fall short of saying what they think as well as this zero point of thinking and saying nothing.

Beckett's work conceives vagabond consciousness as nonuseful and beyond the procedures of rational thought. It is an expression of the vagabond's condition: disturbed by the law, the sound of something in the air, even his own speaking. This is Beckett's turn from Joyce's stream of consciousness and the freedom of association in philosophical speculation. Lucky's speech in act 1 of *Waiting for Godot* is the most noteworthy instance of vagabond thinking in Beckett's work. Commanded by Pozzo to "Think, pig!" Lucky responds by thinking aloud. This thinking begins in exigency rather than choice. The thinking is performed as a spectacle. Lucky's monologue is a ramshackle collection of official-sounding decrees, public oratory. Through Lucky filter the rhetorical formulae from the discourses of medicine, law, science, theology. It is closer to a heterologue (consisting of many voices) than a monologue. From these discourses Lucky preserves only the oratorical debris. He puts the "turns" of these rhetorics into series, arrays, contradictory enumerations: "in short in fine" and "for reasons unknown in spite of the tennis the facts are there but time will tell I resume alas alas" "that as a result of the labors unfinished of Testew and Cunard it is established as hereinafter but not so fast for reasons unknown that as a result of the public works of Puncher and Wattmann it is established beyond all doubt."[5] We get endlessly prefatory proclamations without anything being proclaimed. The gesture of meaning thereby turns into nonproductive gesticulation. This is Lucky's version of vagabond thought, one that lives up to its status as a performance and as an action. True to Vladimir's verdict on Estragon's private nightmare, the characters within earshot of Lucky's speech all find it intolerable: the stage directions specify that Pozzo "suffers," Vladimir and Estragon being to "protest," and it ends with all three "throwing themselves on Lucky who struggles and shouts his text."[6] The mechanisms of what passes for thinking become visible (it is Lucky's "display" of knowledge). Their meaning and rational purpose sapped, these gestures of thought recover their quality of movement: this is the dimension of thought as performance and not just display. The key phrase in Lucky's speech is "I resume," repeated four times in the monologue and the only instances in which Lucky says "I." "I resume" is the *cogito* of the vagabond (a kind of *cogito ergo resume*). This is not synonymous with saying "I repeat," for vagabond thinking is more about struggle than doing the same (reproducing thought). Nor is it "I resume with" because the resumption goes on without any accumulation to thought and almost against speech. The "I" of vagabond thought lurks between discontinuous and fragmentary statements and does little more than continually usher in more of them. He is the siphon, rather than the agent, of speech.

The homeless characters of Beckett's prose do not seek to share their thoughts any more than does Lucky. Instead, their thought seems forcibly and violently extroverted. Vagabond consciousness is always forced out in public because no private or domestic space is available for thinking. Consciousness itself is extruded and unsheltered; reality intrudes upon it at every step. It resembles a hobo's sock, one that is reused by turning it inside out.

Vagabond thought is extravagantly kinetic, characterized by process rather than knowledge. Leo Bersani and Ulysse Dutoit refer to the "learned derelict" and ascribe to this consciousness a familiarity with culture unmoored from meaning. For Bersani and Dutoit this is freeing: "There is no agonized reevaluation of a tradition," they write.[7] They oppose Beckett to the surrealists. Whereas the surrealists "preserved terms" to which their revolutionary project relates, Beckett by contrast preserves nothing. His work "proposes something far more radical: a work cut off from all cultural inheritance."[8] Yet there is little of utopian or redemptive potential in this freedom. What matters is that the consciousness Beckett cares about is rootless, "cut off" but not "free from" inheritance. Bersani describes Beckett's approach to culture as a rummaging: "Much like the learned derelicts of his fiction, he evokes art and philosophy of the past as if he were rummaging through a junkyard, giving an amused kick now and then at some useless and irrelevant relic of a dead imagination."[9]

Bersani and Dutoit use the figure of the vagabond to conceptualize more broadly Beckett's relation to literary history and to the relic of language. What gesture does their "learned derelict," and subsequently Beckett's work, undertake? "Rummaging" suggests that the vagabond relates to junk as if he were shopping for antiques. The "kick" of the derelict likewise evokes the kick a prospective buyer might give a tire on a used car to test its worth. These are owners' gestures. Bersani and Dutoit helpfully focus on how the vagabond mediates the understanding of what Beckett's work does, how it thinks about the past, and its language process. Yet it is also important to understand the nonproprietary nature of vagabond thinking. The homology drawn by Bersani and Dutoit suggests that works of culture have fallen into ruin and that it is the hobo who pores over this inheritance. They saddle the derelict with the critic's ambition. In doing so they miss the nonevaluative nature of the hobo's gesture and deep indifference to thought, either as possession, assessment, or understanding of the world. Vagabond thought is without a proper place and renounces possession of what it says. This is the reason we pause before agreeing with Bersani and Dutoit's description of Beckett's characters as "learned derelicts." Vagabond thought does not stockpile itself or abide in the thinker in the past tense, as if it were a valuable hoard available for display. Walter Benjamin suggests that one reason we mistrust beggars is because we "forget that their persistence in front of our noses is as justified as a scholar's before a difficult text. No shadow of hesitation, no slightest wish or deliberation in our faces escapes their notice."[10] The vagabond mirrors our reading process. His obstinacy is reminiscent of learning. But the beggar is distinguishable from the scholar because he is motivated by desperation and existential need rather than curiosity, dedication, or knowledge.

What kind of thinking does not even bother to refuse reason, as if occurring in a completely different order? This chapter explores this question by discussing *la pensée vagabonde* in terms of its double emergence, both thought itself and a path for thinking. In the spirit of *la pensée vagabonde*, I weave through seven distinct operations of vagabond thought that supplant reasoning as a method for thinking for Beckett's characters: (1) thinking by hearing (by murmur), (2) radiographic understanding, (3) thinking by force (by axiom), (4) thinking by naming or designation of things (as a dictionary or thesaurus), (5) thinking by obligation (the pensum), (6) thinking as extroversion (as terror), and (7) mythic tense: thinking in the permanent present.

Thinking by Hearing: The Murmur

> We were confronting, as it were, a new and infinitely delicate point in the texture of reality, from which something far greater than ourselves seemed to be appealing to us as if seeking help. At the same time and all through the intervening years I believed that that independent sound, taken from us and preserved outside us, would be unforgettable.
> —Rainer Maria Rilke, "Primal Sound"[11]

Beckett's vagabonds substitute *ratio* with listening. Molloy indicates that he hears a murmur *with his head*. This is different both from a sound that is heard either *with the ear* or *in the head*. The murmur Molloy hears is not perceived through usual means, nor is it simply imagined. As an unconventional organ of listening, the exact working of the head is poorly understood. It does not offer simple ways to shut itself off or to stop sound. Unlike the ear, the head cannot be stuffed with cotton or wax. Even the location of this thought is unclear: as a murmur, this thought seems to surround Molloy rather than emanate from him. Molloy can neither interrupt this murmur nor put space between it and himself. The murmur is a kind of thinking that cannot be stopped or owned by the self. Can it even be heard? Molloy observes, "It's not a sound like the other sounds, that you listen to, when you choose and can sometimes silence, by going away or stopping your ears, no, but it is a sound which begins to rustle in your head, without your knowing how, or why. It's with your head you hear it, not your ears, you can't stop it, but it stops itself, when it chooses. It makes no difference therefore whether I listen to it or not, I shall hear it always, no thunder can deliver me, until it stops."[12] The murmur that penetrates everything exists in a state of indeterminate proximity to the listener, and Molloy speaks as if it had the nearness of a radio implant. Molloy says that there is no place, either in silence or in deafening thunder, which is outside its sonic range. He therefore cannot gain perspective on, or possibly even hear, a sound that always persists and cannot be interrupted. A murmur does not present an item for listening, and is unlike the sound of a bell or a gong whose clarity pierces the moment.[13]

Beckett measures a life not by the sound of thought but in terms of the thought to which that life is a mere backdrop. Molloy charts aging as if it were not the development of personality by experience, reason, or understanding but as a transition of sound: beginning as rumor, evolving into murmur and rising to a scream. Commenting on an old man he sees in the street, Molloy observes, "He looks old and it is a sorry sight to see him solitary after so many years, so many days and nights unthinkingly given to that rumor rising at birth and even earlier, What shall I do? What shall I do? now low, a murmur, now precise as the headwaiter's And to follow? and often rising to a scream. And in the end, or almost, to be abroad alone, by unknown ways, in the gathering night, with a stick."[14] Rumor acts prematurely, "rising at birth and even earlier," and this prematurity suggests a moment of possibility, even if this possibility extends no further than *boy or girl?* Molloy suggests that life itself is precipitated by this rumor, and we are never equal to this moment of possibility (rumors being well-known instances of stories that are impossible to both author and stop). He describes, moreover, the time in which the old man was unthinkingly given to this sonic boom after which his life has followed. Molloy formulates aging as a fall from the high velocity of rumor to a waiter's *sotto voce* murmur. In the process, the question about our possibility ("what should I do?") transforms into a choice made within the closed system of a restaurant menu, the future arriving as the next dish.

The precise formulation in which Molloy describes his abandonment to nonrational thought makes his experience of life similar to an animal's. The description of the old man as "unthinkingly given to that rumor" suggests we are intimately tied to noise through our ignorance. This transaction takes place in the passive voice: we are given to it, displaced and uprooted by it. Vagabond thought follows our expropriation by sound. The murmur enjoins Molloy to keep leave wherever he happens to be, to keep moving. In *Malone Dies*, the title character refers to the murmur as a buzzing: "The noises of the world, so various in themselves and which I used to be so clever at distinguishing from one another, had been dinning at me for so long, always the same old noises, as gradually to have merged in a single noise, so that all I heard was one vast continuous buzzing. The volume of sound perceived remained no doubt the same, I had simply lost the faculty of decomposing it."[15] The buzzing Malone hears challenges his "faculty for decomposition," both impossible to hear and impossible to avoid. Like an enormous doorbell it beckons and specifically addresses the listener.[16]

Malone notes that he once found noise to be a source of information and meaning: "worlds" were knowable to him through the sounds that represented them. Noting the loss of this enlightened faculty, Malone asks us to imagine noise without its referential and distinguishing marks. In this sense the sound that Malone hears loses the world. Worldless, this sound becomes what Beckett calls "fundamental." The more Molloy gives himself over to thinking by hearing buzzing and tries to exercise a discerning ear over the noise of his life, the more arthropodic his life becomes. Hearing a swarm of bees is the first step toward becoming a bee. The shift of his language is unannounced and indicates a sense of measure being lost: "I could not help thinking that the notion of a wandering herd was better adapted to him than to me. But I have never thought anything but wind, the same that was never measured to me."[17] A disturbing and decentered restlessness characterizes this brief passage as much as it is its subject. "To think wind" is to think without measure, in such a way that retains the empty sound of the wind and scatters references and distinctions.[18] In another context "to think wind" might designate a kind of transcendental exercise, and expansion of self, but here it denotes a process in which thinking is given over to notions one cannot help thinking. "Helpless thinking" is thinking like an insect or animal. It means several things—involuntary thinking that is determined from an outside, thinking that cannot be assisted by us, thinking that is lost to our charitable efforts at interpretation, thinking that does not help us picture the thinker: "the same that was never measured to me."[19] In some way thinking like an insect qualifies Molloy for one of Augustine's injunctions for sainthood: to engage unthinking, only at the level of base existence, heroically, epically. Molloy is a modern-day Odysseus equipped with an antenna, unable to draw nearer to or farther away from his Sirens. When Malone says that the notion of the wandering herd was "better adapted to [Jackson] than to me," he speaks of the process of metaphor blending with and becoming indistinct from an identity in the same way that one speaks of an insect trying to merge with its environment through adaptation. Here a metaphor does not inscribe an identity so much as it undergoes an evolutionary mimicry and becomes part of a larger camouflage. Beckett's character conceptualizes as an insect rather than as an entomologist.

By way of contrast one could consider the manner in which Franz Kafka formulates the drama of Gregor Samsa becoming a beetle in the heart of the family household, saddled with his old cares, habits, and anxieties. When Samsa is transformed into an insect, he had already lived like one and thought like one—his metamorphosis, though bizarre, is coherent, organic, and the natural consequence of metaphor. Being transformed causes Samsa no suffering. It is his family that suffers. Beckett's characters have no family to suffer any transformation: not only is there no one to knock on their door about their well-being, there is no room, no door. Beckett's characters do not definitively cross the limits of the human form. Instead of becoming analogical, experience swarms in Beckett's prose and is marked by the loss of qualities and the surge of forgotten residues of past experience. Malone compares his acquaintance not to a cow but to a "wandering herd," a multiple grouping. It is a comparison that was originally applied to him: acting like a weather vane for metaphor, he renounces the comparison, turns it backward, and says it suits its maker better. The path a herd suddenly cuts across space, the sound of its hooves, the dust made, the forgetting of the immediate past: these bring us closer to understanding Molloy's manner of speaking than any linguistic analysis.

The murmur that solicits the tramps on stage in *Waiting for Godot* has a different thought function than it does for Molloy. The dialogical structure of the stage neutralizes the murmur's engulfing confinement of the solitary Molloy. What happens when a murmur is perceived by two people instead of the one? What casts Molloy into the confusion of thought seems indisputably present on stage for Vladimir and Estragon and without the imperative function it has for Molloy. The murmur is tellingly drowned out by the banter of Vladimir and Estragon trying to describe it:

VLADIMIR. They make a noise like wings.
ESTRAGON. Like leaves.
VLADIMIR. Like sand.
ESTRAGON. Like leaves.
    Silence.

VLADIMIR. They all speak at once.
ESTRAGON. Each one to itself.
    Silence.

VLADIMIR. Rather they whisper.
ESTRAGON. They rustle.
VLADIMIR. They murmur.
ESTRAGON. They rustle.[20]

The back and forth between Vladimir and Estragon puts their dialogue in close approximation to the murmur: though they do not both "speak at once," they often seem to "speak only to themselves."

The dialogue between the vagabonds usurps the function of the murmur in *Molloy*. The critical success of *Waiting for Godot* depends in part on its successful sublimation of the murmur into voice. In his monologue in act 2, Vladimir speaks of "those cries for help still ringing in our ears."[21] Whereas Molloy claims to have heard voices with his head, Vladimir reclaims the ear as a repository where sound goes to vibrate. This ringing takes on the quality of an ethical alarm rather than the force that decomposes the listener. Where sound compels Molloy into metamorphosis, the cry in *Waiting for Godot* becomes the figuration of the human: "At this moment in time, all mankind is us, whether we like it or not."[22] The animal enters only as an exemplary indifference to sound (the tiger that slinks back into its thicket).

The helplessness of thought and its usurpation by the murmur appears in *Waiting for Godot* only comically, not horrifically. Molloy's encounter with sound as something that thinks through him returns faintly in the dialogue between Vladimir and Estragon. Vladimir states, "What is terrible is to *have* thought." Estragon replies, "Did that ever happen to us?"[23] Vagabond thinking is something undergone, not something that we do but something that happens to us (and, as Estragon suggests, without leaving any traces). In Beckett's landscape, the *cogito* cannot be an active verb. Thought is a deponent of something that happens, something that might not even be happening. Estragon's question about whether thought ever occurred to them is matched only by the certainty that it has ceased:

> VLADIMIR. We're in no danger of ever thinking any more.
> ESTRAGON. Then what are we complaining about?[24]

Radiographical Understanding

> He describes the radiographical quality of his observation. The copiable he does not see.
> —Samuel Beckett, *Proust*[25]

Vagabond thought operates on Beckett's characters radiographically. Molloy is bombarded and surrounded with noise in a manner similar to a radio surrounded by waves. Scraps of sound hit Molloy from indeterminate locations, and the radio replaces the *ratio*. Molloy describes sound in technical terms: "Sounds unencumbered with precise meaning were registered perhaps better by me than by most. What was it then? A defect of the understanding perhaps, which only began to vibrate on repeated solicitation, or which did vibrate, if you like, but at a lower frequency, or a higher, than that of ratiocination, if such a thing is conceivable, and such a thing is conceivable, since I conceive it."[26] Molloy speaks of a channel that is "lower ... or higher" than ratiocination, then credits himself with conceiving the idea. This thinking proceeds not by means of ratiocination but by registration, through waves, frequencies, repetitions, solicitations, and poor reception. Despite a suspected and self-admitted defect in understanding, Molloy is nothing like the "unreliable" narrator in the style of Emily Brontë or Thackeray—characters who offer a partial or biased perspective on the events they narrate. Molloy is rather a *relayable* narrator, involved in a wholly original quest to investigate what can be transmitted, an unbearable situation of listening without comprehension.

Noises for Molloy are not subject to the doubt of the speaker: they are not ambiguous. To the contrary, Molloy says he hears noises with distinct clarity. The clarity is alarming because it is apart from meaning. He continues: "Yes, the words I heard, and heard distinctly, having quite a sensitive ear, were heard for a first time, a second time, and even a third as pure sounds, free of all meaning, and this is probably one of the reasons why conversation was unspeakably painful to me. And the words I uttered myself, and which must nearly always have gone with an effort of the intelligence, were often to me as the buzzing of an insect, And this is perhaps one of the reasons I was so untalkative."[27] Here Molloy returns to discussing his murmur as insectlike. When Molloy claims his ear is "sensitive" he is referring to the precision with which it registers sound and not to an ability to hear nuance or overtone. He is deaf to sense. Unlike those who, hard of hearing, eventually "get" the message upon hearing it repeated a second or third time, he claims that language abandons its sense for him—as it does for words that children repeat—with more frequent repetition. Molloy desists from all habits of listening that make for easy understanding and that are as surely ingrained as habits of speech. Heard as "pure sound" rather than as traces within a differential system, language does not leave any deposits behind after its disappearance.

Molloy speaks of his experience as if he were a radio, a receptive system destitute of interpretive and calculative ability. He supplies an apparatus rather than a metaphor: instead of providing an intelligible figure in which to encapsulate the nonsense of his acoustic world, the description leads through the wires and knobs of an instrument of "nonunderstanding." It leads not into an image but into the box of Molloy's head, right to the working component of his radiophonic ear: a "defect of the understanding." Nonsensical hearing is merely another "station" on the dial with rational understanding and works at a slightly different radio frequency. Molloy thereby places these not in opposition but in continuity with one another. Through this schema Molloy tries to explain how understanding occurs only when its defects are solicited. Understanding remains an elusive experience. "It is true that in the end, by dint of patience, we made ourselves understood, but understood with regard to what, I ask you, and to what purpose."[28] Molloy's question here is drawn from the language of ratiocination, inquiring into the means (understood with regard to what?) and ends (and to what purpose?) of understanding. We are hardpressed to offer an answer. The point, however, may be to rearticulate the question. He implores the reader to think temporarily with terms that the vagabond's discourse has actively impoverished.

Vagabond thinking cobbles together an alternative image of the understanding process, based on the sound, registration, and the radiophonic ear, rather than on reason and the extraction of sense. Molloy asks us to consider about the possibility of an understanding between two people without remainder or higher purpose, and that does not secure anything. Molloy asserts that an understanding transpired but without proof: it remains fictitious. In his quick aside to the reader, he may be asking whether such a thing is conceivable. Our goal is to orient ourselves in such a way toward vagabond thinking, expressed here as a reaction without desire for enlightenment, which one is allowed to say, with Molloy, yes, it is conceivable, because we conceive it.

Molloy exposes the ear as the last outpost of the Enlightenment and submits the rational selectivity of the ear to an acoustic catastrophe: his own words are not spared. Thinking by radiophonic ear rather than by *ratio* raises questions, in other words, about the very basis of a consciousness steered by Enlightenment logic, questions that we perhaps do not hear because we reason. Painstakingly Molloy asks us to interrogate what we hear in the word "understanding," graspable not by quantifying variable terms as by a calculator but by the reception of wave signals as by an audio receiver. "And to the noises of nature too, and the works of men, I reacted I think in my own way and without desire of enlightenment."[29] Molloy's ear, exposed to the vacuous quality of language, asks what understanding can be communicated about a process that leaves nothing behind, where language does not communicate meaning. Molloy says it best: he does not react with the desire for something and does not exchange the sound of language for something to which he can then lay claim. Molloy listens without outcome, and in the process gives expression to the long-standing philosophical incompatibility of analytical enlightened thought and the murmur.[30]

Thought by Force: The Axiom

The murmur that courses through Beckett's work is part of a general radioscopy of consciousness in perpetual withdrawal. Another mode of this withdrawal I call the "axiom." By definition an axiom is a generally accepted or self-evident truth, such as "The whole is greater than the parts." It appears in mathematical or logical arguments as a premise that does not require demonstration. Beckett is not interested in the truth of axioms or in collecting them. He is interested in the "force" of axioms.

In the instances when vagabond thought operates axiomatically, logic is not displaced by noise or sound. It is instead embedded within thought. A solicitation creates a moment of interruption and sudden depropriation, but again the initiative for understanding is missing. The axiom fills the void. Though a drifting character, Molloy's thoughts are not freely adrift in stream-of-consciousness style. Instead his thought process is engaged at all times with multiple categories of necessity, principle, and conceptual rule. A strange evisceration of his thought is palpable even in this simple passage in which Molloy is walking down an alleyway at night: "Espying a narrow alley between two high buildings I looked about me, then slipped into it. Little windows overlooked it, on either side, on every floor, facing one another. Lavatory lights I suppose. There are things from time to time, in spite of everything, that impose themselves on the understanding with the force of axioms, for unknown reasons."[31] Molloy speaks here of his inexplicable subjection to the axiomatic. For the straggler Molloy, even this negligible experience of identifying the lights in the window as "lavatory lights" involves susceptibility, and unusual attentiveness, to the ways a conclusion is imposed. Here "lavatory lights" is a conclusion reached involuntarily, as if it were someone else's. This imposition of a form, the symmetrical arrangement of lit windows, on the understanding does not contradict Molloy's earlier claim that it was always the defect of his understanding that reality made vibrate. This "defect" of understanding is particularly active here where an understanding has been imposed on Molloy. As Molloy says, he cannot grasp the premise of this understanding, and the axiomatic force is imposed "for unknown reasons." Molloy reminds us of what needs to be forgotten before every gesture of identification: its premise. Forgetting this premise endows the identification with its completely natural and "of course" quality, with force. An identity, to have an identity, must silence its basis. Something comparable happens when a person is asked to explain his or her prejudices: their foundation, like that of Molloy's supposition, cannot be stated.

Molloy thinks in such a way that he grasps neither the premise of his "understanding" nor the motivation, the reasons for his logical certainty. The axiomatic nature of this architectural symmetry, what it denotes, is based on a kind of déjà vu (through what experience do I know these to be lavatory lights?) that is not his, however, to remember. The conclusive designation is stated in fact as a supposition ("Lavatory lights I suppose"). Suppositional thinking is the equivalent in logic to homelessness. The supposition is a mode of understanding that seems equally removed from its conclusion as from its occasion: the understanding it offers does not give us means to communicate with its premise, and since it is often made in the absence of all premise, its premise is something that itself must be supposed. There is a homelessness that is endemic to axiomatic society, since its forms do not give us the means to understand how we know what we know. We are in short abandoned to its conclusions.

Molloy is not dazzled by the light. Instead, his thinking becomes a screen that sensitively registers the larger logical operations that society enforces through its individuals. The simple symmetry of small, lit windows overlooking an alley initiates Molloy into a simple conclusion that they were lavatory lights, a knowledge he perhaps did not know he had. What happens when architecture and society in general impose their meanings axiomatically, when their forms bear the force of axioms? It is at this moment that the law becomes immanent to form. The conclusions drawn are deduced through the individual, given an air of self-evidence. Molloy bears witness to the self-alienating effect of this axiomatic moment, since on second reflection he cannot understand wherefrom comes this "of course" feeling.

Molloy's knowledge of architecture comes at the cost of its shelter. This recognition of architecture is uncanny, a testament to his own abandonment by architecture and its interior. His knowledge of this particular aspect of architectural design is disarming because he is not privy to the use of this space in the same way as those who inhabit it. Only for the man unfamiliar with beds, sleeping in the alley with the newspapers and filth, can the lavatory law and expedience of architectural space be lifted into the realm of pure knowledge. For the derelict, the home can only be supposed: its inside is truly hypothetical.[32]

Lexicographic: Supposition as Thinking

A third mode of vagabond thought I call "lexicographical thinking" because it substitutes supposition as word association for *ratio*. In his essay "Two Aspects of Language and Two Types of Aphasic Disturbances," Roman Jakobson distinguishes between the "syntagmatic" and "paradigmatic" aspects of language.[33] A syntagmatic disturbance is structural and occurs on the level of syntax and grammar. The paradigmatic disturbance is operational and on the level of sense or the morpheme. Beckett's characters' lexicographical thinking is unlike the syntagmatic thinking of the true aphasic where disturbance results in incomprehensibility. Nonetheless, the lexicographical thinking that characterizes the vagabond thought is akin to a syntagmatic disturbance in the sense that thinking and speaking become a kind of supposition by substitution of morpheme, a paradigmatic flipping through the dictionary.

Supposition articulates the logical as the condition for Molloy's vagabond thought. This supposition is not a condition in the sense that it becomes the ground for a conclusion. For Molloy supposing is not an activity performed once and for all, waiting in the expectation of verification, but rather continuously, obsessively. Molloy's entire monologue has the tone of a repeatedly made and repeatedly abandoned supposition. The homeless condition that underlies Molloy's surprise at his familiarity—though speculative, from the view in the alley—of an interior space is also inflected in the torrent of words that describes the alley itself. In Molloy's description of the alley in which he is searching for a resting place, language moves laterally and not vertically, tirelessly picking itself up to resume the process. Molloy relates,

> There was no way out of the alley, it was not so much an alley as a blind alley. At the end there were two recesses, no, that's not the word, opposite each other, littered with miscellaneous rubbish and with excrements, of dogs and masters, some dry and odorless, others still moist. Ah those papers never to be read again, perhaps never read. Here lovers must have lain at night and exchanged their vows. I entered one of the alcoves, wrong again, and leaned against the wall, my feet far from the wall, on the verge of slipping, but I had other props, the tips of my crutches. But a few minutes later I crossed the alley into the other chapel, that's the word, where I felt I might feel better, and settled myself in the same hypotenusal posture. And at first I did actually seem to feel a little better, but little by little I acquired the conviction that such was not the case. A fine rain was falling and I took off my hat to give my skull the benefit of it, my skull all cracked and furrowed and on fire, on fire.... At last I began to think, that is to say listen harder.[34]

Far from being a figure that adopts indifference as a way to cope with his existence under siege, the derelict is attuned to the smallest of differences. Molloy overhears his own speaking, and consequently speaks with an incredible finickiness, listening for the more exact word for his experience. First he says "alley," and then "blind alley." "Recess" is replaced with "alcove" and then "chapel." It is important not to confuse dereliction with inebriation: Molloy does not stumble around drunk in his speech but soberly seeks out the right term. The monologue transmits destitution by not allowing meanings to take root despite the profusion of small differences. Molloy is picky with his words, and this scrupulousness requires an empty hand. Being picky means never really allowing your hand to grasp or possess. Contrary to popular wisdom, Beckett's beggar can indeed be a chooser, but only a chooser, and without laying claim to what is chosen.

None of the words toward which his precision tends ever add up—they do not become building blocks for anything. Molloy's search for the "proper" word for his resting place in the alley does not seem to be a search for deeper significance. He does not, for example, find any solace in the religious or ceremonial overtones of the word "chapel." Though he places a chapel in an alley littered with excrement and trash, Molloy never suggests this to be a profane or transgressive gesture. There is no prose that is bowed so low as Molloy's. He seems oblivious to connotation, and in words such as "chapel" he finds the forgotten, literal designation of a hollowed rather than a hallowed space. Molloy's homelessness is conveyed by his ignorance of idiom, by his being out of reach of both the morality and popularity of certain phrases or meanings. He speaks as if he learned the words very long ago, prior to the idiomatic significance they later acquired. Molloy is a lexicographer of the alley who does not grab onto these meanings but quickly lets them go. His substitutive gestures are precise but endless and oblivious to their rhetorical function. It could be said that Molloy uses an architectural dictionary in a way that is, paradoxically, nomadic, as if to exhaust words, run through them, sacrifice them, and abandon them. Closely tied to Molloy's attentiveness to particular words is this neglect of the signification they have for us.

In making thinking synonymous with listening, the final line of this passage above underscores the centrality of the ear in Beckett's conception of homeless existence and recalls the first mode of vagabond thought mentioned above, the murmur. More than the face, the ear is our most open feature. This "listening harder" is not a state of repose but of restless exposure and susceptibility, and I have already described the ways Molloy is subject to endless injunctions, calls to order, and murmurs that compel him to move on. In the above passage it is possible to see the discriminating activity of Molloy's ear.

The sobriety with which words are employed in Molloy's description of the alley is such that these words are striking without our noticing it. One of these is Molloy's use of the word "excrements." In his penchant for specific designations, Molloy has no need of the singular case of this word. His desire to divide and distinguish divorces him from the habit of speech that confers an abstract plural unity upon "excrement" (as upon "trash"). This is a testament to the life lived in the alley. Molloy's speech refers to specific producers, and not just the idea, of excrement.

Another word of surprising precision is Molloy's description of his body posture as "hypotenusal," which means that he is leaning like a hypotenuse facing the right angle formed by the ground and the wall. The word sounds like hypertensional, but this would only designate an antonym to this posture in which Molloy—with one of his legs shortening and the other stiffening—finds rest possible. Moreover, "hypotenusal," unlike "hypertensional," is not an adjective describing a psychological or "inner" state but rather Molloy's posture as it functions in a larger figure, namely, the triangle formed by body, ground, and wall. His posture expresses less a habit than an axiom, less a self in repose than a segment inserted into a larger geometrical function, dictated by the space offered by the blind alley.

Thinking as Obligation: The Pensum

> I have said that we undertake our works on the basis of several kinds of freedom: freedom with respect to material, with respect to size and shape, with respect to time; the mollusk seems deprived of all these—a creature that can only recite its lesson, which is hardly distinguishable from its very existence.
>
> —Paul Valéry, *Sea Shells*[35]

Vagabond thought in Beckett's characters is the substitution of *ratio* with a strenuous search of verbal exactitude. This thirst indicates that his characters labor under a lesson that needs to be learned. Beckett's word for this unremembered lesson is a kind of cognate for the thought itself: the pensum.[36] This word recurs throughout the Beckett oeuvre.[37] The *Oxford English Dictionary* defines "pensum" as "a charge, duty, or allotted task; a school task to be prepared, often imposed as punishment."[38]

The derelict is devoted to the unrecitable pensum as he is to everything unremembered. Beckett's characters abandon their possessions and abjure the world in favor not of spiritual clarity but of the thing they cannot dispense: the imperative to speak. The title character in *The Unnamable* admits,

> Yes, I have a pensum to discharge, before I can be free, free to dribble, free to speak no more, listen no more, and I've forgotten what it is. There at last is a fair picture of my situation. I was given a pensum, at birth perhaps, as a punishment for having been born perhaps, or for no particular reason, because they dislike me, and I've forgotten what it is. But was I ever told? . . . Strange notion in any case, and eminently open to suspicion, that of a task to be performed, before one can be at rest. Strange task, which consists in speaking of oneself. Strange hope, turned towards silence and peace. Possessed of nothing but my voice, the voice, it may seem natural, once the idea of obligation has been swallowed, that I should interpret it as an obligation to say something.[39]

The pensum is described as a punishment for having been born, something he has forgotten ("but was I ever told?"). Beckett pictures this pensum as an interval between Molloy and his existence, between Molloy and his thought. As the imagined key to his silence and as that which always remains to be thought, the pensum addresses the thinking subject from the position where he would no longer be thinking, where his response would be rote, a reflex of habit. This is the manner in which the pensum is significant to Beckett's art of poverty: it is emblematic of the way thought can be directed or assigned without being informed or given content. The pensum is the cause or the task for thinking and speaking that never reveals itself. The pensum is of great interest to Beckett's depiction of the vagabond since it is the vagabond's, but at the same time the vagabond cannot appropriate it. Were he to remember it, Molloy even specifies that he would recite it not in his voice but in "the voice." Molloy frequently frames his monologue with reference to a duty that he has forgotten but that he must nevertheless perform. Interrupting his thought with pedagogical exactitude, Molloy says that just speaking freely cannot be equated with a freedom from the obligation enforced by the pensum: "And truly it little matters what I say, this, this or that or any other thing. Saying is inventing. Wrong, very rightly wrong. You invent nothing, you think you are inventing, you think you are escaping, and all you do is stammer out your lesson, the remnants of a pensum one day got by heart and long forgotten, life without tears, as it is wept."[40] Here the pensum appears as the force that impoverishes expression. Since it cannot be remembered, the pensum cannot be dispensed with, exchanged, or gotten rid of. For that very reason Molloy describes it as the content of his thought: it controls what he says. Even while improvising, Molloy claims he remains under the spell of the pensum, its "remnants." As with Lacan's understanding of the unconscious as an interval that is both unthinkable and ethical, Beckett's pensum is predominantly that which recurs and recurs at odds with what the thinking subject thinks. It is in force when we think ourselves farthest from it. Here we seem to be very far from poverty as it is ordinarily understood. But the pensum pertains to loss, and a loss with which we cannot dispense and cannot overcome. It is the lesson that has been lost: the moment when thinking, expression, meaning, and performance seem to meet in the student in front of the blackboard. The final words of the passage above describe the complete terror of this dispossession: "a life without tears, as it is wept." Nothing would seem more natural than the equivalence, the simultaneity, of weeping and tears. The pensum intervenes between these moments, separating meaning from expression, sign from value. Something is therefore missing from this image of loss, and in Molloy's picture the subject is absent to his own sum, and weeps without crying. Loss and grieving are never relieved in Beckett's work through emotive or sentimental signs. It is always the burden of the reader to discern the destitute state of his characters, as it is registered in their evaporated stares.

The wandering of vagabond thought is not its identity but its torment. Molloy's wandering monologue is a kind of response, a searching for response, to the educational imperative. This imperative—to remember, recite, to speak—originates in an immemorial time, and it is as if the demand of the schoolteacher were the first form to be imposed on the drifter and the last to be abandoned. Some critics regard Molloy's increasing forgetfulness as a philosophical lesson, a renunciation of worldly possessions, and a station on the way to pure reflection. Leo Bersani conjectures,

> The poverty of Molloy's projects and resources creates a dramatic vacuum in which he can develop the logic of a more radical poverty and thus prefigure his later incarnations in the trilogy. The crippled derelict is an ideal image for a philosophical apprenticeship. The trilogy carries the Cartesian process backwards, starting with a bodily *je suis* and ending with a pure *cogito*. Molloy's infirmities give him more time for reflection. Unable to move and to think at the same time, Molloy can enjoy, or suffer, an absolute mental concentration during the pauses between his painful movements.... His thought rarely "reaches" matter, and this provides a grotesquely comic confirmation of that autonomy of mind which Descartes experienced as the strength and dignity of mind.[41]

This is *Molloy* as *bildungsroman*, an educational novel in which knowledge is hoarded in its alienation from the world, and experience is gathered up as a kind of capital. It makes Molloy's resolute dereliction sound downright advantageous as it gives Molloy "more time for reflection." In this sense Bersani misstates the nature of the task—a task as much for us as it is for Molloy—in the thought of the beggar.

Bersani converts the pursuit of thought into a leisurely activity, a kind of hobby in which he can "develop the logic of a more radical poverty." But impoverishment does not obey logic. Its expression—the imperative of the lesson to which the beggar is submitted—is akin to an unconscious structure, something Bersani perhaps misses in trying to understand Molloy as a parodic fulfillment of *Cartesian* philosophy. Molloy presents a more "radical" poverty than is seen in Bersani's model. Molloy's thinking is directed toward an outside in which the self is dispossessed of its presence in thought. Molloy's repeated acknowledgment that he is not where he thinks stands counterposed to Bersani's claim that Molloy offers a confirmation, however grotesque, of "autonomy of mind." The alienation of Molloy from the world does not allow him an opportunity to retreat to the irreducible point of the *cogito*.[42] Rather, his alienation is truly alienated and a sign of his absolute dependence, his helplessness, before the demands of the outside. According to Bersani, poverty creates "a dramatic vacuum," but the pathos of the derelict and the tenor of his thought in his dependency deserve a wider situation, a situation of terror from which no possessions and no self can serve as protection. The alienation of Molloy presents a particular incidence of a situation of *absolute exposure* in which Molloy is turned away, not in a voluntary fashion toward inwardness (as is implicit in the notion of a "dramatic vacuum") but in an involuntary fashion away from himself.

Thinking as Extroversion

> Hearing nothing, I am nevertheless prey to communications.
> —Samuel Beckett, *The Unnamable*

Though it is a type of drifting, dereliction has nothing to do with being free. It means having nowhere to go, but also having nothing to retreat to. In his poem "Enueg" Beckett writes, "Sweating like Judas / tired of dying / tired of policemen / feet in marmalade." This describes three ways in which Beckett's characters are locked into contingent, external situations rather than internal or moral ones. The drifting beggar is not a drowned figure but a forever drowning figure, not a mortal figure but a permanently mortal figure. The vagabond is importantly not "tired to death," or to the point of respite, but rather tired of dying. He is subject to an exhaustion enforced by the law. Beckett does not express the mortality of his characters by saying they have feet of clay. He emphasizes their impoverished and endlessly dying status by remarking that he trudges like a Sisyphus through preserves. The viscous medium through which the character moves is also a jumbled reference to an impoverished literary figure that precedes him. "Marmalade" offers a submerged reference to the derelict Marmaladov in Dostoevsky's *Crime and Punishment*.[43]

Jean-Luc Nancy observes that one is always abandoned to something as much as abandoned by something. "One always abandons to a law," he writes. "The destitution of abandoned being is measured by the limitless severity of the law to which it finds itself exposed. . . . [Abandonment] is a compulsion to appear absolutely under the law, under the law as such and in its totality."[44] In Nancy's description, every day is a court date for the derelict, not because he appears before the court at such and such a time, but because his mere appearance is an appearance before the law, the law "as such." The vagabond experiences the law "as such" because nothing mediates or tempers its exercise over him. There is no recourse for vagabond thought to disappear, to remain silent, to retreat. "If only I were not obliged to manifest," regrets Beckett's Unnamable.[45] The burden on the derelict is not composed of manifesting something particular for the law such as respect or desire. Rather, he remains in an intransitive relation to the law and is obliged to merely manifest. Molloy describes this obligation to manifest as a state of perpetual eviction and of having no place from which to withstand the provisions of the law. He is looking again for a place to sleep:

> But already the day is over, the shadows lengthen, the walls multiply, you hug the walls, bowed down like a good boy, oozing with obsequiousness, having nothing to hide, hiding from mere terror, looking neither right nor left, hiding but not provocatively, ready to come out, to smile, to listen, to crawl, nauseating but not pestilent, less rat than toad. Then the true night, perilous too but sweet to him who knows it, who can open to it like the flower to the sun, who is himself night, day and night. . . . The night purge is in the hands of technicians, for the most part.[46]

There is a strange lack of obviousness to the poverty described in such a passage. Rejecting all sociological references to the phenomenon and the historical plight that produces begging, Beckett's prose nevertheless conveys something about the experience of poverty. Small details accomplish this. "The walls multiply": the city's structure becomes opaque, self-reproductive, active, producing a labyrinth around the life of the beggar. There are no houses, no interiors, no architecture per se, just their rudiments—their walls—that exclude, hunt, and overwhelm Molloy. Molloy is imprisoned paradoxically by being locked out, and his description of this indicates the way in which his experience is strewn before the very etymology of the mur-mur, the sound that grows between walls. Still more delicate and alarming, and characterizing the coup offered by Beckett's prose, is Molloy's use of "obsequiousness." The word denotes deference to authority with the hope of gain or improvement of one's position. This is a surprising term to describe Molloy's life, devoted to loss and subject to permanent eviction. In the beggar the obsequious posture becomes permanent. Even objects such as the wall or a walking stick seem to extrovert Molloy and turn him out of himself in a gesture of complete dependency on the world.[47] Making no great claims for himself, Molloy asserts that he is nearer to the indolence and impassivity of the toad (and by implication the toady, i.e., the obsequious sycophant) than to the animal stereotyped for its survival techniques, the rat. For Beckett the derelict is not a survivor whose instincts carry him past the crisis but rather the permanent inhabitant of that crisis, the sensitive wound registering its demands (always ready to "smile, to listen, to crawl"). Molloy's readiness is the catalyst for his metamorphosis, as if obsequiousness and its bent posture placed him outside the realm of upright creatures. Molloy's state of mind can be summed up with "You never know . . . (what may happen, what may come in the night)." Instead of inaugurating a condition of doubt, however, this inaugurates a state in which the self is readied for constant disintegration.

Vagabond thought is consciousness ransacked by terror. The domination of this consciousness and the experience of terror increases as the trilogy proceeds. In *Molloy*, the conditions for depropriation are embodied in the figure and situation of the derelict. As the trilogy evolves, the vagabond as subject—this most marginal of figures—is chased off and pushed out. In the harassed monologue of *The Unnamable*, for example, we encounter the narrator buried under thinking torn in a process of dispersion: "I only think, if that is the name for this vertiginous panic as of hornets smoked out of their nest, once a certain degree of terror has been exceeded."[48] Badiou remarks of this passage, "like all terror, this one is also given as an imperative without concept, and it imposes an obstinacy that gives no quarter and allows no escape."[49] Badiou exposes the force and duress that scar the monologues of Beckett's characters—an imperative to speak but without any concept or understanding that authorizes the imperative. Badiou goes on to say that Beckett enacts a gradual and literal "torture of the cogito" at the hands of a "terroristic imperative to sustain the unsustainable."[50] But here Badiou overstates the role of philosophy because the absence of concept does not truly account for Malone's terror. Beckett's texts formulate a terror that exceeds philosophy not because of any limit of philosophy but rather because of a limit of the mind. Beckett removes the figure of the mind (and therefore thought), replacing it with a hive susceptible to rapid disinternalization. In other words, vagabond thought occurs in the level of the hive—or at best the brain—rather than in the mind. Forgetting that the basis of vagabond thought is the vagabond risks philosophizing Beckett. The result is that we end by speaking philosophically and generally about terror: "All terror," as Badiou calls it. Taking the perspective of the beggar reminds us that Beckett is no more interested in all humanity than he is in all terror. Rather, Beckett sees and is interested in the difference between all terror and what the vagabond undergoes and what ultimately constitutes his consciousness: daily terror.

Life without shelter is a daily terror depicted with typical understatement by Beckett, though a brutal amputation is taking place. A simple contrast with the beggar of Maurice Blanchot's *La Folie du jour* is instructive in this regard. Blanchot's story is in many ways inspired by Beckett's novel and brings the themes of *Molloy* to explicit theoretical exposition. The narrator reports, "I was beginning to sink into poverty. Slowly, it was drawing circles around me; the first seemed to leave me everything, the last would leave me only myself."[51] The passage that contrasts most strongly with Beckett's approach describes the way the narrator explains his metamorphosis and his vulnerability in his new situation. "Even though my sight had hardly weakened at all, I walked through the streets like a crab, holding tightly onto the walls, and whenever I let go of them dizziness surrounded my steps. I often saw the same poster on these walls; it was a simple poster with rather large letters: *You want this too*. Of course I wanted it, and every time I came upon these prominent words, I wanted it."[52] Blanchot controls the metamorphosis of his character more than does Beckett. Where Blanchot's character turns to the walls for support, no laws of physics intercede to relieve the condition of Beckett's derelict. Vertigo, curable in the former, consumes the life of Beckett's character and becomes almost palpable in the way he says the walls multiply. Above all it is important to notice how comprehensibly social and legible the helplessness of the beggar is for Blanchot. His weakness is signaled by the fact that he is addressed more strongly by the poster, by his inability to resist the function of the advertisement that informs the viewer of his wants.

This can be called, borrowing Beckett's phrase, a resentful indigence because it is replete with desire for what it cannot have. The openness of the narrator to the socioeconomic signifier, *ces mots considérables*, is the openness of a fully functional and employed subject. Like Kant's idea of a law that both needs and commands our attention (*Achtung*) and respect, these considerable letters in the advertisement address the care and consideration of Blanchot's beggar unproblematically. The susceptibility of his desire and imagination to its message is in a way indistinguishable from anyone else's: he occupies the same subject position of any consumer and occupies it more literally, as each time he sees the slogan, in Blanchot's words, *he wanted it*. His destitute condition is there merely to provide his desire with melodramatic value: the beggar is both full (of desire) and empty (of means) before the advertisement. The advertisement's system of socially sanctioned meaning therefore undergoes no distortion under the gaze of the dispossessed.

In Molloy's description, the extroversion of the beggar is not toward a commodity or the letters in its advertisement, but toward the night. Molloy says he is open to the night the way a flower is open to the sun. "Proust," Beckett observes, "assimilates the human to the vegetal. He is conscious of humanity as flora, never as fauna . . . and this preoccupation accompanies very naturally his complete indifference to moral values and human justices."[53] Molloy follows this inverted or chiasmatic natural law: his openness is compared to a heliotropism that directs him toward the sounds of the night. Therefore, the condition of the homeless wanderer is not only focused around an absence—the night that holds his peril—but the necessity and inevitability of this focus is graspable only by the disruption of a natural metaphor.

Advertisement makes little appearance in *Molloy*. Its absence is consistent with the law of his extroversion that follows a second-order natural necessity.[54] Yet it is instructive to note the care with which advertisement does enter the story of the derelict. Molloy is telling one of his countless stories of sleeping in gardens and ditches, and he remarks, "But it is useless to dwell on this period of my life. If I go on long enough calling that my life I'll end up by believing it. It's the principle of advertising."[55] Unlike Blanchot's character, Molloy is not susceptible to the lures of the advertisement and does not mercilessly want what it sells. Rather it is the mythic principle of advertising—the fact that repetition will produce belief—that sustains the structure of Molloy's interior world, his conviction, and his ability to designate his experience as "my life." To tell or write his life, Molloy must resort to exterior equipment: the slogans and reiterations of advertising become for Molloy a kind of self-training that evokes the various methods of *askesis* recommended by Seneca: memorization, abstinences, silence, listening, and, above all, the *hupomnemata* or account books that offered to the self everything that required repetition for the self to take shape.[56]

The Mythic Tense: Thinking in the Permanent Present

> What is it defends her? Even from her own. Averts the intent gaze. Incriminates the dearly won. Forbids divining her. What but life ending. Hers. The other's. But so otherwise.
> —Samuel Beckett, *Ill Seen, Ill Said*

Molloy's touching finickiness, his preference for one low spot on the food chain over another, should not divert our attention from the unbearable source of his pathos and what Molloy himself describes as "hiding from mere terror." "Mere terror" means nothing more than terror, but also nothing but terror. The minimalism of this mereness, which is a part of the process of reduction undertaken by Beckett's writing, suggests that between Molloy and the experience of terror there are no intermediaries, neither rights, nor personality, nor private space. In the figure of Molloy, Beckett asks us to think about the form life assumes when it is made the exclusive object of a technique. Beckett shows us how, paradoxically, the individual abandoned by society becomes its target. The "night purges in the hands of technicians," like the constant injunctions to leave, are part of society's war on poverty.

Critics frequently point out the way in which Molloy's interminable ambulations offer a challenge to the laws of Newtonian physics, an inexhaustible careening of crutches, bikes, and legs in various states of dysfunctionality.[57] Molloy does not cast himself beyond the laws of physics as much as he is cast out of a society that operates according to these laws. Molloy is put instead in a perpetual submission to the law, a perpetual motion machine *in vacuuo:* "suppliant, not a transgressor," as a later character describes himself.[58] The derelict is in a state of mobility more intense than the soldier's. There is no time to think. A "No Loitering" sign hangs at the gates of Beckett's novel—Molloy's one confrontation with the law is his arrest for being in an "obscene state of rest." Sitting is a posture seemingly relegated to a former species: "The desire to sit down came upon me from time to time, back upon me from a vanished world."[59] Molloy speaks of the Salvation Army as if it were just that, a relentless military action against the impoverished: "[Social workers] will pursue you to the ends of the earth, the vomitory in their hands. The Salvation Army is no better. Against the charitable gesture there is no defense, that I know of."[60]

Molloy documents the way in which being helpless has become synonymous with being defenseless, and of the way mere existence has become synonymous with mere terror. Walter Benjamin writes in one of his fragments, "As long as there is a single beggar, there will still be myth."[61] Benjamin's insight is illuminated by the defenseless existence of the beggar. For Benjamin, a single beggar stands between myth and its disappearance. Here Benjamin does not seem to be asserting the popular cliché, namely, that the beggar is the last outpost of a culture's ancient wisdom, its prophet and its storyteller. Benjamin's comment locates the possible sources of myth in the routinely terrorized situation of the beggar. The placelessness and miserable anonymity of the beggar mimic the way the origins of myth are obscured and belong to a time outside history.[62] Molloy himself notes the way in which the familiar markers of time have lost their clarity in his story. Noting how he cannot distinguish between events that have happened, those that are happening, and those yet to happen, Molloy must "speak in a mythological present" that includes all tenses.[63] Molloy's story is not alerted to the passage of time. The routine of the beggar partakes, in fact, of the ambiguous iteration of myth. His habits are at once an expression of his idleness and a force of necessity—the need to find food and a place to sleep has, in a parody of the prehistoric condition, become a routine. The derelict simultaneously has no habits and has only his habits. His routines are the expression of how unfree it is to be out of the loop: Adorno compares the gestures in Beckett's plays to the repetitive and automatic behavior of the prisoner in his cell.[64] The enclosed unconscious space of habit entirely swallows the life of the derelict. Like mythic form, the derelict life is trapped in a state of repetition without memory. The activity of the beggar seems "habitual" because the beggar occupies a space that is both self-enclosed and unfamiliar: his activity designates a loss of self but without the context, the domestic interior, in which this loss is wagered in safety. The self-enclosed space of the beggar excludes the familiar.

The mythic situation of the beggar becomes more palpable as we try to imagine the conditions of Benjamin's statement, the concept of the "single beggar." Without community, beggars are never anything but single. Yet the vagabond inhabits a strangely eviscerated solitude, and his singleness lays claim only to isolation, rather than to differentiation. In the epigraph above from *Ill Seen, Ill Said*, Beckett asks, "What defends her?" Beckett deepens this question as he explains it: "Averts the intent gaze. Incriminates the dearly won. Forbids divining her." Molloy, too, averts the intent gaze of the reader and incriminates the claims that are made on him: in reading *Molloy*, confronted with the derelict existence of its character, every assertion, every attempt to discern the proper space of the beggar and establish his belonging, comes with a receipt. Georges Bataille proposes that *Molloy* is closer to myth than to a novel. This perspective on the work begins with Bataille's realization that no proper terms suitably designate our encounter with the vagabond. This encounter with Molloy in fact seemingly spills over into Bataille's biographical encounters with street people ("I can say something more about him, and that is that both you and I have met him"). Bataille writes,

> There is in this reality, the essence or residue of being, something so *universal*, these complete *vagabonds* we occasionally encounter but immediately lose have something so essentially indistinct about them, that we cannot imagine anything more anonymous. So much so that this name *vagabond*

I have just written down misrepresents them. . . . This thing we name through sheer impotence *vagabond* or *wretch,* which is actually *unnamable* (but then we find ourselves entangled in another word, *unnamable*), is no less mute than death. Thus we know in advance that the attempt to speak to this phantom haunting the streets in broad daylight is futile. Even if we knew something about the precise circumstances and conditions of his life (?) and his wretchedness, we would have made no headway: this man, or rather this being whose speech, sustaining him, might have made him human—whatever speech subsists or rather exhausts itself in him no longer sustains him, and similarly, speech no longer reaches him. Any conversation we might have with him would only be a phantom, an appearance of conversation. It would delude us, referring us to some appearance of humanity, to something other than this *absence* of humanity heralded by the derelict dragging himself through the streets, who fascinates us.[65]

For Bataille the situation of the beggar signals the mythological dimension: language loses its state of possibility, its conversion value. The typography of Bataille's effort to speak of the vagabond creates an obstacle course of italicized terms. Their profusion indicates the foreign nature of each critical designation for Molloy. It also indicates a perpetual need to resume or reestablish emphasis, to enumerate terms to categorize this "essentially indistinct" figure that seems to undo each assertion of emphasis. Molloy does not actively undo or subvert the critic but rather proffers a passivity and destitution that inspire a strange hesitancy or, to use Beckett's terms in the epigraph from the beginning of this section, a sense of the incrimination of the dearly won. Bataille says we name the vagabond only through "linguistic impotence." In the vagabond Bataille notes that language no longer sustains itself or helps him survive, but rather is weakened (*il s'épuise en lui*).

No longer rejuvenated by the speaking "I," language undergoes an exhaustion and emaciation in the derelict. For Bataille this situation signals the mythological dimension of the beggar. Language loses its state of possibility in the beggar, its conversion value: we cannot have a conversation with him, Bataille curiously notes, but only the appearance of one. Language fails to perform another conversion as well: the beggar is not transformed from *l'être* into *l'homme.* Bataille employs an array of figures to mark this demise of language at the terminal self of the beggar: *il ne porte plus,* language no longer delivers, carries, or supports the derelict from a state of "being" to a state of being something (*l'homme*). Language loses its capacities in the impoverished instant of the derelict. The beggar has a mythological status for Bataille because he at once is both this absence of humanity and signifies or heralds this absence. In the following description, Molloy emerges as a kind of phoenix in reverse, as ashes risen from the creature:

> Doubtless the birth we should attribute to Molloy is not that of a scholarly composition, but rather the only one that would be suitable to the elusive reality I have been speaking of, that of myth—monstrous, and arising from the slumber of reason. There are two analogous truths that can only take shape in us in the form of a myth, these being death and the "absence of humanity" that is death's living semblance. Such absences of reality may not indeed be present in the clear-cut distinctions of discourse, but we may be sure that neither death nor inhumanity, both non-existing, can be considered irrelevant to the existence that we are, of which they are the boundary, the backdrop, and the ultimate truth.[66]

Earlier I note the way in which Benjamin asks the reader to think the intrinsically mythological nature of the beggar in which the *presence* of the beggar is the *sine qua non* of myth. This dependent relation of myth on the single beggar is inverted in Bataille's picture in which the beggar is a living *absence* ("death's living semblance"), at a mythological remove from both clear-cut discourse ("scholarly composition") and from our existence as it is. Bataille's approach to Molloy is both tactful (in the hesitancy it marks in what to name this vagabond being) and apocalyptic (in its understanding of the unnamable, a living absence). The emphasis on the latter draws our attention away from Molloy's self-named "mythological present." Benjamin's comment has the effect of forcing us into that present as an eternal present, one without memory and without projects. Bataille paradoxically gives the vagabond a kind of home in the conceptual landscape. He writes, "The profound apathy of death, its indifference to every possible thing, is apparent in him, but this apathy would encounter in death itself its own limit."[67] The vagabond shakes hands with "death itself," and the apathy of the vagabond in turn reminds us of this death limit.

In this gesture the signifying operation of the vagabond—whose apathy Bataille has described as inaccessible, immune to language, and impersonal—becomes rather familiar to us. Bataille draws a conclusion that betrays the observations (pertaining to both Molloy and personal experience) on which it is built. Though there is no proper name for this being that is "no less mute than death," Bataille says that the beggar both announces this absent condition and embodies it. Bataille takes the unnamable and transumes it in the description of the vagabond as a kind of ghost or undead figure. The activity of the vagabond is described as a haunting:

"This horrible figure painfully swinging along on his crutches is the truth that afflicts us and that follows us no less faithfully than our own shadows . . . the spectre that haunts the streets in open daylight."[68] A ghost no longer able to haunt his house, forced to walk the streets by day, a faithful shadow: these figures evoke the drifting situation of the beggar at the same time they force us to ask whether Molloy's dislocation precisely resembles a ghost's. The ghost has a sense of belonging to a place that in fact exceeds the beggar's: its dislocation is specific and imposes a particular debt on the living because the dead has been removed from the final "resting place." Ghosts are restless; beggars are forbidden sleep. Molloy does not seek the place, once and for all, but a place. The final sentence of Molloy's monologue is "I longed to go back into the forest. Oh not a real longing. Molloy could stay, where he happened to be."[69] The contingency of the beggar's resting spot, of resting where he happens to be, is entirely offset by the comma and preceding conditionality: "Molloy *could* stay." Contingency is not a continuous privilege of the beggar as might be suggested if the sentence were written as "Molloy could stay where he happened to be." This unitary statement is interrupted by the comma indicating that "where he happened to be" is a spot that must be sanctioned by his solicitors, the policemen and night watchmen or by their absence.

The restless resumption of this contingency under law differs from the predicament of the undead or unburied. Consider once more the brief litany of Beckett's poem "Enueg": "Tired of dying / tired of policemen / feet in marmalade / perspiring profusely / heart in marmalade." Tired of dying, the vagabond is subject to an exhaustion enforced by the law. The insuperably helpless situation of Molloy is reflected in the fact that everything, even help, contributes to this dying. His situation actively blackmails the common sense of the social management of poverty. Of his mother Molloy complains, "Her charity kept me dying."[70] There is no way for the helpless in Beckett to break with their condition, and not even death is permitted to them. Help, or charity, ends by accelerating and deepening helplessness, so that in trying to keep the vagabond from dying, charity paradoxically condemns him to dying.

Beckett writes to show us the world seen from the standpoint of the helpless, through eyes withdrawn into dying. There is a glimmer there that provides us with an understanding—to which Bataille and Benjamin gesture—of the experiential structure of myth in the situation of need. The figure of need is separated by a gap that the ancients understood to exist between mortals and the immortals. But this gap in Beckett exists between mortals. A few lines from the monologue of Beckett's Unnamable can give a sense of this:

> Et l'autre. Je lui ai prêté des yeux implorants, des offrandes pour moi, un besoin d'aide. Il ne me regarde pas, ne me connaît pas, ne manque de rien. Moi seul suis homme et tout le reste divin.
>
> [And the other? I have assigned him eyes that implore me, offerings for me, need of succour. He does not look at me, does not know of me, wants for nothing. I alone am man and all the rest divine.]⁷¹

It is alarming to encounter the term "other" in Beckett's prose since the monologues of his derelicts are not anchored in the premise of the self. In the transition from Beckett's French to his English, the stance toward the other becomes a question. The other is both something superadded and a question, both an unquestionable surplus or excess (*le reste*) and open to a type of philosophical thinking (and hence the prospect of conceptual assimilation). The truth of the other is in a way expressed as the gap between the two languages and between expressions. The sentences that follow therefore appear as a kind of answer to the simple question of "And the other?" This answer brings the questioner into a quandary of need. The sentences that follow are not answers but rather enumerations, open to infinite incompletion. The French version emphasizes that what follows is not an answer but a list, soberly laid out without Beckett filling in the connection for us.

At first, the figure states that he has lent the other (*prêté*) the signs of need: imploring eyes, a "need of succour." These indices of need are lent to the other, that is to say, given over provisionally, as in a situation of crisis in which one lends another a blanket. The crisis here is precipitated by the question of the other. But lending is always an expectation of a return. It is in this sense that the gesture of assigning the signs of the vagabond to the other, this conversion of the other into a beggar, is an answer to the question of the other. This question ("And the other?") offers no qualifications by which to lead us and does not fill in any blanks for us. It is answered most coercively, therefore, by instituting the state of discernible need in the other. The self secures an answer to the monstrous question about the other by serving a philanthropic function, by making the ego charitable. It has lent to the world the pure sign of its purpose: vagabond signs signifying total need that nevertheless promise "offerings" (*des offrandes*) to that self in return.

The second sentence sounds like it should undo the first, yet it does not hold dialogue with the first gesture and does not aim at contradiction. Here the question of the other approximates the version of the other as posed by Beckett's French, the other as the *unintegratable* surplus and elusive remainder. Beckett's character speaks of the other as one who is *unreciprocal:* the other is indifferent to and ignorant of all relation to the self, is blind to the self. This other does not communicate with us. These sentences do not form a progression, a revision, or even the basis of recognition in the character. They are juxtaposed as discontinuous moments within which Beckett's character catches a glimpse of the human. The last sentence is delivered with the Beckettian mixture of clarity and puzzlement and conveys a sense that is both precise and in the process of evaporating. It connects the vicious circle of need and indifference, their nonexclusive though contradictory nature, to the permanent mortality of the speaker and his exclusion from the divinity.[72] Need and insufficiency are the markers by which the self imagines itself to integrate the other; the impoverishment of the other emerges here as an instrument by which the self acts out its relation to the world before its own poverty, its own absence of relation, is noted. Poverty is not just in "the other," and it is the return of the self to a condition of poverty that marks mortal time for Beckett's character. Beckett's figure says that he is nothing to the one whom he imagines to have nothing and to be in need of him. Yet this turn is already at the heart of the first charitable gesture by which want is discerned in the world, since it is in that first estimation of the vagabond nature of the other that the self has unwittingly testified to the helplessness and truly involuntary aspect of the other, having nothing and yet offering something to us. For Beckett, to be "man" does not mean to join a species but to feel oneself to be the last man, the single beggar.

4

Textual Indigence

THE READER IN AN AESTHETICS OF POVERTY

> So forgive me if I relapse . . . into my dream of an art unresentful of its insuperable indigence and too proud for the farce of giving and receiving.
>
> —Samuel Beckett[1]

Making Less of Less

Critics widely observe that Beckett's work, characterized by broken syntax and a dearth of discernible narrative structure, verges on the unreadable.[2] Much of Beckett criticism tries to deal with this problem. The best criticism of Beckett makes a paradox of this, taking the view that the reader's difficulty is the point. In his essay appropriately titled "Trying to Understand 'Endgame,'" Adorno writes that understanding *Endgame* can only mean "understanding its unintelligibility, concretely reconstructing the meaning of the fact that it has no meaning."[3] According to Adorno, the most we can do is scrupulously take stock of all the ways Beckett frustrates our effort to grasp or anticipate his work. Beckett does not discourage the experience of unintelligibility Adorno finds constitutive of his work. He is famously indifferent to this effort as he is to the struggle of audiences with his drama. "My work is a matter of fundamental sounds (no joke intended) made as fully as possible, and I accept responsibility for nothing else. If people want to have headaches among the overtones, let them. And provide their own aspirin."[4]

In his dialogue with Georges Duthuit, Beckett, perhaps unwittingly given his predilection for almost cruel statements, furnishes an enigmatic key to his work. Beckett says he has a vision, a "dream of an art unresentful of its insuperable indigence." What does this mean? Beckett does not intend to impart a supreme value for humanity or that art should add to the stockpile of cultural monuments. Beckett dreams neither of an art replete with redemptive potential nor, unlike other dreamers, of striking it rich. Rather, Beckett dreams of an art uninterested in giving anything to the spectator, of a literature capable of a forthright and unapologetic expression of its poverty.

Beckett's work is guided by this dream and its surprising and discordant elements. The surprise begins with the terminology itself. Beckett juxtaposes the terms *insuperable* and *indigence*. This conflation challenges us to envision a state of need so needy that it cannot be redeemed, surmounted, or made a positive value through articulation or representation in a novel, a paragraph, or even a word. The ultimate node of Beckett's dream as informative of his own creation may not be of art's indigence (as this for Beckett is perhaps constitutive of art per se) but a thing even more improbable: an attitude toward this condition, that his work express an equanimity, an unresentful disposition toward this inherent and unalienable indigence.

The challenge to Beckett's reader is made more difficult because his dream of an art unresentful of its insuperable indigence does not involve either reader or reading in any stated way. In fact, it is not clear that a reader is welcome, or even necessary. Insofar that Beckett's dream requires the participation of the reader, it is less to do something than to not do something: not to annul, not to distort the carefully stacked poverty of Beckett design.

How can readers insert themselves into so tight a loop? It is not easy to participate in another's dream. The most obvious paths of response are blocked since most interpretations seek to make the text into a resource or a repository of significant traces. Reading in the spirit of Beckett's design means avoiding precisely this making more of less, this cancellation of Beckett's carefully designed poetics of indigence. The reader is asked to encounter Beckett's dream of a work of need—needfully. In other words, the reader should be open to the surprising and unforeseen outcomes that emerge when approaching Beckett's poverty as such without any additional determination or dissemination, without annulling it or transforming it.

Beckett makes no mention of any image within this dream, only of art's relation to itself. This relation is the only one remaining after Beckett shears world (represented object), artist (represented subject), and audience from the work of art. Beckett praises Dutch painter Bram van Velde as the first artist "to submit wholly to the incoercible absence of relation, in the absence of terms or, if you like, in the presence of unavailable terms."[5] Beckett's insistence on negativity and indigence without any repeal or redemption suggests that any attempt to read his work within "the humanities" would annul art's essential indigence. The problem is mirrored in the inaugural address that awarded Beckett the 1969 Nobel Prize in Literature. Beckett's award goes to the "author who has transmuted the destitution of modern man into his exaltation."[6] This is precisely the misunderstanding that Beckett sought to avoid and that Beckett's dream of an insuperable indigence counters so clearly. Yet this charitable negation of the poverty of Beckett's art remains a temptation to all readings of his work. Like the Nobel Committee, commentators see Beckett as a kind of Midas figure equipped with a typewriter. As Steven Connor remarks, the motto "less is more" has become the "standard way of interpreting Beckett's texts."[7] Connor also accurately defines the problem with this approach, when he writes that this interpretative model is "the rate of exchange whereby criticism has been able to move the dwindling 'lessness' of his work from the red into the black of cultural profit."[8]

Taking Beckett at his word requires of his reader both deep familiarity with and also distance from the text. For Jacques Derrida, notably, distance to Beckett was difficult to achieve. Of why he does not write about Beckett, Derrida says, "this is an author to whom I feel very close, or to whom I would like to feel myself close; but also too close. Precisely because of this proximity, it is too hard for me [to write about him], too easy and too hard."[9] Derrida does not feel Beckett to be at the right distance to permit "writing transactions."[10] He claims that this is partly a problem of language itself. Derrida says that he can write about foreign authors such as Joyce, Kafka, and Celan precisely because his own writing, in French, allows him to develop a language in response to the work of these authors. By contrast, Beckett writes in what Derrida calls a "particular French" that makes it difficult to reply: "How could I write in French in the wake of or 'with' someone who does operations on this language which seem to me so strong and so necessary, but which must remain idiomatic? How could I write, sign, countersign performatively texts which 'respond' to Beckett?"[11] Beckett's "operations" on the French language remain, for Derrida, so unassailably idiomatic that they paradoxically cannot be translated into Derrida's French. Without this distance, his treatment of Beckett can only devolve into a mediated discourse, or what Derrida calls "the platitude of a supposed academic metalanguage."[12] Yet Adorno, who has the advantage of writing in a language other than Beckett's French, has a problem similar to Derrida. Of *Endgame,* Adorno writes that a reading of Beckett "cannot pursue the chimerical aim of expressing the play's meaning in a form mediated by philosophy."[13] In the absence of a philosophical narrative about Beckett's work, Adorno proposes a reading that keeps closer to the text: understanding *Endgame,* he writes, "can mean only understanding its unintelligibility, concretely reconstructing the meaning of the fact that it has no meaning."[14] Adorno proposes that the reader treat Beckett's text with the meticulous attention one might give to a crime scene: the most the critic can hope for is recreating, step by step, the way Beckett's language assaults meaning and parts company with our understanding. For both Adorno and Derrida, in other words, critical mediation of the Beckett text requires both nearness and distance, the use of a language at once familiar and unfamiliar.

My purpose here is to avoid both the platitudes of academic language and the imposition of language not "vouched for by the work's imminence."[15] In their *Arts of Impoverishment* to which my study is indebted, Leo Bersani and Ulysse Dutoit observe that Beckett "has given us, by common consent, unforgettably original images of meaninglessness and failure, and reasonably literate people all over the world recognize encounters, spectacles, verbal exchanges they unhesitatingly qualify as Beckettian."[16] Yet Beckett's work also presents a type of impoverishment not so easily recognized, one that the reader can qualify or name only with hesitation. The needfulness of Beckett's work not only renders our "reasonable literacy" insufficient but also requires us to rethink the reading process altogether. To this end, I assemble here six key strategies for reading Beckett's aesthetics of indigence, culled from Beckett's own texts. They are conditions of poverty that characterize Beckett's poetics and that affect our encounter with his work. They are (1) begging the question, (2) the syntax of weakness, (3) writing and abandonment, (4) deliberate provisionality, (5) the hypothetical imperative, (6) worsening as narrative strategy. These six operations call attention to what we do differently on account of the meagerness, both slim yet ineradicable, offered by Beckett's work. I introduce the topic with "A Poetics or an Ethics of Indigence," a perceptively titled chapter from James Knowlson and John Pilling's *Frescoes of the Skull: The Later Prose and Drama of Samuel Beckett.*

A Poetics or an Ethics of Indigence

Beckett challenges the reader to take on his poverty without annulment. Beckett's poverty is a vanishing and incalculable figure, rendered as an abyss ("the inverted spiral of need") or an insurmountable height ("an insuperable indigence"), that seems to call for an ethical problem.[17] Knowlson and Pilling raise this issue in converting indigence into a summary term for Beckett's work. What could be more difficult to isolate, to endow with fetish status, or *possess*, they ask, than poverty? They observe, "perhaps [indigence] is the only word that can encapsulate the obsession with 'need' and 'poverty' that has been at the heart of Beckett's thinking through such a long and distinguished career."[18] For Knowlson and Pilling, Beckett's obsessions with poverty can be brought within a functioning aesthetic. But because they fail to consider the ethical demands imposed by Beckett's work, Knowlson and Pilling risk containing or "encapsulating" the very poverty Beckett sought to leave undomesticated. Ethics questions our implication with an ever-withdrawing figure of need. The homeless narrator of Beckett's short story "The End" allegorizes the reader's predicament when faced by this figure. He describes how his cries for assistance sounded unintentionally like their opposite: "I tried to groan, Help! Help! But the tone that came out was that of polite conversation. My hour was not yet come and I could no longer groan. The last time I had cause to groan I had groaned as well as ever, and no heart within miles of me to melt."[19] Here the character cannot reckon his need to groan with his inability to do so. His last great groan came and went unheard by anyone who might have offered him a sympathetic gesture. Reading Beckett in terms of pure aesthetics runs the risk of fastening its attention only on this tone of polite conversation, the formal conventions of bourgeois society. The groan of Beckett's characters is both untimely and of unrecognizable form. The distress is not imprisoned in the form of the work.[20]

This idea is not necessarily inappropriate for many works of art. In colloquial understanding, the artwork is a cry for help. In this view art becomes a displaced statement of despair (usually the artist's). Here the cry is both audible and legible, and it bears the mark of a strictly psychological or existential distress.[21] But Beckett tends to work within and against this idiom. We need rather to ask: How do we attune ourselves to the groan under, or within, the tone of polite conversation? Beckett conceives of the artist's helplessness as an absolute disenfranchisement of means. Asked by Georges Duthuit why he claims that the artist is "helpless to paint," Beckett replies, "Because there is nothing to paint and nothing to paint with."[22] This startling proclamation deprives us of the means by which to understand the work of art, since for Beckett art happens in a space without objects (things to be painted) and without means (brushes, canvases, paint, but also hands, eyes, and skill). Beckett's comment pulls art away from all the instrumental terms with which it has traditionally been surrounded.

As counterintuitive as it may be for readers who seek to understand the text through interpretation, Beckett seems to ask his reader for an inability to understand, that the readers be defeated by their attempt at understanding rather than have a light go on in the mind. This makes the reader a participant in the poverty rather than a factor for eliminating it. In *Malone Dies*, for example, the reader encounters the title character bedridden and writing in his exercise book. He notes, "For I want to put down in it, for the last time, those I have called to my help, but ill, so that they did not understand, so that they may cease with me. Now rest."[23] Is it not conceivable to think here that the *name of the reader* might be inscribed on Malone's list of those who did not understand his cry for help? Can the reader be a mere bystander here—free to walk? Or are we not as readers inscribed within the novel, as in a necrology, and belonging to those who failed the call?[24] The failure of the reader to respond is not a failure of critical judgment or insight. Rather, it connects us to the cry in the most intimate but also encrypted way. We merge with the work at the point where it cannot communicate with us, cannot get us to respond. Malone acknowledges that his demand for help may not have been apprehended in the first place, since his cry partakes of his distress and is made "ill."[25] In other words, the call to action is itself afflicted, made "ill" instead of made known. Rather than conveying the picture or message of need, language itself is in need. But the error or illness of the imperative does not reduce its urgency: it only eliminates the reader's ability to heed that call, to provide aid or to redeem a need.

In his review of the poetry of Denis Devlin, Beckett himself formulates a theoretical relation between the reader and need. Contrasting art with "opinion" (what Beckett calls an "escape from need"), Beckett describes Devlin's poems as "no more (!) than the approximately adequate and absolutely non-final formulation of another kind [of need]."[26] In other words, poetry's "own terms" are paradoxically those that mark it as unfathomably dispossessed. Beckett goes on to say that "art has always been this—pure interrogation, rhetorical question less the rhetoric—whatever else it may have been obliged by the 'social reality' to appear, but never more freely so than now, when social reality . . . has severed the connection."[27] Beckett does not assert that artworks *state* these needs, but rather that they offer its "approximately adequate and absolutely non-final formulation." Faced with a poem, a reader is not faced with a need *for* something. That is, the terms of poetry are not about need but are instead themselves needy, do not refer to a particular need but are in need of reference, seek out their reality by lacking it. As a "non-final formulation," Devlin's poems offer a need that is unstable and itself in need of articulation. To use the expression of Beckett's narrator, it calls ill. In "Cascando," Beckett refers to "the black want splashing their faces."[28] Want, like need, is never in the expression of the face but running over it, discoloring it, evaporating from it. This is why for Beckett the opposite of need is not fulfillment but opinion, the idea hardened into a position that can be unambiguously appropriated and exchanged.

Beckett's pure interrogation of need and its place in literary articulation suggests for the reader a role beyond the mere divestment of subject (an agency that poses the question) and object (something asked for). The question of art and the responsibility of the reader operated through a constitutive subtraction: *a rhetorical question less the rhetoric*. Beckett defines literature in such a way that the reader approaches it primarily through its dispossession. There are two consequences to this neediest of states in which the rhetorical question has been stripped of its rhetoric. Without the rhetoric, a rhetorical question lacks the means of its enunciation. This question, then, is so close to the being of the artwork that it cannot be distanced, or turned, in order for it to be posed: in short, it loses the material form by which it is recognized. This means there are questions that are not formulated in Beckett's text but posed by the text and weigh on the text through their absence. The title character in Beckett's prose work *The Unnamable*, for example, makes a distinction between *not formulating* questions and conceding their inevitability: "Decidedly it seems impossible, at this stage, that I should dispense with questions, as I promised myself I would. No, I merely swore I'd stop asking them. And perhaps before long, who knows, I shall light on the happy combination which will prevent them from ever arising again in my—let us not be over-nice—mind."[29] Beckett's work constitutes a search for an arrangement that situates or exposes a question rather than simply poses one. This combination is the site where questions insinuate themselves into the text. Beckett does not seek to formulate questions per se; he does not systematically seek the question the way a philosophical treatise might. Beckett's character expresses the hope that he will fall upon the desirable combination that will *obstruct* formulation and make the question-formula fail. Beckett's work dethrones ostentatious form of the question in favor of making its problems ostensible.

There is another potential implication for the reader to Beckett's definition of art. Purified of rhetoric, the question of literature is purified of its rhetorical *function*. Rhetorical questions conventionally lend continuity to arguments: they do not expect a response to be given. Beckett's definition of literature within these parameters requires from the reader a response.

Some of Beckett's best critics have inverted Beckett's statement and insisted that Beckett's minimalism produces an autonomous artwork, art that witnesses the complete disintegration of the dialogic structure of question and response. In his essay on *Endgame,* Adorno writes, for example, "Beckett spells out the lie implicit in the question mark: the question has become a rhetorical one."[30] My point here concerns the way in which Beckett does not offer us the sign that designates a question (the *Fragezeichen,* literally, the question mark) but withdraws that sign in a gesture of radical poverty. Reading Beckett entails nothing other than the search for questions in need of their sign, a search for unwritten questions. Contrary to the picture offered by Adorno, there seems to be in fact considerable urgency, one might say emergency, in the way in which this unasked question needs the reader for its articulation.

Beckett's oeuvre of need seeks to multiply the missing questions and actively *unask* questions in order to implore the readers to realize the question themselves. This clashes with the tendency within modern art and philosophy to define themselves through their struggle to remember questions. Gilles Deleuze and Félix Guattari describe their project as a search for questions that do not already contain their answers. They take Henri Bergson's definition of a false problem to be one rooted in the "badly stated" question: a drive toward its proper articulation guides their thinking all the way up to *What Is Philosophy?*[31] Deleuze and Guattari observe that this question, which entitles their final work, has never been heard because it was always asked too abstractly and "can perhaps be posed only late in life, with the arrival of old age and the time for speaking concretely."[32] When Martin Heidegger writes that "questioning is the piety of thought," he references a disposition (piety) habitually associated with faith and *not* questioning to assert the unquestioned need of the question.[33] He begins *Being and Time* by declaring that we have forgotten the Greek question of Being.[34] Heidegger furnishes us with a way, a lexicon of Greek philosophical language, to access this question. Ultimately, Beckett sides with amnesia rather than with philosophical recollection. Beckett's novels are gerontological in a way that surpasses the scenario furnished by Deleuze and Guattari. Instead of old age's recent arrival and the opportunity to speak concretely, Beckett gives older age and speech frozen into a series of non sequiturs. Beckett's forgetful work functions like a trap into which questions fly in from the outside.

Beckett's tactic of spurring the reader to ask questions works with the assumption that answering and posing of questions is not the difficult task. The decisive moment for Beckett comes earlier: in formulating the conditions for a question. Beckett's disposition toward the rhetorical question in this sense runs contrary to established critical notions about literature. Beckett's literary destitution proposes a model in which the work (and not the author) needs the reader. This dependency is reminiscent and possibly modeled on the predicament of the vagabond. Beckett's active dispossession of the question mark differentiates his work sharply from that state of deferral or suspension, or a state of fundamental ambiguity, that other theorists regard as the defining mark of literature. Roland Barthes writes:

> It is ambiguity which counts, which concerns us, which bears the historical meaning of an oeuvre which seems peremptorily to reject history. What is this meaning? The very opposite of a meaning, i.e., a question. What do things signify, what does the world signify? All literature is this question, but we must immediately add, for this is what constitutes its specialty, *literature is this question minus its answer.* No literature in the world has ever answered the question it asked, and it is this very suspension which has always constituted it as literature: it is that very fragile language which men set between the violence of the question and the silence of the answer.[35]

Whereas Beckett defines literature as a rhetorical question minus its rhetoric, Barthes defines literature (its "specialty") as this question minus its answer. Barthes's math sets literature aside as a space of questioning "for its own sake" and as the perpetual deferment of meaning and answering. Instead of meaning, literature proposes only questions (*What do things signify? What does the world signify?*). Not only is literature for Barthes an endless posing of questions; its ambiguity is itself posed or "set" between "the violence of the question and the silence of the answer." Though its language is unable to resolve its ambiguities and too weak to answer itself, literature for Barthes is protected by its place in a structure between violence and silence.

Fragility in this picture acquires a paradoxical functionality: when Barthes speaks of literature's inability to answer, it is depicted as a silence that is guarded (defended, something "kept" by literature) and not a situation of dumb muteness.[36] For Barthes, the position and suspension of this fragility recuperates its powerlessness and even its value. He describes the language of literature as "set," much like a diamond or a figure in a glass case. Barthes describes this fragile language as a kind of tender membrane separating question and answer. It is not to be disturbed. Beckett's literary indigence takes a contrary route: it breaks with the aesthetics of suspension by exercising and *worsening* the fragility of language and pursues a *provisional* state in which it is unable to found itself. Beckett's work is not set either for permanence (as in stone) or to accentuate its value (like a diamond), but strikes a more provisional posture. *Not* to shelter or *not* to suspend its disability means to pursue an art of broken pieces and in a combination that renders the pieces less distinct.[37] For Barthes, the subtraction process in literature stops at the irreducible questions it poses.[38] Beckett does not stop there and includes asking in the list of activities (among them, answering) literature fails to do.

Begging the Question

> That is typical. I know no more questions and they keep on pouring from my mouth.
> —Samuel Beckett, *The Unnamable*[39]

The expression "begging the question," an idiomatic translation of *petitio principii*, refers to the way an argument takes for proven something that it ought to be proving.[40] A line of reasoning that begs a question therefore assumes possession of what could only be acquired later, namely, through proof. The counterintuitive nature of the begging in this idiom makes the expression pertinent to our understanding of Beckett's work. First, "begging" as it is described here is in no way a loud or imploring gesture of want. In fact, this want is not even uttered. The state of need must be discerned by the listener in the aberrant reasoning. Second, the idiom suggests that the proper response to this begging is not an answer but a question. Ordinarily, begging would seem synonymous with questioning as an asking *for* something. Yet the statement that begs a question asks nothing. Asking for nothing, however, it asks to be asked.

The figure of speech therefore bears this insight into Beckett's work: that an utterance can bear unconscious questions. What Beckett's figure calls "typical" about himself holds true for Beckett's work: that it does not "know" questions and yet questions come forth at each instant. These questions in the text emerge in an encounter with the other, through reading and in the reader, at the place where these questions are refused.

To pose a question not only to Beckett's text but for Beckett's text turns the reader toward what the text does not know about itself and what it cannot ask. Enoch Brater says, "The major dramatic question is not raised by the figures onstage in the language one of them speaks, but is developed instead by the observer: it is we who must postulate a harmony between what we see and the 'sad tale a last time told.'"[41] Yet making sense out of Beckett's work may not require us, as Brater claims, to "postulate a harmony" out of our experience with it. In fact, the true questions with which we respond to Beckett's text may not be restorative of unity between form and content but may in fact be "begged" by their precise ordering: the readers' questions are a reaction to the formal coherence of Beckett's work in which form and content seem forcibly reconciled. If, as Hans Robert Jauss claims, modernist free indirect discourse compels the reader to make *evaluations* of the narrative data, Beckett's hermetic style invites a wholly different reply.[42] This is quite different from Brater's suggestion that the reader is to "postulate" something like a formula for the text, estranging the reader from the irrational silence of Beckett's world.

In *Waiting for Godot*, Beckett's characters do not like to be asked questions. They are existential challenges and mildly disrupt the discursive status quo on stage. In response to Estragon's objection to the treatment of Lucky, Pozzo shouts: "(*violently*) Don't question me!"[43] And yet this objection or deflection of the question results not in its being suppressed but in its being enhanced—acted out. In other words, though Pozzo wants the question of why Lucky does not put down his bags to "go away," it reappears not by being restated but through Estragon's charade: "(*forcibly*) Bags. (*He points at Lucky.*) Why? Always hold. (*He sags, panting.*) Never put down. (*He opens his hands, straightens up with relief.*) Why?"[44] This question goes to the heart of the power dynamic in the play. Estragon wants to know why the slave never stops working, and why he displays a peculiar attachment to his burden. He resorts to pantomime when faced with the futility of more explicit questioning, making each component of his question visible through gesture.

Questions do not disappear on stage. Going unheard, they emphatically reappear as a performance that grabs the eye of the addressee. Pozzo replies to Estragon's performance, "Ah! Why couldn't you say so before?"[45] Yet Estragon's need to corporealize the question offers us an inkling into how Beckett's novels submerge their questions past the point of visibility or the silence of pantomime. This moment in *Godot* signals a fundamental bifurcation of questioning between Beckett's novels and his theater. Beckett's stage will increasingly make questions explicit through the performer's body. In *Rough for Radio II* and *Rough for Theater II* (whose titles indicate both a provisional art form—the rough draft—and the roughness of force applied between the characters) the activity of questioning that befalls the reader of Beckett's novels is aggressively staged. The questions at the heart of *What Where,* "Did you give him the works?" "He didn't say anything?" "Begged for mercy?" allow the Beckettian vectors of work, need, and physical distress to converge in the scene of interrogation.[46]

We measure the impoverishment of Beckett's work in its failure to call or to command the reader, yet at the same time without ceasing to invoke the reader. If it calls on the reader, it calls "but ill." The reader shares Molloy's difficulty in answering the call of an imperative whose voice is always dissipating and that seems to alert the addressee only to its impotence. How does the impoverished text ask questions? In his Beckett study *L'Oeuvre sans qualités,* Bruno Clément states, "In truth, the Beckettian text is outside questions in the traditional sense: it does not ask any, does not ask any of itself any more than it leaves any out."[47] For Clément, Beckett's work neither poses questions in the traditional sense nor leaves questioning off to the side. Beckett does not utilize the question mark with frequency. His writing shows "how it is" (the title of one of his novels) and our route to his work is through the question "How did it get this way?" *How It Is* as a title, for example, seems to cry out for its formulation as a question (How is it?). As Clément observes, a provocation to question lurks even within Beckett's titles: *Watt* is recast by the reader as *What?* and *The Unnamable* as *Why?* Even Beckett's characters seem to deflect questions with a shrug of the shoulders. As the narrator of "Enough" explains, "What do I know of a man's destiny? I could tell you more about radishes. For them he had a fondness. If I saw one I would name it without hesitation."[48] The topic of man's destiny, the convergence of life and questioning, is dropped in favor of talking about radishes. Nevertheless, the seemingly cohesive statement about naming radishes comes apart as it provokes us to ask: What would a radish be named? Are radishes as numerous as mushrooms, and with as many types and species? Could a radish be given a proper name? Talking about radishes is not, for Beckett, the opposite of raising questions. It is precisely this affirmative gesture of Beckett's prose that forecloses questions, but in the process saddles the reader with the responsibility for asking them. This injunction to question *is* man's destiny in the twenty-first century.

And yet the way Beckett's work closes out questioning is not without interest.[49] An example of how *Molloy* begs questioning can be seen in the single encounter Molloy describes with his mother. Here he foregrounds how he "got into communication" with her:

> The room smelled of ammonia, oh not merely of ammonia, but of ammonia, ammonia. She knew it was me, by my smell. Her shrunken hairy old

face lit up, she was happy to smell me. She jabbered away with a rattle of dentures and most of the time didn't realize what she was saying. Anyone but myself would have been lost in this clattering gabble, which can only have stopped during her brief instants of unconsciousness. In any case I didn't come to listen to her. I got into communication with her by knocking on her skull. One knock meant yes, two no, three I don't know, four money, five goodbye. I was hard put to ram this code into her ruined and frantic understanding, but I did it, in the end. That she should confuse yes, no, I don't know and goodbye, was all the same to me, I confused them myself. But that she should associate the four knocks with anything but money was something to be avoided at all costs. During the period of training therefore, at the same time as I administered the four knocks on her skull, I stuck a bank-note under her nose or in her mouth. In the innocence of my heart! For she seemed to have lost, if not absolutely all notion of mensuration, at least the faculty of counting beyond two. It was too far for her, yes, the distance was too great, from one to four. By the time she came to the fourth knock she imagined she was only at the second, the first two having been erased from her memory as completely as if they had never been felt, though I don't quite see how something never felt can be erased from the memory, and yet it is a common occurrence. She must have thought I was saying no to her all the time, whereas nothing was further from my purpose.[50]

This is Beckett's hermetic world, in which there is not enough air to laugh. Our gasps of disbelief, the painful chuckles under breath, even the way we imitatively hit our palms against our foreheads at the proceedings, constitute attempts to decompress the text. Molloy's description of his communicative laboratory, turning his mother's head into a hybrid Morse code receiver and ATM machine, is disarmingly matter-of-fact. Its unperturbed and unalarmed tone requires us, however, to take up questions (and alarm) on our own time.

The brutal abbreviation of Molloy's semiotic system magnetizes our inquiry. Following the logic of the *petitio principii*, we seek the premises overlooked by Molloy's assertions. Our questions interrupt the business-as-usual mood of the passage: we want to learn the costs and profits of this system of "fundamental sounds." If the smell and taste of money anchors its signification to four knocks, by what sensory hinge did Molloy connect "yes" to one knock or "I don't know" to three? Inherited wisdom tells us that money does not smell (*pecuniam non olet*): Does it smell enough to establish a syntax? Is its smell more pungent than the double-knock emphasis of Molloy's claim that her room smelled not only of ammonia but "ammonia, ammonia"?

The mother's forgetfulness becomes the agency for our questioning, a source for questions that the passage is unable to articulate. This forgetfulness calls our attention to the learning scenario described by the narrator. Molloy claims he was "hard put to ram this code into her ruined and frantic understanding, but I did it, in the end." But what end is there to forgetting? By what signal or measure did he estimate that his mother understood this code? Is the institutor of the code merely an institutor of violence? How are we to discriminate between bludgeoning the other and purveying a message to her? Amnesia challenges the Pavlovian principle that repetition produces learning and memory. Amnesia provides the frame for the questions with which we disturb the *fait accompli* of the communicative transaction.

The questions elicited by Beckett's scenario are also literary. To what extent is Beckett returning here to the episode in Marcel Proust's *Nom de Pays: Le Pays*? In this section of *La Recherche*, the narrator Marcel cannot fall asleep in his strange new setting of Balbec. Marcel communicates with his grandmother, who is in the adjoining room, by knocking on the wall between them, signaling his distress in the moments he needs warm milk. Years later he is overwhelmed with an involuntary memory of these transmissions when he sees this wall: the wall, the former obstacle of contact, through time becomes an instrument that still registers and emits those percussive signals between him and his grandmother. In *Molloy*, Beckett sees no need to have a wall. Beckett works with reduced means and the knocking happens directly on the skull. Yet the closed circuit of Molloy's communication invites us to ask about the supposed directness of this communication. Time for Beckett does not arrive, through memory, with the redemptive force it displays in Proust. Forgoing memory, Beckett's character tries to communicate directly with forgetfulness.

Beckett precipitates our questions most intensively around that vault of the unsaid, the cliché. In the passage cited above, "She was happy to smell me" varies only slightly from "She was happy to see me," and constitutes the new idiom for greeting in Beckett's sensory-deprived universe. Another cliché that calls upon our scrutiny occurs in *Malone Dies*. Very open minded, the narrator enumerates his efforts to make friends with a broad array of peoples, including the institutionalized:

> My relations with Jackson were of short duration. I could have put up with him as a friend, but unfortunately he found me disgusting, as did Johnson, Wilson, Nicholson and Watson, all whore-sons. I then tried, for a

space, to lay hold of a kindred spirit among the inferior races, red, yellow, chocolate, and so on. And if the plague-stricken had been less difficult of access I would have intruded upon them too, ogling, sidling, leering, ineffing and conating, my heart palpitating. With the insane too I failed, by a hair's breadth.[51]

In solitude, making a mental list of friends may help us affirm some connection to the world. Malone undertakes a more Beckettian task: a list of failed friendships. He seems to make his attempts according to various taxonomical systems. He offers us, for example, his failure to befriend people with the family name ending in *-son*. The genre of his recollections more closely resembles a phonebook rather than a diary. He itemizes the races using two colors and a flavor. The verbs by which Malone describes his befriending gestures remain intransitive and prepositionless. He sidles but not up next to anyone, ogles without ogling someone. The words he enumerates display the disengagement of a thesaurus entry. He ineffs about how he ineffs, breathing and leaving everything unspoken around his friend-target. With some surprise then we find at the end of this list a measurement, an estimate of how far Malone was from potential friendship. He says he failed with the insane "by a hair's breadth." What would be the signs of successful, rather than failed, friendship with the insane? On what side of the ledger would we put their smiles, or their laughter at our jokes? Does this "hair's breadth" refer to an institutional isolation, the width of a wall that makes the insane "difficult of access"?

In most circumstances we accept an idiom without further inquiry, for we know what it means without having to interrogate its form. Yet after the Linnean systematicity of the passage, we set about measuring and decomposing this expression in order to see how we can situate Malone's effort at relationship. We have here the very opposite of an appropriative discourse, or literature that seizes everyday figures of speech in order to renovate or claim their meaning. Beckett's matter-of-fact presentation sentences what is unsaid in the cliché to appear. Our questions are what get the cliché to confess.

Syntax of Weakness

"Someday somebody will find an adequate form, a syntax of weakness," says Beckett in an interview with Lawrence Harvey.[52] This utterance is surprisingly optimistic for Beckett because weak syntax implies a form and method for expressing the sine qua non of Beckett's literary reality: movement toward a minimum that verges between the adequate and inadequate (as in the phrase "adequate food and shelter").[53] Beckett's own search for this form and syntax becomes apparent in the way he contrasts his work with James Joyce. He describes Joyce's project as seeking an utmost in signifying potential: "[Joyce] was making words do the absolute maximum of work. There isn't a syllable that isn't superfluous. . . . The more Joyce knew, the more he could."[54] Beckett is not interested in clarifying any details (what Joyce knew, what Joyce's work could do). Beckett opposes the direction of Joyce's *more*, the addition of knowledge and the subsequent amplification of literary capacity. By contrast Beckett observes, "I'm working with impotence, ignorance. I don't think impotence has been exploited in the past. . . . I think anyone nowadays who pays the slightest attention to his own experience finds it the experience of a non-knower, a non-can-er [somebody who cannot]."[55] Beckett follows Joyce in the sense that neither is interested in literary realism where expression provides "adequate reference" in forging an inherent and intuitive resemblance between literature and the world.

Throughout his career Beckett experiments with impoverished and broken syntax. *How It Is* is perhaps the best example of this. The story features a character on his way to Pim, who crawls face down in the mud; his only possessions are a sack of tinned food and a can opener.[56] Like the narrator in *The Unnamable*, the subject exists in an acoustic whirlwind of voices: he only says, into the mud, what he hears. The novel begins:

> how it was I quote before Pim with Pim after Pim how it is three parts I say it as I hear it
>
> voice once without quaqua on all sides then in me when the panting stops tell me again finish telling me invocation
>
> past moments old dreams back again or fresh like those that pass or things things always and memories I say them as I hear them murmur them in the mud
>
> in me that were without when the panting stops scraps of an ancient voice in me not mine[57]

Beckett's weakened syntax mirrors the weakened condition of his character. As Christopher Ricks observes, "It is not that such syntax is weak; rather, that it is a 'syntax of weakness,' pressing on, unable to relinquish its perseverance and to arrive at severance."[58] Ricks suggests that the syntax cannot even lay claim to weakness, but emerges from the component incapacities to either continue or stop. The story can be discerned from its syntax. As the removal of grammar leaves words stranded, the character is likewise stranded. Pim is unreachable without a grammar. And without punctuation or grammar to structure the relation between language and experience, their mutual relationship becomes forlorn. How are we as readers to refer to these words scattered across the page? Are they sentences or paragraphs? Are they citations dictated to the narrator by a voice he hears?[59] The words of the text are not domesticated by the sentence that conventionally organizes words into meaningful units (the hierarchy of subject versus object or the main versus subordinate clauses). Consequently, we look at the words before we are able to arrange them into a pattern of meaning. We see the page without being cued as to how to construe its organization. *How It Is* does not look like a novel. The words are arrayed like separate organisms on a microscopic slide, or like the marks in a cutting board.

Beckett's impoverished and broken syntax makes us, as readers, into beggars. The nonrelation between terms on the page forces our eye to take a vagrant itinerant path rather than obeying a syntactic linearity. A period delineates the literary utterance. In the absence of this delineation our eye moves from left to right and from right to left, as if to plumb the orientation each phrase has toward its neighbor. The process is repeated on the morphological level. Here we do not move from word to word as if crossing a river. In place of this transversal *How It Is* gives us those words as if they had been haphazardly dropped into a lake, offering no guidance. We are forced to assess each word by the ripple of water over its form, or by its submersion.

The broken and impoverished syntax in *How It Is* is beyond appeal to Beckett as author because the novel reads as a work of amanuensis rather than authorship. Our reading process acknowledges the fact of each word's inscription before its relational status: as a place in relation to a group of words. Beckett detaches the formal clarity of the statements from their revelatory or communicative function. Philosopher Stanley Cavell characterizes Beckett's writing as having a "hidden literality." By "hidden," however, he refers to the way in which it is the reader who hides what is exposed in Beckett's prose. Cavell locates the language that Beckett has discovered or invented not in its use in dialogue but rather "in its grammar, its particular way of making sense, especially the quality it has of what I will call *hidden literality*. The words strew obscurities across our path and seem willfully to thwart comprehension; and then time after time we discover that their meaning has been missed only because it was so utterly bare—totally, therefore unnoticeably, in view."[60] "Totally, therefore unnoticeably, in view" describes the condition of Beckett's vagabonds both on stage and in his novels (and in our world). Cavell's comment brings to mind Molloy's description of his nightly efforts at finding a place to sleep. He calls this "Hiding, but not provocatively."[61] Like the vagrant Molloy, Beckett's text can hide only in the open. The prose of *How It Is* lives up to its title: it shows us a state of being *thus*. The secret of Beckett's text is not something it willfully keeps but the unremitting problem it poses for us. The provocation of literature that claims an inner lair or fictional reserve (how the court system operates in Kafka's novels, for example) is to be contrasted with Beckett's "invocation," this voice that dictates the novel.

Because the syntax is so broken and scant we as readers have to supply syntactical construction in order to make any sense of the text. Taking the second group of words from *How It Is* as an example: "voice once without quaqua on all sides then in me when the panting stops tell me again finish telling me invocation." Eager to condense the words into larger but more comprehensible units we might join "without" to "quaqua," creating the impression that this voice is "without quaqua" or without nonsense.[62] Yet we have to annul this conclusion because this quaqua nonsense *is* the voice. "Without" designates the locus of the voice.

The syntax we devise for the words we read on Beckett's page has a provisional quality. The text invites us to make errors and then forces us to rescan them. We read in a rocking motion rather than in a strictly forward or prospective one. This is intimately connected to the process of the text itself. What the narrator says is only what he hears. Conventional syntax runs aground on the dispossession of the voice, of language unattached to grammatical subjects. How would the rules of grammar arbitrate this situation in which everything is a citation? The phrase "tell me again finish telling me invocation" suggests, though we cannot be sure, that the voice tells the speaker its invocation. In Beckett's scenario, the speaker does not invoke the voice as he might the wisdom of the ancients (though he calls it an "ancient voice"). Beckett's novel turns this inside out: the voice invokes, literally lodges its voice inside the speaker. Bersani and Dutoit describe the situation in Beckett's text: "He [the narrator] may be just that: not a person with a history, but merely a kind of stopping point for voices, an intersection of extortionary speech acts, a collecting depot for all the words whose source of transmission remains uncertain."[63] The figures offered by Bersani and Dutoit seem to cancel the poverty of Beckett's work. Instead of becoming a *stopping point* for voices, Beckett's personae transmit and disperse the voices they hear; instead of becoming a *collecting depot* for words, the narrator becomes an *aquilex,* a semi-open and unclenched hand through whom language flows. Beckett's weakened syntax presents a record or the invoice of this tale charting the dispossession of voice.

Abandonment

Beckett's text is accessible to his reader through awareness of strategies of textual abandonment. If the typical story of an abandonment begins with presence or ownership and leads through misadventure to abandonment or loss, Beckett is its inversion. For Beckett abandonment is a premise rather than an outcome. Georges Bataille acknowledges this when he writes that a line from Dante's *Inferno*, "Lasciate ogni speranza voi qu'entrate,"[64] "could well be the epigraph for this absolutely striking book [*Molloy*], whose exclamation, uninterrupted by paragraphs, explores with such unflinching irony the extreme possibilities of indifference and misery."[65] Bataille suggests that shedding hope may be a precondition for reading Beckett's work, an imperative we must endlessly undertake. Abandonment in Beckett occurs at the very beginning of the story rather than at its end (where it might have functioned as a gesture of being done with it all).[66] His characters enter the stage, already abandoned, and the abandonment continues as the story unfolds. The economy of abandonment enacts chance and dispossession. The alternative, the more conventional story of being abandoned, is for Beckett a farce. He calls this the "farce of giving and receiving."

Beckett's career, in other words, goes beyond a limited view of abandonment defined as leaving something unfinished or unconcluded. Abandonment is also "to" something: abandonment to the elements, to an uncertain future, to chance, the orphaning of Oedipus rather than just nailing him to a side of the cliff. These measures, which I argue make Beckett's view of abandonment close to impoverished dereliction, commence long after the intention to begin has died ("I don't know when I died") and finish only when the formula for stopping has been given up.[67]

This nonlimited view of abandonment becomes clearer if we consider Beckett's pivotal short story, "From an Abandoned Work." The narrator of the story seems pressed into finishing some arbitrary tale involving, in no particular order, his mother seen waving to him from a window, a white horse, his aimless wandering through thickets, his sore throat, and a man, Balfe, who terrified him as a youngster ("Now he is dead and I resemble him").[68] Cohn's description of the incidents as "unconcatenated" suggests how the story is in fact a collection of contained rather than far-reaching failures.[69] The travails of the hero are productive of one thing: conclusiveness. By being able to push on without being taxed, the narrator leaves his condition of ever-trying intact, as if it just had not hit upon the right means, no matter how irrational, to express itself: "There was a time I tried to get relief by beating my head against something, but I gave it up."[70]

S. E. Gontarski uses the term "abandonment" to describe Beckett's textual history rather than an operative principle to his work: "Abandoned in 1966, 'Le Dépeupleur' was also unabandoned, 'completed' in 1970, and translated as *The Lost Ones* in 1971."[71] Though Gontarski's quotation marks around "completed" hint that even the published work both appeared and was abandoned, he uses the term "abandoned" as little more than a synonym for "unpublished." Abandoned works end up in the Beckett archive, whereas unabandoned ones end up on the shelf. Gontarski's perspective overlooks the paradoxically generative function of abandonment in Beckett's writing. The character Lucky in *Waiting for Godot* may be so named because his thinking, a hymn to labors left unfinished by Testew, Cunard, and others, invites chance. On the surface, Gontarski seems to have it right: if Beckett abandons his work, does this not mean that he stops writing it? The abandonment of literature, the abandonment of something fictional, allows abandonment to seep into the process of its creation. It is not about abandoning something once and for all, but about persistently giving something up, giving it up to an unknown future.

Many of the themes from Beckett's oeuvre make an appearance in "From an Abandoned Work," but only in congealed and almost dead form. The murmuring that envelops Molloy, for example, is reduced to a muttering, "the sound of my voice all day long muttering the same old things I don't listen to, not even mine it was at the end of the day, like a marmoset sitting on my shoulder with its bushy tail, keeping me company."[72] Agonizingly ubiquitous in *Molloy*, the disembodied voice here assumes the same friendly proximity as a captain's parrot, an isolated point of enunciation. Beckett allows the speaker some distant claim of ownership over this voice: "only a voice dreaming and droning all around, that is something, the voice that once was in your mouth."[73] In similar fashion, the ending of *The Unnamable* ("you must go on, I can't go on, I'll go on") atrophies here into a question, an option: "But what's the sense of going on with all this, there is none."[74] The Unnamable never inquires about the meaning or sense of his *going on*, as his speech is wrapped up in this impossibility and necessity of speaking. The coercive state of dereliction in the novel is absent in the short story. Going on *with* suggests an accompaniment and instrument for going on: if he does not go on with this story, the narrator implies, he can go on with something else. The short story appends such prepositions and adverbs to going on in order to cushion its horror. Elsewhere the narrator says that questions come to him when he walks: "How shall I go on another day? and then, How did I ever go on another day?"[75] This question separates a capacity to go on from his understanding. The narrator articulates it as a daily struggle, like a man living from paycheck to paycheck. It is a struggle by sunlight.

At the conclusion of the story the narrator says he just went on, "my body doing its best without me."[76] The separation of body and self is so neat that the body functions fine without him. The isolation of the *cogito* resolves itself. Yet there is no feeling here about the abandonment of one by the other, or of both. It must be the only instance in all of Beckett in which the best is achieved, rather than the worst, or the worse.

Beckett's abandonment of reference is frequently contrasted to the model of the committed artwork as defined by Sartre. In his essay "Commitment," Adorno groups Kafka's work with Beckett's:

> The minimal promise of happiness [Beckett's works] contain, which refuses to be traded for comfort, cannot be had for a price less than total dislocation, to the point of worldlessness. Here every commitment to the world must be abandoned to satisfy the ideal of the committed work of art. . . . This paradox, which might be charged with sophistry, can be supported without much philosophy by the simplest experience: Kafka's prose and Beckett's plays, or the truly monstrous novel *The Unnameable*, have an effect by comparison with which officially committed works look like pantomimes. Kafka and Beckett arouse the fear which existentialism merely talks about.[77]

In Adorno's dialectical understanding, the autonomous work achieves an effect that is the project of its opposite, the committed work. According to this claim, Beckett's work acquires political resonance not through engaged writing but through the reader's "simple experience" of this text that has "abandoned every commitment to the world." Adorno accurately remarks that Beckett does not enter easily into philosophical elaboration and that the truth of Beckett's work is not measured by its stated project (about which Beckett was notoriously silent) but by our experience of his work. At the same time, the simplicity of Beckett's work is not one that strikes the reader as a completed simplicity. And in avoiding all preconceived vehicles of sense, Beckett's text assigns a challenging task of understanding to the reader.[78] We can qualify Adorno's argument that Beckett's writing as "autonomous" in light of the impoverishment that characterizes Beckett's writing. In the above passage Adorno insists on abandonment as the constructive principle of Beckett's work. Adorno understands this more as a gesture of abandonment, however, and less as a condition, more as an operation that is performed (once and for all) than as a task. He says, in short, that Beckett has abandoned "every commitment to the world" in order to "satisfy the ideal of the committed work." Yet Beckett's work clearly raises as a question whether abandonment can be understood dialectically, whether it is—in the derelict existence of his characters, for example—something that can be substituted for or exchanged for its opposite (the hallmark of dialectical thinking). Adorno inscribes the gesture of abandonment within an economy of means: in saying that abandonment serves a project (in fact, the *opposite* project), Adorno suggests that abandonment is something that happens purposefully. But is it possible to ascertain the precise destination and outcome of what is abandoned? This recuperation is something that Beckett's work systematically forecloses as part of its pursuit of abandonment. In *Endgame* this is apparent in a succinct exchange:

> CLOV. Do you believe in the life to come?
> HAMM. Mine was always that.[79]

The words of redemption persist, as in this exchange between Hamm and Clov, but they are used in a context in which they are useless. Hamm's response suggests the way life has and has not always been displaced by the real life, the life to come. Even where the transcendence—the hereafter—is asserted, it does not attain credibility and flusters the reader by turning everyday life into a life still to happen, a life stricken by a great pause, a life in which nothing happens. Beckett draws us in through these words that seem forlorn of meaning. He draws us into a discussion that takes place not only between helpless characters but through the helpless condition of language itself. It asks something impossible of us, namely, to conceive our present life as a life to come, and to conceive this *present* life within the terms of a transcendence that has been *lost*. In this typical Beckettian exchange, the language is preeminently closed, assertive and pithy. At the same time it relies on and needs the reader to complete its sense (a completion it constantly reminds us is impossible). In this exchange between Hamm and Clov, we are asked implicitly to assist the words toward a meaning, a meaning those words deny. Beckett's text does not "cry out" for help: the state of need in his language is balanced by that language's indifference to the interpreter. Therefore, helpless writing is in a strange dependency on the reader, since it is helpless to say *how* it is that it requires our assistance. But fundamentally, Beckett's writings do not, as Adorno claims, simply abjure commitment to the world. Much of Beckett's writing hobbles toward a state of disability that it cannot name, a state that language in fact annuls: "Unable, unable, it's easy to talk about being unable, whereas in reality nothing is more difficult."[80] The opposite of talk, chatter, and discourse, the reality of being unable rips open Beckett's fiction. In the process, Beckett's work disables our normal questioning powers: it makes us sensitive to the way in which this absence of capacity exceeds our temptations to coerce and designate it.

Beckett's literature of need, its tireless effort at being without, is therefore not graspable as an "autonomous" entity that has sworn off every reference to the world. Quite the opposite is true, as its inabilities insert it into a dependent relation on the world. Franz Kafka, whose writing Adorno compares to Beckett's in the above passage, describes just such neediness as the defining characteristic of writing: "Writing's lack of independence from the world, its dependence on the maid who tends the fire, on the cat warming itself by the stove; it is even dependent on the poor old human being warming himself by the stove. All these are independent activities ruled by their own laws; only writing is helpless, does not dwell in itself, is frivolity and despair."[81] The situations that Kafka depicts as being situations of dependency—the maid tending the fire, the cat by the fire, the man by the stove—are not helpless situations in the extreme and singular way that writing is helpless. These needs are met functionally, the way a cold man is dependent on the fire for warmth. By contrast, writing is without tools. Nothing can help writing, and because it does not follow a law of the "self" or subject, it cannot help itself. The absence or need implicated by writing is intolerable. When Kafka discerns the vagrancy of literature in claiming that writing "does not dwell in itself," he means this lack that is writing's is not the possession of writing, something it actively showcases and that we can designate as a "lack." Writing cannot propose its own house rules by which to represent and dispense with its need: it goes elsewhere.[82] As if to prolong or accentuate its helpless condition, writing ends up being dependent for Kafka on relations that seem to leave it out: on the cat, the maid, and the "poor old human being." Writing has no choice but to forfeit its security of self-enclosure.

Hypothetical Imperatives

In his *Foundations of the Metaphysics of Morals,* Immanuel Kant contrasts the "categorical imperative," the imperative declaring an action to be of itself objectively necessary without reference to any purpose or end, with the "hypothetical imperative," which prescribes an action but only as a condition of a possible goal.[83] For Kant, in other words, the categorical imperative involves a good in and of itself. The hypothetical imperative, by contrast, is a good with a purpose—as a means to something. The categorical imperative for Kant is the moral necessity and thus absolute and global. The hypothetical imperative is normative and lacks the absolute. Kant's thinking is structured by this dyad, whereby the morally categorical or necessary is opposed to the morally hypothetical or normative.

For Beckett, morality and rules of conduct cannot be anything other than an impoverished form of the normative. Beckett therefore eliminates the categorical first half of the Kantian dyad. Unhinged from moral necessity, Molloy's hypothetical imperative assumes the urgency, the imperative necessity Kant reserves for the categorical. By moving the imperative mood to the side of the hypothetical, Beckett simultaneously impoverishes it. Thus a critique of Kant's categorical can be glimpsed: if Beckett's hypothetical imperative indeed retains the force of the categorical, then it impoverishes grammar and even perhaps the Kantian system of moral distinction. Furthermore, Beckett's hypothetical imperative is an imperative mood made poorer even than Kant's normative nonnecessity. It is actually hypothetical—an imperative estranged from any premise, any goal. Kant's figures are always endowed with necessary resources for thought, philosophical and aesthetic contemplation,[84] but Beckett's characters lack the mind, status, and full stomach to be anything other than hobos and desperados.

In Beckett's world of impoverished means, the imperative is less a grammatical mood than a loose signifier, liberated from obligation to meaning and flapping in the wind. In the novel *Molloy* the character claims to detect in a murmur, his only companion, something other than white noise: "In its framing I thought I heard something new. For after the usual blarney there followed this solemn warning, Perhaps it is already too late. It was in Latin, nimis sero, I think that's Latin. Charming things, hypothetical imperatives."[85] For Molloy, interpretation of the murmur is vital and faithlessness to it unthinkable. He receives the hypothetical imperative of the murmur like a gong signaling a lost thing, a marking of the passage of time more than a command. The hypothesis has swallowed the imperative, yet without producing a merely undecidable world of ambiguities, a world in which contraries flourish. Shorn from its end, the hypothesis becomes strangely *categorical*. In the totality of its supposition, the hypothetical imperative becomes a parody of an activity done for its own sake.

Theodor Adorno sums up the rationale of Beckett's world in writing that "the senselessness of an action becomes the reason for doing it."[86] Molloy refers later to his "so-called imperatives."[87] Between the French *soi-disant* and the "so-called" lies the difference between the imperative's self-saying authority (its diction intrinsic to its event) and its so-called (by Molloy, via Kant) or supposed or rumored status. Molloy experiences ongoing uncertainty about what the imperative says, whom it addresses and in what language, and about whether an imperative has been enunciated at all. This imperative follows an irrational or kettle logic.[88] Molloy notes that only a slight shift separates what he hears from the usual "blarney" or prattle of the murmur: he is addressed by the sudden "framing" of the murmur, which marks Molloy as the addressee without providing any content to the frame. The murmur deposits only a fragment of sense, an urgent but enigmatic marker of time: *nimis sero*.[89] Molloy can translate the Latin for us but cannot offer a reference for the imperative: late for what? The demanding nature of this imperative is that the reference of the imperative has been cut off, so that instead of being late for something, Molloy is late, period.

Address without reference is the subject of endless experimentation in Beckett's work. Beckett is interested in the hypothetical demand because the impoverished artwork communicates to the reader through need. The artwork may be needy because it can in fact only make hypothetical demands: the inability of literature to enact something or to authoritatively enter the practical world of action is the source of its vagrancy and poverty. Beckett's work to this end reorients the conventional separation of performative speech acts from constative or descriptive ones.[90] Throughout his late novella *Worstward Ho*, Beckett employs the imperative "say":

> It stands. What? Yes. Say it stands. Had to up in the end and stand. Say bones. No bones but say bones. Say ground. No ground but say ground. So as to say pain. No mind and pain? Say yes that the bones may pain till no choice but stand. Somehow up and stand. Or better worse remains. Say remains of mind where none to permit of pain. Pain of bones till no choice but up and stand. Somehow up. Somehow stand. Remains of mind where none for the sake of pain. Here of bones. Other examples if needs must. Of pain. Relief from. Change of.

All of old. Nothing else ever. But never so failed. Worse failed. With care never worse failed.[91]

The text commands us to resuppose these elements, to say bones, say ground, say mind, to say everything in short that might be supposed of a character who stands. The imperative "say" is hypothetical because it truly asks us to suppose something where there are literally no grounds for supposing it. The imperative transpires in the face of its impossibility. On the one hand, "say" enlists us to mouth the words in succession, the way the lips of readers sometimes mimic what the eyes see. On the other hand, the verb entails a wholly provisional demand, active only within the supplementary space of the example (as encountered in such phrases as "say you are walking down the street and . . . ").[92]

The hypothetical imperative prolongs the poverty discerned by the text in its opening sentence. Disavowing that anything can be supposed or taken for granted, or *as* granted, around it, the text demands us to suppose these things. The text asks us—tentatively, yet imperatively—to concede something to the representation. In a way our interest in the text is sustained by a sequence of charitable gestures sustaining a sentence that only apparently stands on its own. This "say"—directed at the reader as well as at the author—asks that something be given or granted that the text does not possess. The reader's charity is implored by a double movement in Beckett's text, a back-and-forth movement that renders the feeling that the text is unable to get started, cannot stand or push off from any sure ground. At the same time there is the feeling of there being only premise, an abyss of presuppositions. Presupposing is an endless task, not because anything can be presupposed but because nothing can be presupposed. Nothing is taken for granted in the simplest of predicates: it must be shown to be supposed and then, once this is withdrawn, must be conceded by the imagination of the reader.

Predication becomes a technocratic activity. Though the narrators of *The Unnamable* and *How It Is* both ascribe their words to a situation of dictation, *Worstward Ho* assumes the cadence of an office memo: "Other examples if needs must. Of pain. Relief from. Change of." Abbreviation is not just the method of this text but its very subject. The imperatives to rescind, to undo, to correct, are executive decisions on the text itself. Every predication seems submitted to official review in order to excise all excess. Though it aspires to the brevity of an office memo, Beckett's text is not merely a formal exercise. Such strange phrases as "Old and yet old" barely seem to inch forward. Yet the phrase suggests that there is a strange residue to even the term "old," as if the old had changed in the moment of its assertion, and this quality had to be reasserted. Did we forget that this image of "it stands" was "an image of old" as soon as it was described as such? This is the memorial function of this memo. What makes a "picture of old," an "old picture," this cliché of a thing standing, is our forgetting how it was made. And Beckett's text scrupulously labors through the discrete components of this picture (the pain, the bones, the mind) as if they were a set of weary joints that needed to be aligned just for the first sentence to become possible. The very syntax of the passage is gerontological.

Beckett once served as James Joyce's amanuensis, taking dictation as Joyce composed *Finnegan's Wake*. In his biography of Joyce, Richard Ellman recounts the well-known but possibly fictitious moment during this dictation in which there is a knock at the door that goes unheard by Beckett. When Joyce says, "Come in," Beckett dutifully notes it down as part of the text. Beckett recollects the moment for Ellman: "Joyce thought for a moment, then said, 'Let it stand.'"[93] Joyce says "*Stet.*" *Worstward Ho*'s disaggregation of "it stands" into its missing components serves both as a reply to and an undoing of Joyce's fiat, his royal permissiveness to let the error stand. Joyce's nod to the error signals the mythic inclusiveness of the Joycean text that absorbs the errors of its own transcription, the accidents of the world. Joyce proclaims "come in" to accident and absorbs it into his text.

By contrast, Beckett's text presents us with a different source of error and a different readerly relation to it. *Worstward Ho* invites us not to "come in" but to knock again on language in order to disperse and excise its excesses. Subjecting "it stands" to a withdrawal of all support, Beckett's prose cuts back and forth between the poverty of the predication and the provision of what it needs. The supposition "say" concedes something to the reader and to the author himself, something that is necessary so as to go on. It is in this sense that I call the supposition a provisional form: the supposition, in the absence of a ground, does not manufacture a ground as much as it temporarily offers us one. It is the offering of a state of crisis, and to one in a state of crisis. Colloquially, "provisions" denote supplies meant to help endure a temporary crisis: etymologically, these are resources that look toward a future after the crisis and toward a time of permanence. In Beckett the provisional never ends. Even the provisional gestures are helpless: each provisional supposition in the passage I have been discussing seems exposed to a need for further supposition and further assistance. A state of temporariness has become final in Beckett's prose, as if it had no future to look forward to. Beckett's work everywhere testifies to a condition very different from Baudelaire's description of the modern artist as one who distills the eternal from the ephemeral: "Il s'agit de dégager de la mode ce qu'elle peut contenir de poétique dans l'historique , de tirer l'éternel du transitoire."[94] Instead of merging opposites dialectically so that the one (the eternal) appears in the guise of the other (the ephemeral), Beckett's provisional mode seems without alternative and without opposition, and yet at the same time threatened.

The Provisional

Beckett's work can be characterized by its provisionality, its temporality of need. The microscopic adjustments and incisions performed on words such as "worse" or "less" (resembling the minutes of an office meeting) suggest the meticulousness of the process by which Beckett writes worstward (or by which he wrote *Worstward Ho*). Its economy (both in the sense of its minimalism and in the transactions it enters into with the reader) is not laissez-faire. Returning to the passage quoted above from *Worstward Ho:* "It stands. What? Yes. Say it stands. Had to up in the end and stand. Say bones. No bones but say bones. Say ground. No ground but say ground. So as to say pain. No mind and pain? Say yes that the bones may pain till no choice but stand."[95]

In Beckett's difficult prose, the reader lands with initial relief on the predication "It stands," one of only a handful of complete sentences in the entire book. The sense of relief is quickly dispelled since it becomes clear that this is provisional. Beckett, whose stage direction in a play discussed earlier prompts "no verticals," feels that even this brief "it stands" should not in fact be allowed to stand. It says too much. "It stands" implicates an entire anthropological and semiotic history: the two-word statement suggests something standing as well as something to stand on, a ground for the figure. "It stands" reflects the relation of figure to ground in its most architectural moment: it holds a position and can become the basis of the narrative of assertions, even if that position is of an abstract/formal nature (as in the phrase "it stands to reason"). This passage proceeds neither to empty out nor fill in the first sentence, but rather sets "it stands" adrift and turns it into a shipwreck.

The entire passage exposes the provisionality of the first assertion. The text proceeds to deny the existence of everything connoted in the statement and all the suppositions that seem necessary to it. The question "What?" following the first sentence of the quotation indicates a sense of surprise internal to the text, as it constitutes not an accommodating question, as in "*What* stands?" but rather "What do you mean, 'it stands'?" The text itself therefore seems shocked that things were progressing or were being built up so rapidly. It is intent on reminding us of the void that its own utterance cannot presume to dispel. There is a total absence of what is supposed to be in the predication "it stands," and against this absence of what it asserts.

Beckett subjects "it stands" to such thorough examination because the task of failure seizes upon any error (and for Beckett, all saying is missaying). The text's flaws, its lacks, its absence of bones, ground, etc., its needfulness, are the moments at which we are addressed by the text. Simultaneously transcribing, dictating, and recording, the text employs the "narrow writing" etymologically denoted by the term "stenography." *Worstward Ho* narrows and reduces the space between such antinomial terms as the worst and the best, the less and the more. In bringing the *mere* nearer to the *most* in the goal of the meremost minimum, Beckett forces us to redraw the graphs of value and quantity around new axes.

What lies behind Beckett's aesthetic interest in the provisional? Written in 1946 while he was a volunteer for the Irish Red Cross hospital in France, Beckett's radio broadcast "The Capital of the Ruins" provides insight into the way we are addressed by the hypothetical imperatives of *Worstward Ho*.[96] In this piece, Beckett writes about the hospital in Saint Lô, a city "bombed out of existence in one night." Unexploded bombs continued to go off after the conclusion of the war and the hospital, which was no more than a group of ramshackle huts, nursed the military and civilian wounded from both sides. In saying that the hospital would need to be in service for years after the end of the war, and that its function could not be a temporary measure, Beckett writes these striking words: "'Provisional' is not the term it was, in this universe become provisional."[97]

The provisional therefore does not become "universal" for Beckett the way Charles Baudelaire speaks of the ephemeral being substituted for the eternal. For Beckett, the meaning of "provisional" is unrecoverable now that it is has ironically become the condition of the universe itself. The provisional can no longer be grasped dialectically, in contrast to the permanent or the necessary, because it has become our condition and our misery. The antonym of provisional has died. Man's attempt at technological mastery over the world has ushered in a state of his total helplessness and his perpetual hospitalization. The observation here exacerbates the joke encountered frequently in Beckett's work in which a pair of haphazardly patched pants is compared to the world.[98] It is against the backdrop of the bottomless need of the war's victims at the clinic that we need to understand the utterly provisional form of Beckett's literature. Beckett takes the urgency and frailty overheard in the word "provisional" when applied to governments or hospitals and renders it the status quo of his work. We should not be misled by the etymology of provisional that suggests that such a work might look to the future, to recovery. In Beckett's work, there is no future for the provisional to look forward to. His work seeks out—with a poor memory—what is irreparable in the present, caught not between the provisional and the permanent but between the provisional and the obsolescent.

Beckett's provisional retains something of a memory—not the possession of the man with a memory capable of resentment, but a memory nevertheless. Beckett's dialogue with Georges Duthuit, the editor-in-chief of the magazine *transition* in which Beckett publishes several translations, took place in 1949. It is strongly informed not only by the aesthetic debates raging in the circles of *transition*, but by Beckett's experience as a hospital volunteer in 1945. Through his discussion of the artwork with Duthuit, the memory of his radio report runs softly but pronouncedly. The paradoxical title of Beckett's address, "The Capital of the Ruins," elevates the provisional and proposes a formal center to disaster, the highest ruin of the ruins. It reminds us that the "insuperable indigence" he speaks of elsewhere in his dialogue with Duthuit is perhaps best understood as another form of the provisional. In this radio address, Beckett sums up what passes in the charitable moment between volunteers (the "we") and sufferers (the "they"): "What was important was not our having penicillin when they had none, nor the unregarding munificence of the French Ministry of Reconstruction, but the occasional glimpse obtained, by us in them and, who knows, by them in us (for they are an imaginative people), of that smile at the human conditions as little to be extinguished by bombs as to be broadened by the elixirs of Burroughes and Welcome,—the smile deriding, among other things, the having and the not having, the giving and the taking, sickness and health."[99] The condition of the hospital is not what Beckett finds enduring. It is the smile deriding everything eternal and even that which mocks the eternal. The last line in the citation above is reminiscent of his comment to Duthuit on how the impoverished artwork is "too proud for the farce of giving and receiving."

Beckett ultimately discovers the provisionality of the place and function of art in a temporary hospital set up in a landscape of desolation following the war. At first glance both Beckett's art and the smile he glimpses belong to a system of meaning and associations that he is in fact critiquing. Though some critics read the radio address as an indication that Beckett believed charity to "be our salvation as we await Godot," the above passage shows that Beckett is *not* saying that this smile is the signpost of eternal humanity or the expression of an understanding.[100] To a certain extent our reading of this radio address (and through it, of his conversations about art) needs to retain the nonintegrated remainder that "humanist" readings of the address (as of his work) would brush over. What is alarming about Beckett's report from Saint Lô is the way the smile seems to have a strange inaccessibility and can neither be "wiped off" nor intensified into laughter. Beckett says this smile is not widened by charity nor reduced by suffering. In the context of suffering Beckett finds the death's rictus, the smile of the skull, on the face of the living. There is an obtuse feeling of stasis in this smile since it is out of order, outside exchange, and derides among other things the "having and not having, sickness and health." This smile is therefore not a reaction to circumstances, suggesting neither relief nor thanks, and is paradoxically both immune and helpless. Outside the particularities of historical circumstance, it merits that name given to the slight lift at the corners of the mouth on ancient Greek statuary: the archaic smile. This smile does not end. For all of its momentum toward the worst and its impulse to amputation, Beckett's work is in fact exclusively dedicated to such negligible and irreducible expressions. Beckett does not look for a particular expression in the face of the suffering or the poor (there is no face in his radio address) but rather for what is inaccessible, the indelible residue, in the face of catastrophe. Beckett pluralizes the expression "human condition" (words not native to the Beckett lexicon) as if to suggest the loss of a common condition following this catastrophe. At the same time, this impoverished smile is on the faces of both doctors and patients. As a novelist and as a reporter, Beckett was attuned to that which could not be imparted, that impassive and truly helpless thing on the face of helper and helped alike.

Worsening

In his last work, *Worstward Ho,* Beckett devises a final strategy of textual indigence. Despite the almost total absence of verbs in the text, *Worstward Ho* assiduously grinds out a figural and lexicographical reduction. From three figures called *shades:* a kneeling woman, an old man and a child, and a skull, the text systematically withdraws all recognizable and distinctive features. The kneeling woman undergoes this process first:

> First one. First try fail better one. Something there badly not wrong. Not that as it is it is not bad. The no face bad. The no hands bad. The no—.

174 • CHAPTER 4

> Enough. A pox on bad. Mere bad. Way for worse. Pending worse still. First worse, Mere worse. Pending worse still. Add a—. Add? Never. Bow it down. Be it bowed down. Deep down. Head in hat gone. More back gone. Greatcoat cut off higher. Nothing from pelvis down. Nothing but bowed back. Topless baseless hindtrunk. Dim black. On unseen knees. In the dim void. Better worse so. Pending worse still.[101]

A praying woman is a fragment or shade (no face, no hands, no—). Yet, as if this image was already too complete or too rich, not sufficiently impoverished, that image of the woman is further reduced and "defigured." The text passes a verdict ("Enough.") over the initial state of want of the figure. The text proceeds to scrape away any qualities we might impute to the figure. This process occurs on the figural level (the image of the woman) as well as on the linguistic level (the language used to describe her). It issues a fiat on surplus ("Add? Never.") and removes the head in hat, everything below the pelvis, and "more back." The greatcoat is hemmed. Yet the reductions in the text ultimately resemble neither an amputation nor a tailoring but rather a deprivation of the image via language. Words such as "hindtrunk" bring the human carcass suddenly into view, but the impression is aesthetic, as if Beckett were operating on words, figures, values rather than flesh and bone.

King Lear lurks in the background of *Worstward Ho*. Beckett's "Sottisier" notebook contains his notations to Shakespeare's play, most notably Edgar's lines, "Who is't can say, I am at the worst." And "The worst is not so long as one can say, This is the worst."[102] Beckett is different from Shakespeare in the sense that Shakespeare makes language into the simultaneous barrier and capacity that separates us from the experience of the worst. According to Edgar, we are not in the worst as long as it bears speech, and as long as we can discourse about it. Edgar's first observation casts doubt on the ability of the worst to be synonymous either with its assertion or with a state of being, the *I am*. The worst occupies a hyperbolic register for Edgar beyond language and existence. When we merge with the worst, presumably, it will be designated only by the absence of speech and by some default of our existence (our capacity to say, "I am").

Worstward Ho constitutes Beckett's literary reply to the theatricality of Edgar's antithesis of speech (saying) and the worst, of language as a refuge from the extreme conditions of misery. Beckett's text works on the impoverishment of both poles: the emphasis on missaying and saying less over saying, and on worsening over the worst.[103] It is not enough, according to Beckett, to say, "this is the worst." *Worstward Ho* begins with the "mere bad" and recedes from there. Alain Badiou observes that the void in Beckett is something named rather than encountered: "Existence is the generic attribute of what is capable of worsening. What can worsen exists. . . . What exists is what lets itself be encountered. . . . Neither void nor dim designate something that can be encountered."[104] Beckett agrees with Edgar insofar as the text can only designate the worst. Though pointed in the direction of the worst, Beckett's text never arrives there: this separation of the address from the destination of the worst is part of Beckett's textual impoverishment of the term.

Implied by Edgar's attention to language is a sense that "the worst" occupies a spectrum or escalating quantity of worseness. Beckett introduces aesthetic criteria to propel poverty past this method of measurement. Instead of an opposition between the more and the less or the good and the bad (as Edgar implies), in which the no sum and degree zero become the apex of poverty, there is a flattening, and a shuffling back and forth rather than a direct linearity: "Worse less. By no stretch more. Worse for want of better less. Less best. No. Naught best. Best worse. No. Not best worse. Naught not best worse. Less best worse. No. Least. Least best worse. Least never to be naught. Never to naught be brought. Never by naught be nulled. Unnullable least. Say that best worse. With leastening words say least best worse. For want of worser worst."[105] The nursery-rhyme simplicity of this passage hypnotizes us with its monosyllabic terms, but does not state its principles but works by force of them, instead enacting them. This plays into its point. "Worse less" sets a phonetic trap for our ear, sounding vaguely like *worthless*.

Beckett's texts do not seek an absence of worth but a diminishment of quality, a best worse. They monitor a movement toward the less and the worse. In *Worstward Ho*, experimental superlatives and comparatives collide. ("Less best. No. Naught best. Best worse. No.") There is an arraignment, rather than an arrangement, of terms in which the hierarchy of measure is put on trial. All this incandescent coupling and decoupling of the worse and less calls attention to the ultimately uncontrolled dimension of the remainder. The text above makes the hairline fracture between "Naught best" and "Not best worse." Worse, being in want of the worst (a kind of negative satiation) thereby becomes the preferable condition.

For Badiou, Beckett's worsening process involves stripping language of consequence. He asserts that Beckett's words are there in order to have their implications dismissed. Worsening is "the exercise of the sovereignty of saying with respect to the shades. Therefore, it is both saying more about them and restricting what is said. This is why the operations are contradictory. Worsening is saying more about less. More words to better leasten."[106] Badiou subverts the commonplace of Beckett criticism, that less is more and that saying less means more meaning. Badiou points out that Beckett is in fact inverting this interpretation, saying more about less. We can push this farther. Beckett's work confronts its own interpretation by inserting its own discussion into our response. Here, less is *worse,* not more. The text thereby forecloses any strictly quantitative measurement of poverty. In this way Beckett's operations are not quite "contradictory" as Badiou claims. Instead of a counterlogical movement (the more becoming less) Beckett entwines two hyperbolic systems. Beckett introduces a third element (varieties on the worse) in order to create a constellation of poverty rather than a conceptual dyad. Badiou's "sovereignty of saying" refers to the exceptions, the distinctions, the forceful separations that Beckett's text seems to decree. Beckett's text proposes a different sovereign: the concept. The text makes two statements against this king: "Pox on bad" and "Pox on void."[107] If Beckett's text enacts sovereignty, it also says down with it, let the face of the void be covered in acne, let us dethrone the mere bad. Beckett pithily denounces the nominal authority of these terms precisely because they arrest poverty: "bad" because it embodies a criterion that is too preliminary, and "void" because it names something too ultimate. "Void" exists only in name, an effigy of what remains *in absentia,* not as textual process. The word would seem to represent the apex of poverty, the achievement of total desolation without remainder. Yet the "unmoreable unlessable unworseable evermost almost void" cannot be transformed, reduced further. The void constitutes the direction of the text, but not its step-by-step operation. Conceptual designations for impoverishment are subverted here in favor of a literary examination of language from the standpoint of an ever-slimming remainder. This remainder afflicts, in the end, the void itself (it is an evermost *almost* void).

As an era of unremitting crisis, modern history provides multiple instances in which the worst has come into view but not yet into language. The conditions of our existence have repeatedly tested our capacity for speech.[108] We have been pushed past Edgar's predicament in which the worst is seemingly yet to come.[109] In his review of John Hersey's *Hiroshima,* Georges Bataille describes the challenge issued by distress on a nuclear scale. He notes the injunction the sovereign individual derives in the face of such suffering: "The man of sovereign sensibility, face-to-face with misfortune, no longer immediately exclaims, 'At all costs let us do away with it,' but first, 'Let us live it.' Let us lift, in the instant, a form of life to the level of the worst. But no one, for all that, gives up doing away with what they can."[110] For Bataille, the sovereign sensibility asks not how to live accordingly after Hiroshima but how to live up to Hiroshima. How can our life bear a form that somehow stands before and does not deflect the radiance of this catastrophe? Beckett, by contrast, does not suggest that we could ever really share the level with the worst. The "form of life" in Beckett's last work is perpetually being unmade, unassumed, and unspoken on its way to the worst, without ever getting there. Beckett seems to be closer to Bataille's description of the default of sovereign sensibility, what he calls the reaction of "no one," an unending "doing away with what they can." This is a good synopsis of Beckett's subtractive attitude. For Beckett, the relentless drive toward the worse requires diligence—a perpetual emptying out of capacity, like water from a sinking boat.

Though the texts themselves focus on the process of leastening and worsening, Beckett's work is put on a level with the worst in its performance. In prison, Sarajevo, and New Orleans, Beckett's form of life, his dramatic persona, are put in balance with the surrounding devastation. Beckett's work appeals to audiences in crisis situations precisely because the worsening process neither ends nor, like Edgar, calls attention to the impossibility of its expression and therefore its validity. Instead of being on a level with the worst, Beckett's work levels or reduces it to a worst worse. Beckett's worsening submits its forms of life to disintegration and thereby opens up something ineradicably inconsolable but also something deeply and ineradicably present.

Afterword

Staging *Godot* in Zuccotti Park

The transition from diagnosis (critical reading) of Beckett to prognosis (seeing Beckett in the world) is obstructed by a persistent Beckettian *agnosis*, an indifference to ideas and knowledge. Marcel Proust compares *À la Recherche du temps perdu* to a telescope that enables readers to bring into focus the disparate details of a world of the past, distant in both time and space.[1] Beckett's work, by contrast, has the reader looking into an inverted telescope, where even proximate things reappear to us as alienated and distant, reduced in size and yet not for the purpose of study. Reading Beckett does not lead the reader to an appreciation of the world but rather to its depreciation and diminution. Beckett's work teaches us to look up from his page with the gaze of the prospector—but in reverse gear. Reality through an inverted telescope appears smaller, untranscendent, and as if the whole world were dumped into the bottom of a well—in short, a place where things are condemned to wait.

The homeless vagabonds in *Waiting for Godot* beg the question of how to stage a world down a well. Godot has been imprisoned, placed under the siege of Sarajevo, cast off with the jetsam in post-Katrina New Orleans. Under what circumstances might *Godot* be performed again? What theatrical stages are being forged within the contemporary political landscape?[2] What new stress might be found within *Godot*'s monotony were the play to unfold, for example, in the shadow of technological disaster, an information meltdown, a failed prediction for the world's end, or during a workers' strike?[3]

The Occupy Wall Street movement of 2011 sought to call attention to the iniquities of the financial system in the United States and worldwide that benefitted a few at the expense of the many. The insight of Occupy Wall Street and related squatter communities that arose in Oakland, Boston, Chicago, Cleveland, London, and other cities across the world was that marginal existence had left the margins and become the status quo. The movement's slogan "We are the 99%" highlighted the statistical gap separating the majority from the wealth and power of the highest and slimmest tier (the 1 percent) of privileged society.

In researching this book, my goal was not to add yet another analysis to the heap of Beckett scholarship. I instead wanted to do something Beckettian, something *less*—to let go of analysis and see what would happen at the intersection of *Godot*'s "country road" with Wall Street. Despite its variegated production history and its appeal to communities in crisis, *Godot* had never been staged with a backdrop of financial crisis. The vagabonds resonated allegorically with displaced inhabitants of the Lower Ninth Ward, with convicts, and with people under siege, yet never with the victims of a financial tsunami, the unemployed, the financially ruined, or, in the language of the Occupy movement, the 99 percent. So in October 2011, along with Jonathan Bernstein and Harold Dean James, I coproduced *Waiting for Godot* in Zuccotti Park at the heart of the protest movement as a kind of "road test" for the concepts I had been developing while writing this book. Though not a play of protest, what might *Godot* become while unfolding in the middle of one? Would the squatters of the Occupy movement feel an affinity with Didi and Gogo? What pressure might the staging of a protest exert on the staging of a play?

As in San Quentin, Gentilly, and Sarajevo, the situation in Zuccotti Park that beckoned the production already seemed Beckettian. Addressing the global movement of capital, the protest assumed an obstinately immobile form, as if the bodies of the participants had nothing in common with the mobility and liquidity of labor, stocks, and indexes. Instead of marching in the street, the protest more closely resembled an effort to live there, in full view and subject to the vicissitudes of weather and circumstance, like vagabonds. The movement de-escalated the Gandhian tactic of passive resistance into impassive endurance or perhaps something more closely resembling the prolonged inertia seen onstage in *Godot*. Descriptions of the Occupiers notably sounded like unwitting descriptions of Beckett's stage-

FIGURE 1
PROTEST SIGNS AT ZUCCOTTI PARK DURING OCCUPY WALL STREET, OCTOBER 2011
(PHOTO BY STACEY MICKELBART)

craft. Ross Douthat, for example, wrote about the "ragtag theatricality" of the movement.[4] The parallels continued and multiplied right up to the night of November 15, when at 1 A.M., without warning, the police cleared all protesters in a very carefully planned raid under Klieg lights, arresting some who resisted. One eyewitness reports, "The sanitation department collected anything left behind and barricades were placed to limit access to the park."[5] The words of Molloy, Beckett's vagabond character, come as close as any to a description for the end of the Zuccotti encampment: "The night purge is in the hands of the technicians."[6]

Occupy Wall Street was not just demonstrating against homelessness and the mechanisms behind it (subprime mortgages, the collapsing housing market, foreclosures), it was also demonstrating homelessness. The rags of the squatters were not mere show: in sharp contrast to previous social movements that divided across class lines,[7] Occupy was permeable to society's most bereft. New York City's homeless population entered the ranks of the protest. Activist Rebecca Solnit observes, "One of the complicating factors in the Occupy movement was that so many of the thrown-away people of our society—the homeless, the marginal, the mentally ill, the addicted—came to Occupy encampments for safe sleeping space, food, and medical care. These economic refugees were generously taken in by the new civil society, having been thrown out by the old uncivil one."[8] Rather than "complication," the inclusion of the homeless is a measure of the movement's complexity. It was not the protest that integrated the homeless but vice versa: the homeless introduced the protest to the day-to-day crisis of their existence, to sleeping on pavement, hunting for food, and the unrestrained intrusion of policemen. Writer Chris Hedges claims that protesters received their "master class in occupation" and learned their tactics for survival from drifters.[9] But even a writer as deeply sympathetic to the movement as Solnit regards the homeless less as participants and more as intruders. These outcasts do not seem to have place even within our political spectrum: they live the condition others protest.

The Occupy movement at times looked like a sit-down strike for the unemployed: they seemed to be striking against the conditions of un- or underemployment, and could do so only by enacting the vagabondage into which the 99 percent had been cast. To dramatize this, the movement raised inutility to the level of public spectacle. Zuccotti Park had neither utilitarian nor symbolic value. Occupying it did not block access to the financial centers, and the park had none of the iconic value of spaces seized in earlier protests (the president's office at Columbia University, the ROTC headquarters, the monument at Wounded Knee).[10] Hunkering down in the park for four months was as absurd as occupying a stage for two acts, waiting for a character who never arrives. This has alarmed Beckett's audiences since *Godot*'s 1953 debut. At the Brussels premiere of *Waiting for Godot* a patron yelled "Why won't they work?" as she stormed toward the exit; "Because they don't have time," replied another.[11] In these early performances the emphatic dereliction of Beckett's figures grated on the work ethic of the audience. Not only were the figures on stage not doing anything but the play was not doing anything—and not doing anything with that fact. "Nothing to be done" signals both that there is no work to do and that much work on the nothing remains to be done (and therefore can be postponed).

Some popular objections to Beckett's theater echo those leveled at the Occupiers. The question "Why won't they work?" is testimony to a desire to place delinquent bodies elsewhere, to make them leave the haphazard collective in the park and disappear into solitary labor. Of course, the failure to disappear in this way, the growing absence and inadequacy of work, was what prepared the ground for the movement. But this condition does not spontaneously generate demands. Indeed, journalists took the movement to task for what Todd Gitlin called "demandlessness," a refusal to formulate objectives that would accommodate existing political discourse and address the platforms of the major political parties.[12] In a speech delivered at the park, Judith Butler observes similarly, "Saying there are no demands leaves your critics confused."[13] Likewise, Beckett replaces "demand" with "need." His work confronts readers with an impoverished and worsening situation rather than a theme or thesis. Beckett describes the work of art as a confluence of two needs, "the being which is need and the necessity of being in need, hell of unreason from which rises the blank scream, the series of pure questions, the work of art."[14] The artwork's scream is blank: need is not sublimated into protest, objection, or articulation. Readers instinctively want to make their job easier by making this scream into a demand, to make it a need *for* something (truth, philosophy, meaning, anything). Yet the poverty of Beckett's work maintains only a need for need: it cannot even imagine the quenching object.

We had a busy week preparing for the performance at Zuccotti Park. We scouted the performance location, met with the improvised and fluid leadership of the Occupy movement, held a casting call for professional actors, rehearsed, found props, scoured thrift stores for costumes, and made flyers and advertising material. In turning to the Salvation Army, that limbo for castaway items, we honored a tradition for *Godot* performances that began at the world premiere of the play at the Babylon Theater in 1953. The props department at the Babylon Theater did not possess an adequate suitcase for the character Lucky, which, director Roger Blin specified, should be old and battered looking. Two days before opening night, the costume lady resolved this problem by asking her husband, a garbage collector for the city of Paris, to find such a suitcase. As in the original production, the Zuccotti *Godot* featured abandoned objects, rather than prefabricated representations of them.

On the day of the show we walked from our rehearsal space to Zuccotti Park. Our troupe, The 99% Theater Company, entered the busy streets of New York like actors for hire, in search of a stage (rather than an author), seeking to claim a performance space, rather than be delivered to one. The actors walked to work in both costume and character, passing out flyers for the performance on the way. People stared at Lucky, a man grunting with a suitcase, a chair, and a rope around his neck. As Pozzo swung the whip, shouting "Think Pig!" "Up Pig!," passersby were confused and alarmed.

Whatever scene we made walking down to Wall Street, upon arriving at Zuccotti Park the actors in their makeup and bowler hats did not stand out but actually blended in with the Occupy crowd. There were so many signs and performances of protest and mini-scenarios on view that we merely took a place next to everyone else. Didi carried the tree made of a few oversized hundred-dollar bills from a "Big Bucks" note pad for leaves and snapped dowels for branches. The barren money tree, which could have been devised for the protest rather than the play, aroused no astonishment.

The protest and the procession of signs and homemade statuary gave a different nuance to the blasted tree in *Godot*. Instead of simply designating a barren wasteland, it became accusatory, less destroyed icon than icon of destruction, like the Styrofoam drone in the photo. In the years prior to the economic collapse, money seemed indeed to grow on trees: capital, even the promise of capital, begat more capital. Labor fell out of the picture. The tree that grew in Wall Street seemed therefore to represent the breakdown of a financial illusion.

Each performance of *Godot* was countenanced by protesters' signs. Didi and Gogo delivered lines such as "No use wiggling" and discussed how Godot had to consult his agents, his correspondents, his books, his bank account "before taking a decision," while staring out into a sea of placards bearing phrases such as "Up against the Wall Street" and "I can't afford a Politician." Quite fittingly, our first performance of Beckett's play took place beneath and out of reach of an enormous red sculpture titled *Joie de Vivre*. The performance space shifted according to the movement of the crowd standing around, many of them with signs.

FIGURE 2
ACTORS BEAR BECKETT'S TREE INTO ZUCCOTTI PARK (PHOTO BY ALEX LUKENS)

Our production of *Godot* took place in a landscape scattered with written imperatives, denunciations, political puns, and lines drawn from Beckett's text. *Godot* is both experimental and extraordinarily unperturbed, unagitated: it does not wince at the horror. The constellation of urgent messages that ringed our stage seemed defined by their collision with the deadpan expression of Beckett's play and the elongated gesture of its emptiness. "It's a Scandal!" uttered by Vladimir in shock at Lucky's condition, is the only line in which the character raises his voice. Printed on a sign, this line hung over each movement on the stage.

The production revealed how Wall Street is a land of capital and for capital and as such a "no-man's-land." The space provided not only an uninhabitable stage for *Godot* but a uniquely inhospitable one as well. This was a protest of the Facebook era—everyone had a voice, but no one a microphone. We immersed the deamplified voices of Beckett's characters into a setting where the prevailing logic seemed to be that if you want to be heard, get louder. It was possibly the windiest *Godot* ever: through the cavernous streets, strong breezes whipped across the park and blew an array of small street debris at the actors and across the stage. Never have the actors in a Beckett play seemed so acoustically and visually dwarfed. Their anxiety

FIGURE 3
LUCKY (DAVID YASHIN) PERFORMS MONOLOGUE NEAR "UN-REPEAL GLASS-STEAGALL"
(PHOTO BY STACEY MICKELBART)

FIGURE 4
DIDI (HAROLD DEAN JAMES) AND GOGO (KATIE SCHWARZ) WAIT IN FRONT OF SIGNS READING
"IT'S A SCANDAL"; "THINK, PIG"; "AT LEAST LUCKY HAS A JOB"; AND "DON'T BE A GASHOLE"
(PHOTO BY ALEX LUKENS)

sharpened in the shadow of the colossal financial buildings surrounding the park, so much so that at times it seemed to tear their huddle apart.

The classical themes of work and worklessness were overshadowed by the real presence of icons of capital. In this setting Pozzo cannot appear except as the incontestable boss, not of Brecht's production (a rational capitalist) but more like one of the occasionally steamed passersby trying to get to work. Pozzo complains, "[Lucky] imagines that when I see how well he carries I'll be tempted to keep him on in that capacity. . . . In reality he carries like a pig. It's not his job."[15] Beckett here pegs the way the impression of usefulness (its performance) has exceeded the value of use. Lucky appears as a laborer who has taken on jobs exceeding the terms of his contract merely to keep that job. The play also shows how Vladimir and Estragon undertake their unemployment like a task, a burden. *Waiting for Godot* dramatizes Sisyphean labors: each activity is ended no sooner than it has begun and produces an unclear outcome—not even the wry smile Camus attributes to the man as he trudges back down the hill is possible. For Beckett's characters the smile is only a slim consolation following the ban on laughter, a "dreadful privation."[16] Adorno's observation that Beckett's plays are filled with a "jargon of a universal disrespect" came out in Zuccotti Park in the owner-worker relation.[17] Unlike on the Brecht stage,

FIGURE 5
DIDI (HAROLD DEAN JAMES) AND GOGO (KATIE SCHWARZ) HUDDLE TOGETHER
(PHOTO BY ALEX LUKENS)

there is no stable universal sense of good work as a value. The desperation of two characters for the seeming lowest of occupations resonates with our age in which unions have suffered and a surfeit of labor makes even humiliating labor appealing. Didi and Gogo are not the solid proletariat, as designated within Brecht's rewriting of the play, but rather are workers whose labor and productivity have been outsourced. Didi and Gogo and even Pozzo appear eager to possibly take Lucky's place, the place of the slave, merely because he is actually paid, albeit in bones and other scraps of food.

Other resonances emerged within the performance itself; as in New Orleans, certain phrases rang more determinedly in our ears. When Pozzo says to Vladimir and Estragon, "The road is free to all," the actor (Cezar Williams) waved his arm toward Broadway, which ran next to the performance space on the edge of the park and which was patrolled by New York City police repeating "Move along!" "Keep moving!" to pedestrians gathering to see the performance. Cezar's improvised gesture illuminated something about that street, and simultaneously inflected a different dimension of the "country road" in Beckett's play. Indeed, throughout the performance the words of the actors are punctuated and intermingled with the words of the police. The unspoken condition for Beckett's play, as for Wall Street, is that this road and that street are not free, are not available to all, and do not constitute a space of opportunity.

A police presence is not an unfamiliar accompaniment to productions of *Godot*, but the requirements of the law in relation to the Occupy production are idiosyncratic and instructive. In the *Godot* in Belgrade, the cops faced the exit to prevent people from entering. In San Quentin and Raiford, police faced inward to keep prisoners from escaping the auditorium. In Zuccotti Park the police cut the audience in half, forcing half of it to be immobile and the other half mobile. A police cordon created a strange moat of human traffic around the inner audience. The barricades they erected prevented newcomers from stopping for too long to peek in either at the play or the happenings inside the park. Although this must have been annoying for some of the audience, a totally supervised space is in fact perfect for a Beckett play. Guns, badges, blue uniforms, and barked orders formed the outer barrier of the production. Adorno calls walking in place "the fundamental motif of the whole of [Beckett's] work."[18] The police enforced this futility of going nowhere, of being unable to stand freely and watch from the sidewalk or leave the park except at prescribed exits. (Our play unfolded not far from two men peddling stationary bikes that powered the electrical generators inside Zuccotti.) Like a performance in a prison yard, every movement of freedom is strangely insularized. The police were perhaps more vital here than they were in the other performances of this book.

The disciplinary force encircling Zuccotti Park actively transformed potential spectators of the production into bystanders, literally standing by or contiguous to the play. This mode of stand-by, even temporary, suggests a mode of witnessing already enwrapped in waiting. But this waiting is more impatient, less meditative, than the expectations cultivated in the traditional spectator. The bystander is marked by the happenstance event, an accident or an unannounced theatrical performance: nobody intends to become a bystander and one cannot purchase tickets to bystand. This simultaneous contingency and contiguity of the audience to the play enabled, however, something customarily denied to spectators: they could get involved. At the very first performance, before any lines had been uttered, an event transpired underneath the *Joie de Vivre* that illustrates this. Katie Schwarz, as Gogo, heartily struggles with her boot at the beginning of the play. Without a curtain to signal the start of the play, a bystander or protester walked forward to do something, to offer his help.

Each performance of *Godot* in this book assaults theatrical decorum in its unique way, breaching the line between the play and its surroundings. The dissolution of that line is never an instance of Beckett entering the world but testimony to how the world recognizes that it has become theatrical, Beckettian. At the inaugural edge of the Zuccotti *Godot,* at that moment when the actor is acting but has not spoken her lines, a man steps forward making an emphatic gesture of assistance. Before Katie could deliver the play's ominous first line, the bystander discerned that something had to be done. By this empathic gesture the man became an actor not only because he had unwittingly entered the stage but because he was acting on this empathy, and thereby exceeding—as most of the occupiers sought to do—the passivity of the traditional spectator. This cleft within the spectator's position also affected the protesters themselves, who were divided between being passive gawkers (in a protest but only there to gawk at it, to photograph it, looking for something to take home with them) and being bystanders, or subjects who intervened and risked arrest.

Transpiring almost without notice and almost before the play began, this transfigurative moment took measure of what it meant to bring this play to the protest. Not only did the context of the Occupy movement make the poverty of Beckett's play more apparent, it created the conditions under which someone could respond to it differently, with an offer of help rather than seizing it as an opportunity for catharsis. This bystander saw a state of need on Beckett's stage, but not the stage. His intervention threw the stage, and the play, off course. In the time I spent at Occupy Wall Street, and in spite of the loud shouts for solidarity, the songs and chants, a drum circle, and weed generously shared, this marked in fact the one time I saw someone try to help another, another who happened to be a fictional character. Alas! Nothing to be done.

Notes

Introduction

1. Samuel Beckett, *Proust and Three Dialogues with Georges Duthuit* (London: Calder, 1987), 122.

2. Beckett assumes poverty through the writing process in his work rather than through a vow, a Franciscan promise to align existence with a spiritual model. For an excellent analysis of Beckett's early relation to resignation and stoicism see Matthew Feldman, "'Agnostic Quietism' and Samuel Beckett's Early Development," in *Samuel Beckett: History, Memory, Archive*, ed. Seán Kennedy and Katherine Weiss (London: Palgrave Macmillan, 2009), 183–200.

3. Anthony Cronin, *Samuel Beckett: The Last Modernist* (New York: Harper Collins, 1997), 389.

4. Idiomatic translation of *petitio principii*.

5. Beckett's poverty focuses on evicted and vagabond characters and recognizes architecture's containing (imprisoning) function rather than the sheltering function. In his essay "Experience and Poverty" Walter Benjamin discusses the glass architecture as the forerunner of the new poverty. The domestic interior is put brutally on view, a situation that appeals to Benjamin via Brecht: "A neat phrase by Brecht helps us out here: 'Erase the traces!' is the refrain in the first poem of his Reader for City Dwellers.... This has now been achieved by Scheerbart, with his glass, and by the Bauhaus, with its steel. They have created rooms in which it is hard to leave traces." *Selected Writings*, vol. 2, *1927–1934*, ed. Michael Jennings, Howard Eiland, and Gary Smith, trans. Rodney Livingstone et al. (Cambridge, MA: Harvard University Press, 1999), 734.

6. This tenacity of inquiry overhangs even Kafka's correspondence, particularly as it comes to us today, because none of the answers have survived his questions: all of Felice's replies have been lost.

7. Beckett, *Proust and Three Dialogues*, 122.

8. Roland Barthes calls Brecht's theater "a moral theater, that is, a theater which asks, with the spectator: what is to be done in such a situation? . . . Brechtian invention is a tactical process to unite with revolutionary correction. In other words, for Brecht the outcome of every moral impasse depends on a more accurate analysis of the concrete situation in which the subject finds himself." Roland Barthes, "The Tasks of Brechtian Criticism," in *Critical Essays*, trans. Richard Howard (Evanston, IL: Northwestern University Press, 1972, 76.

9. Clas Zilliacus, "Three Times 'Godot': Beckett, Brecht, Bulatovic," *Comparative Drama* 4, no. 1 (Spring 1970): 3–17. Brecht makes Estragon's German more colloquial through the addition of idioms (changing Tophoven's translation from "Schweigen wir ein wenig, ja" to "Halten wir das Maul") and the abbreviation of Estragon's verbs (*hätt', heut', werd'*). Ibid., 6.

10. Beckett's characters are too far gone for cooptation. The contrast between the authors becomes apparent through a consideration of Brecht's poem, "Belonging to a Reader for Those who Live in Cities." Here Brecht advises his readers to erase their traces, cover their tracks ("Verwisch die Spuren"). To the underground political worker reading his poem, Brecht issues the imperative to pass by your parents as if they were strangers; to not show your face; to go in any house when it rains; to see to it that you do not have any gravestone inscription to betray you. Yet Beckett's figures already comply with these suggestions. The distance between Beckett and Brecht becomes apparent in the difference between unwanted anonymity (the state of Beckett's characters) and going incognito (Brecht's proposed strategy). *Poems 1913–1956*, ed. John Willet, Ralph Manheim, and Erich Fried (New York: Routledge, 1987), 131–40.

11. Zilliacus, "Three Times 'Godot,'" 8.

12. Elin Diamond, "Re: Blau, Butler, Beckett, and the Politics of Seeming," *TDR/The Drama Review* 44, no. 4 (Winter 2000): 38.

13. Since the author's death, the Beckett estate has continued as the official arbiter separating approved from outcast productions.

14. Everett Frost, "Letter to the Editor," *Beckett Circle* 16, no. 1 (Spring 1994): 5.

15. Ibid. Frost revealingly observes that liberties taken with the play in a performance at Lincoln Center are liberties taken with "Beckett's 'Godot.'"

16. Darko Suvin, *To Brecht and Beyond* (Sussex, UK: Harvester Books, 1984), 225.

17. Though Suvin does not elaborate the point any further here, "camps" refers most likely to refugee camps, detention camps, or concentration camps. The relevance of Beckett's work echoes in these laboratories of the modern world wherein the subject is dispossessed of rights, agency or movement, and human status.

18. Samuel Beckett, *Waiting for Godot* (New York: Grove Press, 1982), 27.

19. Vivian Mercier, "The Uneventful Event," *Irish Times*, February 18, 1956, 6.

20. Beckett, *Waiting for Godot*, 60.

21. Ibid., 7, 60.

22. Martin Esslin, *The Theatre of the Absurd* (New York: Anchor Books, 1961), xvii.

23. Herbert Blau, "On Directing Beckett," in *Sails of the Herring Fleet: Essays on Beckett* (Ann Arbor: University of Michigan Press, 2004), 63.

24. David Bradby, *Samuel Beckett: "Waiting for Godot"* (Cambridge: Cambridge University Press, 2001), 163.

25. Ibid.

26. Quoted in Deirdre Bair, *Beckett, a Biography* (New York: Harcourt Brace Jovanovich, 1978), 640.

27. George Craig, Martha Dow Fehsenfeld, Dan Gunn, and Lois More Overbeck

eds., *The Letters of Samuel Beckett 1941–1956* (Cambridge: Cambridge University Press, 2011), 594.

28. Suvin, *To Brecht and Beyond*, 225.

29. Samuel Beckett, "The Capital of the Ruins," in *Complete Short Prose, 1929–1989*, ed. S. E. Gontarski (New York: Grove Press, 1995), 278.

30. Samuel Beckett, *Worstward Ho* (New York: Grove Press, 1983), 43.

31. Ibid., 9.

32. Samuel Beckett, Whoroscope notebook, Nd MS 4000/1. Beckett Collection, University of Reading.

33. Georges Bataille, "Concerning the Accounts Given by the Residents of Hiroshima," in *Trauma: Explorations in Memory*, ed. Cathy Caruth (Baltimore: Johns Hopkins University Press, 1995), 232.

34. *The Kittredge Shakespeare's King Lear*, ed. George Lyman Kittredge, Irving Ribner, and Scott Foresman (New York: Blaisdell, 1968), 4.1.27–28.

Chapter 1

1. Quoted in James Knowlson, *Damned to Fame: The Life of Samuel Beckett* (New York: Simon & Schuster, 1996), 369.

2. Rick Cluchey, telephone conversation with author, September 20, 2011.

3. Esslin, *Theatre of the Absurd*, xvii.

4. Ibid., 142.

5. Ibid., 7.

6. Ibid.

7. Ibid., xv.

8. Ibid., 309. He claims that the reality given on stage in the dramas he discusses "is a psychological reality expressed in images that are the outward projection of states of mind, fears, dreams, nightmares, and conflicts within the personality of the author" (304).

9. Ibid., 305.

10. Ibid., xxiv.

11. Alden Whitman, "In the Wilderness for 20 Years," *New York Times*, October 24, 1969, 32.

12. Without explicitly referencing prison, Mary Bryden describes *Godot* as "wall to wall maleness." "Gender in Transition: 'Godot' and 'Endgame,'" in *"Waiting for Godot" and "Endgame": A New Casebook*, ed. Steven Connor (Basingstoke, UK: Macmillan, 1992), 151.

13. David Smith, "In Godot We Trust," *Observer*, March 7, 2009, 8.

14. See Giorgio Agamben, *Homo Sacer: Sovereign Power and Bare Life*, trans. Daniel Heller-Roazen (Stanford, CA: Stanford University Press, 1998). See also Theodor Adorno's discussion of "das bloße Existenz" in describing the life we see on Beckett's stage, "the absurdity into which mere existence is transformed when it is absorbed into naked self-identity" ("zu einem Absurden, in das bloße Existenz umschlägt, sobald sie *in ihrer nackten sich selbst Gleichheit aufgeht*"). "Versuch, das Endspiel zu verstehen," in *Noten zur Literatur* (Frankfurt: Suhrkamp, 1974), 287.

15. Samuel Beckett, "J. M. Mime," in *Samuel Beckett: An Exhibition*, ed. James Knowlson (London: Turret Books, 1971), 117. Roger Blin describes how this nudity of Beckett's work inspires both wonder and discretion: "*Waiting for Godot* struck me as so rich and unique in its nudity that it seemed to me improper to question the author

about its meaning." Quoted in Ruby Cohn, *From Desire to "Godot": Pocket Theater of Postwar Paris* (Berkeley: University of California Press, 1987), 150.

16. Jean Anouilh believed this point crucial enough to use it as the title of his review, "'Godot' or the Music-Hall Sketch of Pascal's Pensées as Played by the Fratellini Clowns," in *Casebook on "Waiting for Godot,"* ed. and trans. Ruby Cohn (New York: Grove Press, 1967), 12–13.

17. Adorno, "Trying to Understand 'Endgame,'" in *Notes to Literature II*, trans. Shierry Weber Nicholsen (New York: Columbia University Press, 1991), 268.

18. Beckett, "Capital of the Ruins," 278.

19. Beckett, *Waiting for Godot*, 58.

20. Beckett, *Proust and Three Dialogues*, 19.

21. Martin Puchner, *Stage Fright: Modernism, Anti-Theatricality, and Drama* (Baltimore: Johns Hopkins University Press, 2002), 159.

22. Tjebbe Westerdorp describes the apparatus Beckett constructs in order to keep actress Billie Whitelaw still as she performs Mouth in *Not I*. These resemble the devices employed to hold sitters immobile during the long exposure times of early photography. "All sorts of complicated constructions were used in the stage play to keep the head of the actress in its place—bars for the arms, for instance, formed a kind of iron trap." The speed of the performance tests these restraints at another level: Whitelaw says she "felt like an athlete crashing through barriers while chained and physically impeded." Westerdorp, "Catharsis in Beckett's Late Drama: A New Model of Transaction?" *Samuel Beckett Today/Aujourd'hui* 1 (1992): 109.

23. Jonathan Kalb, *Beckett in Performance* (Cambridge: Cambridge University Press, 1989), 79. Beckett also railed against productions that exceeded the haiku-like simplicity of *a country road, a tree, evening*. The Miami premiere, for example, set the play in a junkyard full of plumbing debris. As Beckett complained to Charles Marowitz about Peter Hall's 1955 production, "the stage was so cluttered the actors could hardly move." Quoted in Dougald McMillan and Martha Fehsenfeld, *Beckett in the Theatre*, vol. 1, *From "Waiting for Godot" to "Krapp's Last Tape"* (London: Calder, 1988), 82.

24. *The Theatrical Notebooks of Samuel Beckett*, vol. 1, *"Waiting for Godot,"* ed. Dougald McMillan and James Knowlson (New York: Grove Press, 1994), 185.

25. C. Bandman, "The Play's the Thing . . . ," *San Quentin News*, November 28, 1957, 2.

26. Quoted in McMillan and Fehsenfeld, *Beckett in the Theater*, 80.

27. Erin Koshal, "'Some Exceptions' and the 'Normal Thing': Reconsidering 'Waiting for Godot's' Theatrical Form through Its Prison Performances," *Modern Drama* 53, no. 2 (2010): 197.

28. McMillan and Fehsenfeld, *Beckett in the Theater*, 97.

29. Knowlson, *Damned to Fame*, 436.

30. Samuel Beckett, *Notes Diverse Holo*, ed. Matthijs Engelberts and Everett Frost with Jane Maxwell (Amsterdam: Rodopi, 2006), 215.

31. Michael Harris, "Godot Presented at Quentin," *San Francisco Chronicle*, November 24, 1957, 23.

32. Richard Strayton, "Inmates Waiting for 'Godot,'" *Los Angeles Herald Examiner*, May 8, 1988, 9.

33. Harris, "Godot Presented at Quentin," 23.

34. Sidney Homan, *Beckett's Theaters: Interpretations for Performance* (Lewisburg, PA: Bucknell University Press, 1984), 57.

35. In her negative review of the first Broadway production, the stage littered with debris from a dump, Marya Mannes collapses the play into the absent character and

puts the audience on stage, too: "Everybody recommends a hit. Everybody, that is, except that very special group, so proudly divorced from all others, that would wait for *Godot* here too, dump and all." Marya Mannes, "Two Tramps," in Cohn, *Casebook on "Waiting for Godot,"* 31.

36. Gregory's staging of *Endgame* channels the trapped situation of *Godot*. A chicken-wire fence encircled the stage, and the stage lighting made it difficult to see the characters through the fence. For details of this production see Walter Kerr's review, "Oh Beckett, Poor Beckett!" *New York Times,* February 11, 1973, 146.

37. Etaoin Shrdlu, "Bastille by the Bay," *San Quentin News,* November 28, 1957, 3.

38. Bandman, "The Play's the Thing . . . ," 2.

39. "I was waiting for Godot and didn't realize it," says inmate Rick Cluchey. Quoted in Herbert Blau, *As If: An Autobiography* (Ann Arbor: University of Michigan Press, 2011), 230.

40. Bandman, "The Play's the Thing . . . ," 2.

41. "Workshop Players Score Hit Here: San Francisco Group Leaves S. Q. Audience Waiting for Godot," *San Quentin News,* November 28, 1957, 1. The prisoner's angle on realism differs from that of Daniel Albright. Commenting on how Vladimir pictures sleep in Godot's loft, he writes, "Godot hovers in the wings like the unrealizability of Realism, a tantalizing ghost. When Beckett told Roger Blin that Godot might be 'a pair of old army boots,' he suggested how strongly he identified Godot with a domain of earthy, comforting objects, as opposed to the spoof-objects present on stage." Daniel Albright, *Beckett and Aesthetics* (Cambridge: Cambridge University Press, 2003), 51.

42. Colin Duckworth, ed., "Introduction," *En Attendant Godot* (London: Harrap, 1966), lxiii.

43. Esslin, *Theatre of the Absurd,* xvii.

44. Kalb, *Beckett in Performance,* 157.

45. Beckett, *Waiting for Godot,* 24.

46. "Letters to the Editor," *San Quentin News,* November 28, 1957, 2. Adjacent to the reviews of *Godot* in the *San Quentin News* are columns on what privileges (improved cell assignments, for example) are open to prisoners with certain ratings. Medium-A inmates are allowed these privileges. The article continues, "Inmates with Medium A classification who have refused job assignment and who have never maintained a reasonably good work or conduct record will not be considered." "North Honor Block Now Open to Medium-A Inmates," *San Quentin News,* November 28, 1957, 1.

47. This letter of the curious prisoner should be contrasted with a letter to the editor of *Le Monde,* written by someone in recent attendance at the premiere of *Godot*. Titled *Manifestation au Théâtre de Babylone,* the writer describes how the director, Roger Blin, had to drop the curtain before the end of act 1 because of "sifflets, insultes, rien'ny manqué"["whistles, insults, the works"]. The letter writer continues, "A l'entre'acte des discussions entre partisans et adversaires prirent un ton élevé, et ce n'est qu'auprès le depart en masse des mécontents, au début du second acte, que l'on eut loisir d'écouter tranquillement la suite de la pièce de Samuel Beckett." ["At intermission the discussion between the supporters and adversaries of Beckett's play took on a heated tone, and only with the discontented crowd's departure en masse at the start of the second act could one listen to the rest of Beckett's play in peace."] "Letter to the Editor," *Le Monde,* February 2, 1953, 36. The disappointed sophisticates make a show, or even a strike (*une manifestation*) out of their disappointment. By contrast, the prisoner who is forced to leave makes a plea to read the part he could not see.

48. For an essay illuminating the differences between *Godot* and *Huis Clos,* see Lois Gordon, "'No Exit' and 'Waiting for Godot': Performances in Contrast," in *Captive*

Audience: Prison and Captivity in Contemporary Theater, ed. Thomas Richard Fahy and Kimball King (New York: Routledge, 2003), 166–88.

49. Jean-Paul Sartre, *Bariona, or the Son of Thunder*, in *The Writings of Jean-Paul Sartre*, vol. 2, *Selected Prose*, ed. Michel Rybalka and Michel Contat (Evanston, IL: Northwestern University Press, 1985), 85.

50. Piouk says, "Here it is. I would prohibit reproduction. I would perfect the condom and other appliances and generalize their use. I would create state-run corps of abortionists. I would impose the death sentence on every woman guilty of having given birth. I would drown the newborn. I would campaign in favor of homosexuality and myself set the example. And to get things going, I would encourage by every means the recourse to euthanasia, without, however, making it an obligation. Here you have the broad outlines." Samuel Beckett, *Eleuthéria* (London: Foxrock, 1998), 43.

51. Sartre, *Bariona*, 87.

52. Ibid., 136. Earlier a character in the play, similarly with an eye toward the audience, says, "You should not keep from having children. For even for the blind and the disabled and the unemployed and the prisoners there is joy" (131).

53. Adorno, "Trying to Understand 'Endgame,'" 249.

54. The word, originally misprinted as "explication," appears in *Catastrophe*. Samuel Beckett, *The Collected Shorter Plays*, ed. S. E. Gontarski (New York: Grove Press, 1984), 299.

55. Joseph Roach, "All the Dead Voices," in *Land/Scape/Theater*, ed. Elinor Fuchs and Una Chaudhuri (Ann Arbor: University of Michigan Press, 2002), 88.

56. James Knowlson, "Beckett's Production Notebooks," in *Beckett: "Waiting for Godot": A Casebook*, ed. Ruby Cohn (London: Macmillan, 1987), 52. This theme is also struck by Lois Gordon: "Imprisoned in a universe they cannot understand, Vladimir and Estragon are dressed as quasi prison inmates." Lois Gordon, *Reading "Godot"* (New Haven, CT: Yale University Press, 2002), 137.

57. "Beckett the poet successfully evades abduction by worthy causes as a condition of his austere, ironic compassion. But *Waiting for Godot* does not evade history. As soon as the refugees that Peter Hall was the first to call 'tramps' begin to take stock of their rotten tubers along 'a country road' in an 'abode of stones,' history and memory come into play. They proliferate in the dramatic silences that *sensitized listeners* cannot but hear as choric" (emphasis added). Roach, "All the Dead Voices," 91.

58. Hugh Kenner puts this sharply when he says of the rapport between Vladimir and Estragon that "the reasoning behind the ritualistic dialogue . . . is of merely idiotic transparency, very appealing." Hugh Kenner, *Samuel Beckett: A Critical Study* (Berkeley: University of California Press, 1973), 73. Kenner's insight is that the transparency of the dialogue is onto something other than common sense.

59. Blau, "On Directing Beckett," 63.

60. Alan Mandell in a telephone conversation with the author, August 19, 2011.

61. Shrdlu, "Bastille by the Bay," November 28, 1957, 3.

62. Knowlson, *Damned to Fame*, 422. Knowlson also notes "[Beckett's] natural sympathy for those who were incarcerated" (566).

63. Ibid., 566.

64. Ibid.

65. Mark Nixon, *Samuel Beckett's German Diaries, 1936–1937* (London: Continuum, 2011), 163. The iron bars of prison seem to fall somewhere between a window and the famed windowlessness of Leibnitz's monad.

66. See Beckett's brief contribution to Avigdor Arikha's exhibition catalogue: "Siege laid to the impregnable without . . . back and forth the gaze beating on unsee-

able and unmakeable. Truce for a space and the marks of what it is to be and be in face of. Those deep marks to show." Samuel Beckett, "For Avigdor Arika," in *Disjecta*, ed. Ruby Cohn (London: Calder, 1983), 152.

67. Enoch Brater notes that "Havel's 'subversive activities' included his membership in the Committee for the Defense of the Unjustly Prosecuted (VONS) as well as his signature on the Charter 77 manifesto, of which he was one of the three original spokesmen." *Beyond Minimalism: Beckett's Late Style in the Theater* (Oxford: Oxford University Press, 1987), 139. Brater's chapter "'Other Only' Images" remains the definitive piece on *Catastrophe*.

68. Brater, *Beyond Minimalism*, 144.

69. Ibid., 145.

70. Blau, *As If*, 229.

71. Strayton, "Inmates Waiting for 'Godot,'" 9.

72. Bryden, "Gender in Transition," 152.

73. It is often because of what is missing rather that what is there that dictates the executive decisions around Beckett's play. Roger Blin, for example, was pondering which of Beckett's plays to stage in the Babylon Theater: *Godot* or the surreal multicharacter drama *Eleuthéria* (Greek for "freedom"). Blin chooses *Godot:* "I was poor, I didn't have a penny . . . and I thought I'd be better off with the *Godot* because there were only four actors and they were bums. They could wear their own clothes if it came to that, and I wouldn't need anything but a spotlight and a tree." Thus *Godot* premiered over freedom. Quoted in Bair, *Samuel Beckett*, 403.

74. Yet the desires of the audience cannot be managed, or predicted. The warden, focusing on the women absent from Beckett's stage, overlooked the boy who appears there. Blau writes that during the performance, as Vladimir took the boy downstage to question him about Godot, "there was an absolute silence in the audience, the men still and staring, then some beckoning hisses, before a voice from the back growled, 'C'mere, boy.'" Blau, *As If*, 230.

75. Adorno, "Trying to Understand 'Endgame,'" 248. "Gewacht wird darüber, da es nur so und nicht anders sei, ein fein klingelndes Alarmsystem meldet, was zur schweigt aus Zartheit das Zarte nicht minder als das Brutale" (Adorno, "Versuch," 289).

76. Herbert Blau, "In Memoriam," in *Sails of the Herring Fleet,* 24.

77. Samuel Beckett, *Murphy* (London: Calder, 1993), 43. The horseleech reference is from Proverbs 30:15: "The horseleech hath two daughters, crying, Give, give."

78. Kenner, *Samuel Beckett,* 182. N. Katherine Hayles defines entropy in these terms: "The first law of thermodynamics, stating that energy is neither created nor destroyed, points to a world in which no energy is lost. The second law, stating that entropy always tends to increase in a closed system, forecasts a universe that is constantly winding down." N. Katherine Hayles, quoted in David Houston Jones, *Samuel Beckett and Testimony* (London: Palgrave Macmillan, 2011), 152.

79. Samuel Beckett, *Murphy,* 5.

80. Kenner, *Samuel Beckett,* 182. Herbert Blau drops into the middle of his essay on Beckett how *Godot* counteracts this law: "Someone cries, another weeps—by the sorcery of form Beckett defies the Second Law of Thermodynamics. Energy is pumped back into the dead system by having it come back from the other side of the stage, crippled and much the worse for wear, crying pitiably for help." Herbert Blau, "Notes from the Underground," in *Sails of the Herring Fleet,* 31.

81. Suvin, *To Brecht and Beyond*, 211. This raises the question whether *Terra Beckettiana* is an island or a universe, an island within a universe, or an island that constitutes a universe.

82. Ibid., 212.

83. David Houston Jones brilliantly describes the science behind his literary analysis in *Samuel Beckett and Testimony,* 152–62.

84. Ibid., 155.

85. Ibid., 159.

86. Ibid., 161.

87. Rick Cluchey, "My Years with Beckett," in *Theatre Workbook 1: Krapp's Last Tape,* ed. James Knowlson (London: Brutus Books Limited, 1980), 120. Cluchey might be misremembering *closed place* (*Endroit clos*), the first words of Beckett's *Fizzles 5,* since "closed system" only appears in criticism of Beckett, not within Beckett's work. This may be a creative misremembering since Beckett's term suggests a space you cannot enter, rather than one that keeps you in. For a discussion see C. J. Ackerley and S. E. Gontarski, eds., *The Grove Companion to Samuel Beckett* (New York: Grove Press, 2004), 99.

88. Alan Mandell in a telephone conversation with the author, August 19, 2011.

89. Edmund Burke, *A Philosophical Enquiry into the Origin of Our Ideas of the Sublime and Beautiful* (Oxford: Oxford University Press, 2009), 43.

90. Ruby Cohn observes that Beckett's characters undergo "playlong dying." *A Beckett Canon* (Ann Arbor: University of Michigan Press, 2005), 229.

91. The monadological nature of the institution transforms Beckett's play even before the performance begins. The San Quentin Drama Workshop begins with but a single copy of *Godot.* They use the version printed within the August 1956 edition of *Theatre Arts Magazine,* held by the prison library. Because of a mishap in the printing process, however, the pages are properly numbered but do not follow Beckett's script. Pages from act 1 have been improperly exchanged with pages from act 2. Though this disturbs the rhythm of the play, it does remarkably little to disturb its sense. A turn of the page entirely recasts who is or who is no longer on stage. At times the sequencing error creates a new dialogue and a different structure of call and response. In this recut version of Beckett's play, Pozzo's suggestion that Estragon invite him to sit down is followed by Estragon's statement as he looks at the tree, "Pity we haven't got enough rope." This demonstrates how performances in prison, like those during the siege and after the flood, must be measured by a standard other than fidelity or infidelity to Beckett's text.

92. Houston Jones, *Samuel Beckett and Testimony,* 153.

93. Cluchey, "My Years with Beckett," 121.

94. Adorno, "Trying to Understand 'Endgame,'" 251.

95. Cluchey, "My Years with Beckett," 121.

96. Sidney Homan, *The Embarrassment of Swans,* unpublished memoir, 19.

97. Blau, "Notes from the Underground," 33 (emphasis added).

98. Cluchey, "My Years with Beckett," 121.

99. Cluchey remembers his cellmate saying "everyone was puzzled until one guy came in with a rope around his neck and another guy whipping him and guess what his name was? Lucky! That spoke to everyone in the audience." Smith, "In Godot we Trust," 8.

100. "Two shapes then, oblong like man, entered into collision before me. They fell and I saw them no more. I naturally thought of the pseudocouple Mercier-Camier." Samuel Beckett, *Three Novels: Molloy, Malone Dies, The Unnamable* (New York: Grove Press, 1991), 297.

101. Jonathan Boulter, *Beckett: A Guide for the Perplexed* (London: Continuum Press, 2008), 31. Like many critics, Boulter uncouples Beckett's compound word and inserts a hyphen to create the new word "pseudo-couple." Some exceptions to this tendency

to pseudo-ize the couple exist. In his gloss on the homosocial dynamics in Beckett's world, for example, Peter Boxall observes: "Like Holmes and Watson, [Vladimir and Estragon] may have breakfast together, but in the critical imagination they have remained resolutely straight." Peter Boxall, "Beckett and Homoeroticism," in *Samuel Beckett Studies*, ed. Lois Oppenheim (London: Palgrave, 2004), 110.

102. The quote continues, " . . . the little gasp of the condemned to life, rotting in his dungeon garroted and racked, to gasp what it is to have to celebrate banishment, beware." Beckett, *Three Novels*, 325.

103. Craig et al., *Letters of Samuel Beckett, 1941–1956*, 524.

104. Samuel Beckett quoted in Craig et al., *Letters of Samuel Beckett, 1941–1956*, 504.

105. See Walter Benjamin's argument about the importance attached by Dada to "its uselessness for contemplative immersion" and Benjamin's own project to introduce concepts into the theory of art "that are completely useless for the purposes of Fascism." *Illuminations*, trans. Harry Zohn (New York: Schocken, 1969), 237, 218.

106. Knowlson, *Damned to Fame*, 369.

107. Ibid.

108. "Let this same Lucky, the caricature of intellect with the white clown face, pound home fruitless insights into the ductile, malleable, impressionable force which may create, but never command the respect of the promoter-master." Bandman, "The Play's the Thing . . . ," 2.

109. "The stage, with its windows high up on the back wall, has been interpreted as the interior of a human skull." Bair, *Samuel Beckett*, 467. The metaphor imposes itself over much of early criticism of Beckett. When the curtains are drawn in *Endgame*, writes Hugh Kenner, "this is so plainly a metaphor for waking up that we fancy the stage, with its high peepholes, to be the inside of an immense skull." Kenner, *Samuel Beckett*, 155.

110. For a discussion about how catharsis is theorized in *Hamlet*, see Stephen Orgel, "The Play of Conscience," in *Performativity and Performance*, ed. Andrew Parker and Eve Kosofsky Sedgwick (New York: Routledge, 1995), 133–51.

111. The meshing of the criminal past with the theater is one of the recurring themes of *Shakespeare behind Bars* (Hank Rogerson, 2005). This documentary film, about a production of *The Tempest* in a Kansas prison, gathers its energy from the way confessions made by prisoners acting on stage are intercut with, and implicitly service, their confessions to the camera about their crimes.

112. The New Testament uses the term *skandalon* to describe an unforgiveable crime that throws a stumbling block (*skandalon*) before our judgment. These were crimes in excess of everyday trespasses (*harmatanein*). See Matthew 18:7.

113. Bandman, "The Play's the Thing . . . ," 2.

114. "Weighing the pros and cons" is a citation from Vladimir's monologue about coming to the aid of his fellow man: "It is true that when with folded arms we weigh the pros and cons we are no less a credit to our species." Beckett, *Waiting for Godot*, 51. Unlike Vladimir, Bandman weighs this decision within the context of prison rather of species. Etaoin Shrdlu also picks up on this line from the play and doesn't bat an eye in literally weighing the cons in the audience: "The trio of musclemen, biceps overflowing . . . parked all 642 lbs. on the aisle and waited for the girls and funny stuff." Shrdlu, "Bastille by the Bay," November 28, 1957, 3.

115. See Martha Nussbaum, *The Fragility of Goodness*, rev. ed. (Cambridge: Cambridge University Press, 2001), 388–91.

116. Sergei Tretiakov, "Bert Brecht," in *Brecht: A Collection of Critical Essays*, ed. Peter Demetz (Englewood Cliffs, NJ: Prentice Hall, 1962), 27 (emphasis added).

117. See Ciaran Ross's argument, contrary to my discussion here, that "the negative is always positive" in Beckett. *Beckett's Art of Absence: Rethinking the Void* (London: Palgrave Macmillan, 2011), 130.

118. Quoted in Jean-Michel Rabaté, "Philosophizing with Beckett: Adorno and Badiou," in *A Companion to Samuel Beckett*, ed. S. E. Gontarski (Malden, MA: Wiley-Blackwell, 2010), 102.

119. Bandman, "The Play's the Thing," 2. Bandman's opinion here echoes Beckett's opening statement to George Duthuit in their discussion of art: "Total object, complete with missing pieces, instead of partial object." Beckett, *Proust and Three Dialogues*, 101.

120. The errancy encouraged by Beckett also includes Bandman's response to it. He speaks oxymoronically, creatively, of how Didi and Gogo "finalize into precursors of doubt and death" (how does one finalize into a precursor?). Bandman, "The Play's the Thing . . . ," 2.

121. Regarding pilgrimage in character: the first time Cluchey and Beckett arrange to meet, Cluchey arrives early at the Deux Magots in Paris. The "noticeable thing" Cluchey wears so that Beckett can single him out of the crowd is a bowler hat. "Do you always wear that hat?" Beckett asks. Cluchey, telephone conversation with author, September 20, 2011.

122. The warden concedes to a twenty-five-dollar yearly budget for makeup, almost ensuring that the workshop devote itself to Beckett's bare-boned productions. The San Quentin Drama Workshop is still active today.

123. "Lenin liked to think of prison as a university for revolutionaries." Michael Hardt, "Prison Time," in *Genet: In the Language of the Enemy*, ed. Scott Durham, *Yale French Studies* 91 (Spring 1997): 64.

124. Skip Kaltenheuser, "The Prison Playwright," *Gadfly*, September/October 1999, 5.

125. Years later Cluchey enumerates the minute sounds of man, machine, and object on stage as evidence for Beckett's detailed "orchestration" of the stage of *Krapp's Last Tape*. He speaks of orchestration rather than direction because Beckett was concerned with the relation between the weaker notes. "The opening of tins, the clink of a bottle, the opening and closing of the book, the sound of slippers on the floor." Cluchey calls these "every essence of the play." Cluchey, telephone conversation with author, October 18, 2011.

126. Ibid.

127. Rick Cluchey and Michael Haerdter, "*Krapp's Last Tape:* Production Report," in *Theatre Workbook 1: Krapp's Last Tape*, ed. James Knowlson (London: Brutus Books, 1980), 127.

128. Ibid.

129. Ibid., 121.

130. In an interview, Cluchey says, "In practice, what happened to me in prison left such a lasting mark, I never get away from it. I'm condemned to that, you could say." Amanda Fazzone, "Walls within Walls," *Washington City Paper*, http://65.79.227.222/articles/17051/walls-within-walls. "What happened," that is, the overlap of theater and prison, left a kind of tattoo, a double mark on Cluchey.

131. Cluchey, *The Cage* (San Francisco: Barbwire Press, 1970), 8.

132. Ibid., 9.

133. Beckett, *Waiting for Godot*, 34.

134. Cluchey, *The Cage*, 32.

135. In his play, Cluchey wants prison to structure the theater. The stage directions for his play are issued through a PA system, not submerged quietly within the script.

Preceding the rise of the curtain and before the lights are dimmed, a voice loudly announces the types of things one might hear in a prison: "The following men have visits. Shirley 09742, Bowen 09582, Rced 09827 . . . etc." and "Attention on the yard. Attention on the yard. Warden Duffy has issued the following memo. 'Cell robberies in the North and West honor units are increasing. Any man caught in another inmate's cell will be brought before the Captain's line for disciplinary action. There will be no exceptions." Cluchey's name and number are listed among those men who are to "report to the laundry-room for work assignments." Ibid., 6.

136. Ibid., 13.
137. Homan, *The Embarrassment of Swans*, 2.
138. Blau, "On Directing Beckett," 96.
139. Ibid., 95.
140. Cohn, *Casebook on "Waiting for Godot,"* 14.
141. McMillan and Knowlson, *Theatrical Notebooks of Samuel Beckett*, 1:239, 293.
142. McMillan and Fehsenfeld, *Beckett in the Theater*, 140.
143. Beckett's play (*Waiting for Godot*, 14) notes how its own dialogue cannot progress dialectically forward. Instead, each statement counteracts the previous one, and answers are jarringly misaligned with questions:

> GOGO. Funny, the more you eat the worse it gets.
> DIDI. For me it's just the opposite.
> GOGO. In other words?
> DIDI. I get used to the muck as I go along.
> GOGO. Is that the opposite?

144. Homan, *Embarrassment of Swans*, 7.
145. Alain Robbe-Grillet, *For a New Novel: Essays on Fiction*, trans. Richard Howard (New York: Grove Press, 1965), 115.
146. Ibid., 121. Robbe-Grillet quickly adds, "Of course, this freedom is without any use."
147. Koshal, "'Some Exceptions,'" 188.
148. Cluchey, "My Years with Beckett," 121 (emphasis added).
149. Homan, *Embarrassment of Swans*, 12.
150. In his illuminating article "The Body as Object of Modern Performance," Jon Erickson leads us through a careful elaboration of the corporeal status of actor in role in Brecht's work. He writes, "Brecht's form of schizoid acting, designed to separate in performance the actor from the role, is meant to draw attention to the role, its socially constructed nature, and not so much to the actor himself. In that the disembodied style of the role is to be maintained throughout, the actor must maintain a critical attitude towards his role, even acknowledging dislike for the character he plays." Jon Erickson, "The Body as Object of Modern Performance," *Journal of Dramatic Theory and Criticism* (Fall 1990): 234. In their moments of address to the characters, the prisoners seem to heal the schizoid potential of the moment. The roles acquire body in turning toward the summons of the audience.
151. Blau, *As If*, 230.
152. "To which another spectator evidently yelled, 'Because they don't have time.'" Alan Simpson, "First Dublin Production," in Cohn, *Beckett: "Waiting for Godot": A Casebook*, 34.
153. Knowlson also reports that spectators eagerly suggested "give him some rope" when Estragon asks Vladimir if he hasn't some rope with which to hang themselves. Knowlson, *Damned to Fame*, 374.

154. Homan, *Embarrassment of Swans*, 13.
155. Koshal, "'Some Exceptions,'" 203.
156. See Fahy and King, *Captive Audience*.
157. Kenner, *Samuel Beckett*, 13. Emmett Kelly was a circus performer who created Weary Willie, based on scruffy hobo types from the Depression.
158. Beckett, *Eleuthéria*, 141.
159. Ibid., 136.
160. Samuel Beckett, "German Letter of 1937," in *Disjecta*, 172.

Chapter 2

1. Knowlson, *Damned to Fame*, 439; Jean Baudrillard, *Screened Out*, trans. Chris Turner (New York: Verso, 2002), 45.
2. In *On War*, Carl von Clausewitz coins the expression to "denote properly such a portion of the space over which war prevails as has its boundaries protected, and thus possesses a kind of independence. . . . Such a portion is not a mere piece of the whole, but a small whole complete in itself." *On War*, trans. J. J. Graham (London: N. Trübner, 1873), 94.
3. Susan Sontag, "Waiting for Godot in Sarajevo," in *Where the Stress Falls* (New York: Picador, 2001), 299.
4. Ibid.
5. Martin Esslin, introduction to *Samuel Beckett: A Collection of Critical Essays*, ed. Martin Esslin (Englewood Cliffs, NJ: Prentice Hall, 1965), 4.
6. Bradby, *Beckett: "Waiting for Godot,"* 139.
7. Ibid.
8. Kalb, *Beckett in Performance*, 92.
9. Adorno, "Trying to Understand 'Endgame,'" 248.
10. Theodor Adorno asserts that "today this is the capacity of art: Through the consistent negation of meaning it does justice to the postulates that once constituted the meaning of artworks. Works of the highest level of form that are meaningless or alien to meaning are therefore more than simply meaningless because they gain their content through the negation of meaning." *Aesthetic Theory*, ed. Gretel Adorno and Rolf Tiedemann, trans. Robert Hullot-Kentor (Minneapolis: University of Minnesota Press, 1997), 154.
11. Adorno, "Trying to Understand 'Endgame,'" 248. Despite Adorno's reservations about Beckett as a political witness, recent scholarship has explored how "Beckett's testimony consists precisely of 'writing differently,' and above all anti-referentially." Houston Jones, *Samuel Beckett and Testimony*, 2.
12. Adorno, "Trying to Understand 'Endgame,'" 249.
13. Rosette C. Lamont writes about Beckett's one revision to the original manuscript of *En Attendant Godot:* the erasure of the name "Levy" and its replacement with "Estragon." Lamont remarks that Beckett "obviously decided to give this central character a vaguely universal name, rather than a pointedly Jewish one." "Letter to the Editor," *Beckett Circle* 16, no. 1 (Spring 1994): 4.
14. Beckett, *Waiting for Godot*, 40.
15. Ibid., 28.
16. Heidegger's title is a partial citation of Friedrich Hölderlin's "Wozu Dichter im durftiger Zeit?" ("What Are Poets for in Time of Need?").
17. Martin Heidegger, *Poetry, Language, Thought*, trans. Albert Hofstadter (New York: Harper & Row, 1971), 91.

18. Ibid., 93.
19. "Sottisier" notebook, Beckett Collection, MS2901, University of Reading.
20. McMillan and Fehsenfeld, *Beckett in the Theatre*, 139.
21. Juan Goytisolo, *Landscapes of War, from Sarajevo to Chechnya*, trans. Peter Bush (San Francisco: City Lights, 2000), 11.
22. Erika Munk, "Sontag Stages 'Godot' in Sarajevo," *Beckett Circle* 15, no. 2 (Fall 1993): 1.
23. Beckett, *Waiting for Godot*, 17.
24. Ibid., 25, 55. The grey twilight is the celestial backdrop to the poverty on Beckett's stage. Trying to tell time through observation of the stage set is a recurring moment of failure in Beckett's work. The moment in which Vladimir and Estragon struggle to describe the sky for the blind Pozzo echoes a situation in Beckett's early uncompleted piece, *The Gloaming* (dusk), featuring a blind beggar with a violin. This figure reappears in *Rough for Theater I*, and asks his companion in a wheelchair, "Will it not soon be evening?" The reply: "Day . . . night . . . It seems to me sometimes that earth must have got stuck, one sunless day, in the heart of winter, in the grey of evening." Beckett, *Collected Shorter Plays*, 72. In Shakespeare, beauty beggars description; in Beckett, it is the sky that does this and for a blind beggar.
25. Gilbert Moses, John O'Neal, Denise Nicholas, Murray Levy, and Richard Schechner, "Dialog: The Free Southern Theater," in *A Sourcebook of African-American Performance: Plays, People, Movements*, ed. Annemarie Bean (New York: Routledge, 1999), 102.
26. Ibid., 107.
27. John O'Neal, "Motion in the Ocean: Some Political Dimensions of the Free Southern Theater," in Bean, *Scourcebook of African-American Performance*, 118.
28. Beckett, *Waiting for Godot*, 42.
29. John O'Neal notes how all the questions posed to the Free Southern Theater "presumed education as a prerequisite for intelligence. The uneducated may lack certain specific skills but they are no less intelligent. Often the very absence of those skills forces people to greater application of creative facilities simply in order to survive competitively in a system loaded against their specific deficiencies." "Motion in the Ocean," 118.
30. It is easy to overlook how humorously colloquial Beckett makes his dialogue as it debunks theatrical tradition. For example, when Vladimir is trying to recall what he wanted to say, ("This evening . . . I was saying . . . I was saying . . . ") Estragon replies with "I'm not a historian." Beckett, *Waiting for Godot*, 42. The historian on Beckett's stage is merely one who remains unafflicted by the forgetfulness of his fellow vagabond, and who can remember what the other person was saying. This is to say that there are no historians on Beckett's stage.
31. O'Neal, "Motion in the Ocean," 115.
32. Gilbert Moses, executive producer of the Free Southern Theater, recalls, "We wanted to see what would happen. We chose it because it's a great play, and we thought *Godot* would act as a barometer of the limits, the ceiling of this audience. It didn't operate that way. All we learned was that our audience can take *Godot*." Moses et al., "Dialog," 107.
33. Ibid., 108.
34. Ibid., 106.
35. Ibid., 108.
36. Ibid.
37. Ibid.
38. Goytisolo, *Landscapes of War*, 10.

39. Susan Sontag, interview by Omer Hadžiselimović and Zvonimir Radeljković, "Literature Is What You Should Re-Read: An Interview with Susan Sontag," *Spirit of Bosnia* 2, no. 2 (April 2007), http://www.spiritofbosnia.org/volume-2-no-2-2007-april/literature-is-what-you-should-re-read-an-interview-with-susan-sontag/.
40. Sontag, "Godot in Sarajevo," 300.
41. Ibid., 313.
42. Beckett, *Waiting for Godot*, 51.
43. Sontag, "Godot in Sarajevo," 326.
44. Ibid., 327.
45. Beckett, *Complete Short Prose*, 234.
46. Beckett, *Collected Shorter Plays*, 316 (emphasis added).
47. Sontag, "Godot in Sarajevo," 300.
48. Ibid., 302.
49. Ibid., 304.
50. Erika Munk, "Notes from a Trip to Sarajevo," *Theater* 24, no. 3 (1993): 28.
51. Sontag, "Godot in Sarajevo," 305.
52. Baudrillard, *Screened Out*, 45.
53. Director Haris Pašović encounters this in the process of organizing a film festival. He reverses the question in order to call attention to the way it sides with the aggressor. When asked, "Why a film festival during the war?" Pasovic replies, "Why a war during our film festival?" Quoted in Kenneth Turan, *Sundance to Sarajevo: Film Festivals and the World They Made* (Berkeley: University of California Press, 2002), 105.
54. Sontag, "Godot in Sarajevo," 304.
55. Beckett, "Dante . . . Bruno. Vico. Joyce," in *Disjecta*, 24.
56. Ibid.
57. About *Work in Progress*, Beckett observes, "Here form *is* content, content *is* form. You complain that this stuff is not written in English. It is not written at all. It is not to be read—or rather it is not only to be read. It is to be looked at and listened to. His writing is not *about* something; *it is that something itself.*" Ibid., 27.
58. Ibid., 25.
59. H. Porter Abbott, "Samuel Beckett and the Arts of Time: Painting, Music, Narrative," in *Samuel Beckett and the Arts*, ed. Lois Oppenheim (New York: Garland, 1999), 11. Porter writes, "In Beckett's hands, such winnowing declares its arbitrary nature . . . just as the events recovered declare their gratuitous autonomy." Ibid.
60. Beckett, *Waiting for Godot*, 46.
61. Estragon could also be asking "How would I know?" since Vladimir is wearing the thinking hat. In act 1, this hat instigates Lucky to "think aloud" when he puts it on and grows silent when it is removed from his head.
62. E. M. Cioran, "Encounters with Beckett," in *Samuel Beckett: The Critical Heritage*, ed. Lawrence Graver and Raymond Federman (New York: Routledge & Kegan Paul, 1979), 334.
63. Ibid.
64. Erika Munk, "Reports from the 21st Century: A Sarajevo Interview," *Theater* 24, no. 3 (1993): 13.
65. Ibid.
66. Frost, "Letter to the Editor," 5.
67. The flurry of letters to the *Beckett Circle* all accuse Sontag of selfish exhibitionism. Rosette Lamont writes, "The trouble with Sontag (and Munk is a co-conspirator) is that everything is always: ME! ME! ME! She does the very opposite of what a great artist does. . . . The fine artists I have had the good fortune to meet never stand center stage . . . in order to call attention to themselves." Lamont, "Letter to the Editor," 4.

NOTES TO CHAPTER 2 • 205

68. Sontag, "Godot in Sarajevo," 309.
69. Sara Villiers, "Beware of the Snipers," *The Herald* (Glasgow), August 20, 1993, 20.
70. Sontag, "Godot in Sarajevo," 312.
71. Munk, "Sontag Stages 'Godot,'" 2.
72. Ibid.
73. Kenner, *Samuel Beckett*, 155.
74. Beckett, *Waiting for Godot*, 42.
75. The Sarajevo Youth Theater, where the performance takes place, is in a precarious state from the shelling. Sontag has the audience sit near the actors on stage because the auditorium is a potential death trap: "the nine small chandeliers could come crashing down if the building suffered a direct hit from a shell, or even if an adjacent building were hit." Sontag, "Godot in Sarajevo," 312.
76. For discussion of a prisoner, Ed Realart, forced to leave for work detail at intermission, see chapter 1.
77. Knowlson, *Damned to Fame*, 711.
78. Ibid.
79. According to Blin, Giacometti would come every night before the beginning of the play and, back stage, "change the position of a twig a little bit and then Sam would come later and he would change it." McMillan and Fehsenfeld, *Beckett in the Theatre*, 80.
80. Beckett, *Waiting for Godot*, 55.
81. See illustration in Ferdinand de Saussure, *Course in General Linguistics*, trans. Wade Baskin (New York: Philosophical Library, 1959), 66–68.
82. Sontag, "Godot in Sarajevo," 313.
83. Munk, "Sontag Stages 'Godot,'" 2.
84. Sontag, "Godot in Sarajevo," 313.
85. Beckett, *Waiting for Godot*, 45.
86. Ibid., 11.
87. Where Sontag says that performing the entire play would be too much to ask of the audience, Erika Munk says that the reduction of the play does not demand enough, thereby counterbalancing Sontag's use of the term: "Given the topical references added throughout . . . even the candlelight, this reduction made for too—easy pathos. Perhaps that sounds odd, considering where we were. But in a whole city of Vladimirs and Estragons (and Luckys and black-marketeering Pozzos), pathos doesn't demand *enough* of its audience." Munk, "Sontag Stages 'Godot,'" 2 (emphasis added).
88. Beckett, *Waiting for Godot*, 44.
89. Adorno is at his most Beckettian when he observes, "A thinking man's true answer to the question whether he is a nihilist would probably be 'Not enough'—out of callousness, perhaps, because of insufficient sympathy with anything that suffers." *Negative Dialectics*, trans. E. B. Ashton (New York: Continuum, 1973), 380.
90. Paul Chan, "Waiting for Godot in New Orleans: An Artist's Statement," in *Waiting for Godot in New Orleans: A Field Guide* (New York: Creative Time Books, 2009), 26.
91. Cauleen Smith directs a science fiction video, *The Fullness of Time* (2007), using sites in New Orleans abandoned after the flood: the empty spaces on which homes once stood, an abandoned and rusted amusement park, a ruined solarium.
92. Chan, "Waiting for Godot in New Orleans," 26.
93. Ibid.
94. Sigmund Freud, "The 'Uncanny,'" in *Writings on Art and Literature* (Stanford, CA: Stanford University Press, 1997), 193–233.

95. Ibid., 210, 215.
96. Ibid., 213.
97. Ibid.
98. Chan, "Waiting for Godot in New Orleans," 28.
99. See Spike Lee's *When the Levees Broke* (2006) for a discussion of the term "refugees" used for denizens of New Orleans.
100. Chan, "Waiting for Godot in New Orleans," 26.
101. Bert O. States, *The Shape of Paradox: An Essay on "Waiting for Godot"* (Berkeley: University of California Press, 1978), 35.
102. Ibid., 34.
103. Mannes, "Two Tramps," 31.
104. Andrea Boll, "Puking My Puke of a Life in Waiting for Godot in New Orleans," in Chan, *Field Guide*, 241.
105. See Sontag, "Godot in Sarajevo," 305.
106. Boll, "Puking My Puke," 241.
107. Black actors playing Vladimir and Estragon, and white actors playing Pozzo and Lucky, was also the distribution in the 1980 Capetown production by Donald Howarth. See Bradby, *Beckett: "Waiting for Godot,"* 167–70.
108. Boll, "Puking My Puke," 240.
109. Ibid., 241.
110. Sontag, "Godot in Sarajevo," 312.
111. Ibid., 315.
112. Ibid., 309.
113. Ibid.
114. Erika Munk, "Only the Possible: An Interview with Susan Sontag," *Theater* 24, no. 3 (1993): 31.
115. Vivian Mercier, *Beckett/Beckett* (Oxford: Oxford University Press, 1977), 48.
116. Ibid., 48, 49. In his taxonomical mania, Mercier counts Molloy's mentioning the *Times Literary Supplement* as an "unambiguously learned reference" yet ignores the fact that Molloy says he likes the *Times* because, using it to wipe his behind, it absorbs his farts better. Mercier mistakes this swipe of the *Times* with a swipe *at* the *Times*. Homeless people know newspapers more intimately than their subscribers do.
117. Ibid., 55.
118. Beckett, "Dante . . . Bruno. Vico. Joyce," 19.
119. Beckett, *Waiting for Godot*, 9.
120. Paul Chan and Kathy Halbreich, "Undoing: A Conversation between Kathy Halbreich and Paul Chan," in Chan, *Field Guide*, 308.
121. Chan, "Waiting for Godot in New Orleans," 26.
122. Lois Oppenheim, *The Painted Word: Samuel Beckett's Dialogue with Art* (Ann Arbor: University of Michigan Press, 2000), 59.
123. Goytisolo, *Landscapes of War*, 11.
124. Franz Kafka, "The Silence of the Sirens," in *The Complete Stories*, ed. Nahum N. Glatzer, trans. Willa and Edwin Muir (New York: Schocken, 1971), 430.
125. Samuel Beckett, *Proust and Three Dialogues*, 93.
126. See Adorno's observation that in *Endgame* a "historical moment unfolds, namely the experience captured in the title of one of the culture industry's cheap novels, *Kaputt*." "Trying to Understand 'Endgame,'" 244.
127. Sontag, "Godot in Sarajevo," 310.
128. The arrival of theatrical night is not part of a natural cycle of inevitability: its arrival seems as unlikely as Godot's. The gray dusk sky of *Godot* is the celestial

backdrop to poverty on Beckett's stage. The difficulty of describing this sky suggests how it "beggars description." Beckett reworks an early uncompleted piece, *The Gloaming* (dusk), as *Rough for Theater I*. This features a blind beggar with a violin. He asks his companion in a wheelchair, "Will it not soon be evening?" The reply: "Day . . . night . . . It seems to me sometimes that earth must have got stuck, one sunless day, in the heart of winter, in the grey of evening." Beckett, *Collected Shorter Plays*, 72. The blind beggar's question will emerge as Pozzo's in *Godot*.

129. Quoted in Bradby, *Beckett: "Waiting for Godot,"* 170.

130. Carrie Lambert-Beatty, "Essentially Alien: Notes from Outside Paul Chan's 'Godot,'" *Parkett* 88 (2007): 78. The second line is part of funerary custom of the New Orleans area: marchers move methodically in sync to the burial. The second line moves more idiosyncratically and festively in returning from the cemetery.

131. Jed Horne suggests that the play's setting only provides the differences in class and race to assert themselves again: "Whites ventured into a part of town that many of them, at least until Katrina, wouldn't have visited in a million years. Tickets were free, and so the poor were able to walk to the performance, while the gentry ventured downriver in limos and fancy rigs that were lined up along blocks now emptied of all but the scraped concrete slabs where houses once stood." "Is New Orleans Waiting for Godot?" in Chan, *Field Guide*, 242.

132. See Wolfgang Iser, "Counter-sensical Comedy in 'Waiting for Godot,'" in Connor, *A New Casebook*, 56.

133. Joseph Roach uses Blau's term while attributing critical origin of the term *tramp* to Peter Hall: "As soon as the refugees whom Peter Hall was first to call 'tramps' begin to take stock of their rotten tubers along 'a country road.' . . . " Joseph Roach, "The Great Hole of History," in *Reflections on Beckett: A Centenary Celebration*, ed. Anna McMullan and S. E. Wilmer (Ann Arbor: University of Michigan Press, 2009), 148.

134. "To call it site specific seems so limiting." Nato Thompson, "Destroyer of Worlds," in Chan, *Field Guide*, 58.

135. Emmanuel Levinas, *Existence and Existents*, trans. Alphonso Lingis (Pittsburgh: Duquesne University Press, 2001), 61.

136. Ibid.

137. Ibid., 63.

138. Beckett, *Waiting for Godot*, 44.

139. Adorno, "Trying to Understand 'Endgame,'" 251. "Die eiserne Ration an Realität und Personen, mit denen das Drama rechnet und haushält, ist eins mit dem, was von Subjekt, Geist und Seele im Angesicht der permanenten Katastrophe bleibt." Adorno, "Versuch," 292.

140. Antonin Artaud, *The Theater and Its Double*, trans. Mary Caroline Richards (New York: Grove Press, 1958), 24.

141. Beckett, *Waiting for Godot*, 14.

142. *Rough for Theater II* remains Beckett's most Kafkan stage piece. Two men facing each other at a table read aloud from the sorry and confused life testimonies of the man standing on the window ledge in the room. The decision of the suicide leap must first pass a review board. *Rough for Theater II* in Beckett, *Collected Shorter Plays*, 77–89.

143. Beckett, *Waiting for Godot*, 44.

144. Chan, "Waiting for Godot in New Orleans," 28.

145. Sontag, "Godot in Sarajevo," 316.

146. Residents of Gentilly, "What Are You Waiting for?" in Chan, *Field Guide*, 283–84. Following Katrina, Ray Nagin hires Ed Blakely as the executive director of Recovery Management for the City of New Orleans. As overseer of the recovery and re-

building process, Blakely earns the title of "Recovery Tzar." Road Home is a housing recovery program designed to provide compensation to Louisiana homeowners affected by the hurricane.

147. Ibid., 283. The Gentilly residents save the expression "waiting on" to describe money: "Waiting on my insurance company to give me more than a nominal amount of money; living in a damaged home because of unfair treatment by the insurance company" (ibid.). Credit that is forthcoming seems essentially nearer than Godot, who only issues vague promissory notes. Money has both a more luminous fantasy component and a more generalized application than Godot. Waiting on Godot would suggest a leisureliness that accompanies waiting on a friend (the Rolling Stones song of that name sounds, paradoxically, like a stroll).

148. Ibid., 284.

149. "People that are there are in the trenches, and you shouldn't be in the trenches in your retiring years." Ibid.

150. Ibid.

151. Maurice Blanchot, "Literature and the Right to Death," in *The Work of Fire*, trans. Charlotte Mandell (Stanford, CA: Stanford University Press, 1995), 329.

152. Sontag says that a side effect of coming to Sarajevo "would make it clear that [working here] was possible." When the interviewer asks, "Possible, or desireable?" Sontag replies, "It's only the possible that I can show." Munk, "Only the Possible," 31.

153. Tim Griffin, "Waiting for Godot," *Artforum International* 46, no. 4 (December 2007): 51.

154. Beckett, *Waiting for Godot*, 11.

155. Ibid., 10.

156. Ibid., 11.

157. Ibid., 10.

158. Ibid., 39.

159. Beckett's stage directions are simple and precise: "Bare interior. Grey light. Left and right back, high up, two small windows, curtains drawn. Front right, a door. Hanging near door, its face to wall, a picture." Samuel Beckett, *Endgame* (New York: Grove Press, 1958), 1.

160. See Kalb, *Beckett in Performance*, 79–81. Beckett issues an angry statement to the ART. Printed within a program insert, Beckett's disclaimer reads, "Any production of *Endgame* which ignores my stage direction is completely unacceptable to me" (ibid., 79). Akalaitis's provision of a corpse demonstrates the risk of the directorial effort to incarnate meaning on stage. In *Endgame* Clov looks out over the audience through his telescope and intones, "All is . . . corpsed" (30). He does not say he *sees corpses* but rather the world struck in the image of one: the earth become posthumous. Akalaitis responds impatiently to Clov's line. The staging blurts out "a corpse!" as if it were submitting to Beckett's play as to a polygraph test.

161. Ilan Ronen, director of the *Waiting for Godot* production in Haifa, explains the situation that inspires him to stage *Godot* within the context of the Israel-Palestine conflict: "Nearly all the construction workers in Israel were Palestinians from the West Bank or Gaza. Each day, in the early morning hours, they left their homes, travelling in convoys to the cities of Israel. . . . This created an absurd situation in which the country, including the Jewish settlements in the occupied territories, was being built almost exclusively by Palestinians under the rule of Israeli occupation." "'Waiting for Godot' as Political Theater," in *Directing Beckett*, ed. Lois Oppenheim (Ann Arbor: University of Michigan Press, 1994), 240. As for the directors under discussion here, Ronen's inspiration comes from a moment of irreconcilable absurdity in the world. Ronen spec-

ifies a moment that resonates strongly with the contemporary border policy of the United States: the military enforcement of national borders combined with dependency on stateless and rights-deprived immigrant laborers.

162. Bradby, *Beckett: "Waiting for Godot,"* 176. Bradby gives an excellent overview of what he calls "the play's special relevance in oppressive circumstances" (162). The *sans-papiers* are foreign laborers who work in France but without documentation, and hence they lack an identity in the eyes of the state. See Jacques Derrida, "Derelictions of the Right to Justice: But What Are the 'Sans-Papiers' Lacking?" in *Negotiations,* ed. and trans. Elizabeth Rottenberg (Stanford, CA: Stanford University Press, 2002), 133–46.

163. "To restore the image of drifters, of people excluded from the France of the 1990s." Bradby, *Beckett: "Waiting for Godot,"* 176.

164. Ibid., 168.

165. Sontag, "Godot in Sarajevo," 322.

166. Anne Gisleson, "Godot Is Great," in Chan, *Field Guide,* 235.

167. *When the Levees Broke* is an anthology of this graffiti. "AS NOT SEEN ON TV" reworks the advertising phrase "As Seen on TV." The graffiti reads like the reverse of such promotion, suggesting the unadvertised, uncirculated, and undocumented extent of the damage to New Orleans.

168. Lois Oppenheim, "Playing with Beckett's Plays: On Sontag in Sarajevo and Other Directorial Infidelities," *Journal of Beckett Studies* 4, no. 2 (Spring 1995): 39.

169. Oppenheim takes issue with Sontag's claim that *Godot* is "about abandoned people, weak, vulnerable people, waiting for something to happen that they go on hoping against hope will happen, and yet it's perfectly clear it's not going to happen and that's the situation of the people of Sarajevo." Quoted in Oppenheim, "Playing with Beckett's Plays," 38.

170. Theodor Adorno, "Notes on Beckett," trans. Dirk Van Hulle and Shane Weller, *Journal of Beckett Studies* 19, no. 2 (2010): 178.

171. Alain Badiou approaches Beckett's reduction philosophically, in a way that authorizes the philosophical thinking of his work, and speaks of the need to "grasp the questions proper to Beckett's work, those that organize the fiction of a humanity treated and exhibited by a functional reduction oriented towards the essence or the Idea." *On Beckett,* ed. Nina Power and Alberto Toscano (Manchester, UK: Clinamen Press, 2003), 4.

172. Oppenheim offers *Catastrophe* as an example of Beckett's parabolic vision. She describes the "facile political interpretation" of the play as a "depiction of life under a communist regime" as myopic. She approvingly cites Antoni Libera's reading of the "mythological context" of *Catastrophe.* Libera understands *Catastrophe* as Beckett's "interpretation of the origins of totalitarianism" and the "philosophical diagnosis of its real nature." Oppenheim, "Playing with Beckett's Plays," 39. Parable then may suggest something closer to a parable of interpretation, a parable of the reading activity, rather than an opaque mirror held up to the world.

173. Elin Diamond argues that *Godot* explores the oppressive effects of identification's mirror relations. She says that Beckett's rejection of political identification entails a study of how one always falls short of that mirror image. That falling short is the basis of Lacan's notion of an asymptotic relation of self and image: "Thus [the infant's] identification with that image [in a mirror] is both self-fulfilling and self-alienating. Because the mirror image invites idealization, it dooms the infant to a frustrating rivalry at which it can only fail. The maturing subject will 'rejoin' its image only 'asymptotically'—that is, never." Diamond, "The Society of My Likes," in Samuel

Beckett Today/Aujourd'hui (series), *Samuel Beckett: Endlessness in the Year 2000*, ed. Angela Moorjani and Carola Veit (Amsterdam: Rodopi, 2002), 383.

174. Paul Chan, "Provocation: Next Day, Same Place. After 'Godot' in New Orleans," *TDR/The Drama Review* 52, no. 4 (Winter 2008): 3.

175. The intervention of logic, a predetermined course of failure, is ubiquitous in the Katrina disaster. The failure of the levee, and not the hurricane per se, should classify the flood as an engineering (and not a natural) disaster. Chan also refers to the "wholesale contradiction" between the neighborhoods around Tulane University left intact and those that are decimated by the hurricane. Chan, "Waiting for Godot in New Orleans," 25.

176. Sontag, "Godot in Sarajevo," 321.

177. Walter Benjamin, "The Author as Producer," in *Reflections*, ed. Peter Demetz, trans. Edmund Jephcott (New York: Schocken, 1986), 231. Benjamin also speaks of "the procedure of a certain modish photography whereby poverty is made an object of consumption" (ibid.).

Chapter 3

1. Beckett, *Waiting for Godot*, 11.
2. Ibid.
3. Beckett, *Waiting for Godot*, 49. Ruby Cohn remarks on the similarity between Estragon's pose and yoga positions. Noted in McMillan and Fehsenfeld, *Beckett in the Theatre*, 119.
4. Beckett, *Three Novels*, 374. The expression "la pensée vagabonde" comes from *L'Innommable* (Paris: Editions de Minuit, 1953), 145. The confusion of the term has been multiplied in the first English translation of *The Unnamable*. There it reads "your thought's wander." The typo brings the wandering of thought into possession by thought. It has since been corrected to "your thoughts wander."
5. Beckett, *Waiting for Godot*, 28.
6. Ibid.
7. Leo Bersani and Ulysse Dutoit, *Arts of Impoverishment* (Cambridge, MA: Harvard University Press, 1993), 19.
8. Ibid.
9. Ibid.
10. Walter Benjamin, "One Way Street," in *Selected Writings*, vol. 1, *1913–1926*, trans. Edmund Jephcott, ed. Marcus Bullock, and Michael W. Jennings (Cambridge, MA: Harvard University Press, 1996), 486.
11. Rainer Maria Rilke, "Primal Sound," in *Where Silence Reigns: Selected Prose*, trans. G. Craig Houston (New York: New Directions, 1978), 52.
12. Beckett, *Three Novels*, 40. Molloy sets his descriptive powers on the noise a little later: "It was a night of listening, a night given to the faint soughing and sighing stirring at night in little pleasure gardens, the shy Sabbath of leaves and petals and the air that eddies there as it does not in other places, where there is less constraint, and as it does not during the day, when there is more vigilance, and then something else that is not clear, being neither the air nor what it moves, perhaps the far unchanging noise the earth makes and which other noises cover, but not for long. . . . And there was another noise, that of my life become the life of this garden as it rode the earth of deeps and wildernesses. Yes, there were times when I forgot not only who I was, but that I was, forgot to be" (49). As in all of Beckett's writing, a certain

sobriety is used in describing movements of great discontinuity, underscoring the jarring pastiche of Molloy's expressions. The noise he hears is none other than the sound of a metamorphosis of his life merging with the life of the garden. Molloy here specifically does not speak of merging with the garden (two identities, in a sense). Beckett instead asks us to accommodate the idea of the garden being the space of a life independent of Molloy's. This is not a pastoral retirement. Prescient of the way we understand the earth's plates to shift over the surface of the planet, Molloy describes the garden in motion, riding the earth, with him as its oblivious passenger. For the purposes of this chapter, it helps note the way this sound is said to elude the vigilance of the day.

13. Molloy, looking forward to the murmurs again, hears instead a gong. "A horn goes well with the forest, you expect it. It is the huntsman. But a gong! Even a tom-tom, at a pinch, would not have shocked me. But a gong! It was mortifying, to have been looking forward to the celebrated murmurs if to nothing else, and to succeed only in hearing, at long intervals, in the far distance, a gong . . . " Ibid., 89.

14. Ibid., 10.

15. Ibid., 207.

16. Throughout Beckett's work, characters are split by the very pronouns by which the murmur addresses them (as well as the pronoun proper to the murmur itself: is it "they" or "it," the anonymous plural or the neuter singular?): "Now I'm haunted, let them go, one by one, let the last desert me and leave me empty, empty and silent. It's they murmur my name, speak to me of me, speak of a me, let them go and speak of it to others, who will not believe them either, or who will believe them too. Theirs all these voices, like a rattling of chains in my head, rattling to me that I have a head." Samuel Beckett, "Texts for Nothing," in *Complete Short Prose*, 120.

17. Beckett, *Three Novels*, 207.

18. In *Malone Dies*, Malone reports how the organization of the journal he is keeping is dictated by the wind: "But my fingers too write in other latitudes and the air that breathes through my pages and turns them without my knowing, when I doze off, so that the subject falls far from the verb and the object lands somewhere in the void, is not the air of this second-last abode, and a mercy it is. And perhaps on my hands it is the shimmer of the shadows of leaves and flowers and the brightness of a forgotten sun." Ibid., 234.

19. The character Malone will insist not only on his own absence to his thought but also on not even being where thinking seeks him out: "Somewhere in this turmoil thought struggles on, it too wide of the mark. It too seeks me, as it always has, where I am not to be found." Ibid., 186.

20. Beckett, *Waiting for Godot*, 40.

21. Ibid., 51.

22. Ibid.

23. Ibid., 41.

24. Ibid.

25. Beckett, *Proust and Three Dialogues*, 83.

26. Beckett, *Three Novels*, 50.

27. Ibid.

28. Ibid.

29. Ibid.

30. Hegel describes the simultaneous inception of Western art and the historical subject in the Greeks' turning their ears away from the murmurs of the natural world and toward the sound that is made by the ear itself *in listening to* these sounds: "Eben-

so horchten die Griechen auf das Gemurmel der Quellen und fragten, was das zu bedeuten habe, die Bedeutung aber ist nicht die objective Sinnigkeit der Quelle, sondern die subjecktive des Subjekts selbst, welches dann weiter die Najade zur Muse erhebt. Die Najaden oder Quellen sind der äußerliche Anfang der Musen. Doch der Musen unsterbliche Gesänge sind nicht das, was man hört, sondern sie sind die Produktionen des sinnig horchenden Geistes, der in seinem Hinauslauschen in sich selbst produziert." Georg Wilhelm Friedrich Hegel, *Vorlesungen über die Philosophie der Geschichte* (Stuttgart: Phillip Reclam, 1961), 336. "On the same principle the Greeks listened to the murmuring of the fountains, and asked what might thereby be signified; but the signification which they were led to attach to it was not the objective meaning of the fountain, but the subjective—that of the subject itself, which further exalts the Naiad to a Muse. The Naiads, or Fountains, are the external, objective origin of the Muses. Yet the immortal songs of the Muses are not that which is heard in the murmuring of the fountains; they are the productions of the thoughtfully listening Spirit—*creative* while *observant*." G. W. F. Hegel, *The Philosophy of History*, trans. J. Sibree (New York: Dover, 1956), 235.

31. Beckett, *Three Novels*, 60.

32. In their analysis of capitalism, Deleuze and Guattari describe something similar to Beckett's suppositional universe. They write, "Unlike previous social machines, the capitalist machine is incapable of providing a code that will apply to the whole of the social field. By substituting money for the very notion of a code, it has created an axiomatic of abstract quantities that keeps moving further and further in the direction of the deterritorialization of the socius." Gilles Deleuze and Felix Guattari, *Anti-Oedipus*, trans. Mark Seem (Minneapolis: University of Minnesota Press, 1986), 33.

33. See Roman Jakobson, "Two Aspects of Language and Two Types of Aphasic Disturbance," in *Language in Literature*, ed. Krystyna Pomorska and Stephen Rudy (Cambridge, MA: Harvard University Press, 1987), 95–120.

34. Beckett, *Three Novels*, 60.

35. Paul Valéry, *Sea Shells*, trans. Mary Oliver (Boston: Beacon Press, 1998), 73. Adorno compares Beckett's characters to mollusks: "Modern ontology lives off the unfulfilled promise of the concreteness of its abstractions, whereas in Beckett the concreteness of an existence that is shut up in itself like a mollusk, no longer capable of universality, an existence that exhausts itself in pure self-positing, is revealed to be identical to the abstractness that is no longer capable of experience." "Trying to Understand 'Endgame,'" 246.

36. *Pensum* refers to a weight of wool given to female slaves to work off as a day's labor in Roman times. In Beckett's "Sottisier" notebook, he notes the following quotation from Schopenhauer: "Das Leben ist ein Pensum zum Abarbeiten: in diesem Sinne ist defunctus ein schöner Ausdruck." "Sottisier" notebook, 13r. ("Life is a pensum to work off: in this sense is defunctus an attractive expression.") Beckett is keen on the "zum Abarbeiten," materially worked off rather than "durcharbeiten" or worked through in the psychoanalytic sense.

37. Beckett ends his essay on Proust by commenting on the way in which the artwork in Proust's work reveals life to be a pensum, a rote lesson whose meaning is not entirely grasped because it is so mediated by habit: the experience of the narrator Marcel is one that bears witness to art, "sees in the red phrase of the Septuor: . . . the ideal and immaterial statement of the essence of a unique beauty, a unique world, the invariable world and beauty of Vinteuil, expressed timidly, as a prayer, in the Sonata, imploringly, as an inspiration, in the Septuor, the 'invisible reality' that damns the life of the body on earth as a pensum and reveals the meaning of the word: 'defunctus.'" *Proust and Three Dialogues*, 93. As with the word "defunctus" it seems that Beckett's at-

traction to the pensum is in fact its part in a dead language, a language that goes dead on the tongue and in which the image of our life is made.

38. See also the definition of "pensum" in the *Encyclopedia Acephalica:* "Few painters produce pictures other than by way of pensums, works imposed on them by an alien, and often hateful, hand. How many writers harness themselves to their novel and voluntarily reduce themselves to the rank of plough-horses, or asses, loaded, now with cereals, now with relics." George Bataille, Michel Leiris, et al., *Encylopedia Acephalica* (London: Atlas Press, 1995), 67. Leiris, the author of this entry, bemoans the pensum as a strictly rote task, a function of habit. For Molloy the pensum is the first and the last task, the impossible task to fulfill, because it is inaccessible to memory.

39. Beckett, *Three Novels,* 310.

40. Ibid., 32.

41. Leo Bersani, *Balzac to Beckett: Center and Circumference in French Fiction* (Cambridge, MA: Harvard University Press, 1972), 59.

42. Beckett always distrusted the effort to redeem poverty and the viewing of failure as an opportunity. Praising the painter Bram van Velde, Beckett wrote, "The numerous attempts made to make painting independent of its occasion have only succeeded in enlarging its repertory. I suggest that van Velde is the first whose painting is *bereft, rid if you prefer, of occasion in every shape and form,* ideal as well as material, and the first whose hands have not been tied by the certitude that expression is an impossible act." *Three Dialogues,* 121 (emphasis added).

43. I want to thank Arkady Plotnitsky for drawing my attention to this reference.

44. Jean-Luc Nancy, *The Birth to Presence,* trans. Elizabeth Rottenberg (Stanford, CA: Stanford University Press, 1993), 44.

45. Beckett, *Three Novels,* 296.

46. Ibid., 67.

47. In *Malone Dies* the title character is bedridden and relies on a walking cane to pull objects from around the room nearer to him. He then observes, "How great is my debt to sticks! So great that I almost forget the blows they have transferred to me." Ibid., 185.

48. Ibid., 350.

49. Badiou, *On Beckett,* 12.

50. Ibid.

51. Maurice Blanchot, *The Madness of the Day,* trans. Lydia Davis (New York: Station Hill, 1981), 9.

52. Ibid.,12.

53. Beckett, *Proust and Three Dialogues,* 89.

54. Molloy does not turn toward things that appear before his eyes. The game he plays is one of turning away from that which is disappearing: "From things about to disappear I turn away in time." Beckett, *Three Novels,* 12.

55. Ibid., 53.

56. Foucault discusses these *hupomnemata* in his essay titled "Self Writing." He summarizes: "The *hupomnemata* served as memory aids. Their use as books of life, as guides for conduct, seems to have become a common thing for a whole cultivated public. One wrote down quotes in them, extracts from books, examples, and actions that one had witnessed or read about, reflections or reasonings that one had heard or that had come to mind." Michel Foucault, *Ethics: Subjectivity and Truth,* ed. Paul Rabinow (New York: New Press, 1998), 209.

57. Hugh Kenner pursues this line of thought in the chapter "The Cartesian Centaur," in *Samuel Beckett: A Critical Study.* A typical observation: "The Beckett bicycle can orchestrate all the great themes of human speculation" (126).

58. Beckett, *Three Novels*, 326.

59. Ibid., 22.

60. The full quote: "Let me tell you this, when social workers offer you, free, gratis, and for nothing, something to hinder you from swooning, which with them is an obsession, it is useless to recoil, they will pursue you to the ends of the earth, the vomitory in their hands. The Salvation Army is no better. Against the charitable gesture there is no defense, that I know of." Ibid., 24.

61. Benjamin, *Selected Writings*, 2:668. Benjamin also writes in his *Berlin Chronicle* that a wealthy child of his generation "could picture the poor, it was, without his knowing either name or origin, in the image of the tramp who is actually a rich man, though without money, since he stands—far removed from the process of production and the exploitation not yet abstracted from it—in the same contemplative relation to his destitution as the rich man to his wealth." In *Reflections*, 11.

62. In *The Myth of the Birth of the Hero* (New York: Vintage, 1959) Otto Rank employs the term "abandonment myth" to describe those stories (i.e., about Moses and Oedipus) that achieve mythical status because their figures survive an exposure to death at an early age, after being abandoned and "given up for dead" by their parents. Rank describes abandonment as a condition that cannot be overcome or diminished. This is relevant to the way in which Beckett's characters are exposed. Rank observes that the figures of myth are exposed to not only the "natural elements" but to the merciless judgment (the "ecce homo") and laws of peoples and divinities.

63. Malone connects the understanding of time to the question of utility: "use" creates the idea of a future, a purpose, a goal. Accumulation and ultimate expenditure structure time for us. In contrast to this, Malone says he is speaking of a character who "could not employ [what he has accumulated], since he feels so far from the morrow. And perhaps there is none, no morrow any more, for one who has waited so long for it in vain. And perhaps he has come to that stage of his instant when to live is to wander the last of the living in the depths of an instant without bounds, where the light never changes and the wrecks look all alike." Beckett, *Three Novels*, 233.

64. Adorno, "Trying to Understand 'Endgame,'" 268.

65. Georges Bataille, "Molloy's Silence," in *Modern Critical Interpretations: Samuel Beckett's Molloy, Malone Dies, The Unnamable*, ed. Harold Bloom (New York: Chelsea House, 1988), 14.

66. Ibid., 20.

67. Ibid., 16.

68. Ibid., 20. "Cette horrible figure se balançant douloureusement sur ses béquilles est la vérité dont nous sommes malades et qui ne nous suit pas moins fidèlement que notre ombre nous suit . . . spectre qui hante le plein jour des rues." Georges Bataille, "Le silence de Molloy," *Critique* 7, no. 15 (1951), 394.

69. Beckett, *Three Novels*, 91.

70. Ibid., 22. This sentence is not translated in the French version of Beckett's novel. Perhaps Molloy's existence inhabits that same space of ethical impossibility as the current debates about assisted suicide.

71. Beckett, *L'Innommable*, 22; Beckett, *Three Novels*, 300.

72. See the second section of *Molloy*: "Gaber, Gaber, he said, life is a thing of beauty, Gaber, and a joy for ever. He brought his face nearer mine. A joy for ever, he said, a thing of beauty, Moran, and a joy for ever. He smiled. I closed my eyes. Smiles are all very nice in their own way, very heartening, but at a reasonable distance. I said, Do you think he meant human life?" Beckett, *Three Novels*, 152.

Chapter 4

1. Beckett, *Proust and Three Dialogues,* 112.
2. Leo Bersani and Ulysse Dutoit title their chapter on Beckett "Inhibited Reading" in *Arts of Impoverishment,* 11–92.
3. Adorno, "Trying to Understand 'Endgame,'" 243.
4. Quoted in McMillan and Fehsenfeld, *Beckett in the Theatre,* 15.
5. Beckett, *Proust and Three Dialogues,* 125. Beckett's creation of an art withdrawn from any economy with reader, society, or artist stymied Brecht's attempts to enlist *Waiting for Godot* into the class struggle.
6. Quoted in Bair, *Samuel Beckett,* 606.
7. Steven Connor, *Theory and Cultural Value* (Cambridge, MA: Blackwell, 1992), 81.
8. Ibid.
9. Quoted in Peter Boxall, ed., *"Waiting for Godot" and "Endgame": A Reader's Guide to Essential Criticism* (New York: Palgrave Macmillan, 2003), 97.
10. Ibid., 98.
11. Ibid., 97.
12. Ibid.
13. Adorno, "Trying to Understand 'Endgame,'" 243.
14. Ibid.
15. Ibid.
16. Bersani and Dutoit, *Arts of Impoverishment,* 15.
17. Beckett, *Disjecta,* 145, 55.
18. James Knowlson and John Pilling, *Frescoes of the Skull: The Later Prose and Drama of Samuel Beckett* (New York: Grove Press, 1980), 255.
19. Samuel Beckett, "The End," in *Complete Short Prose,* 91.
20. In an interview with Tom Driver, Beckett describes how he was once pestered at a party about "why I write always about distress. As if it were perverse to do so! He wanted to know if my father had beaten me or my mother had run away from home to give me an unhappy childhood." Beckett decides to leave the party as soon as possible and gets into a cab. He says, "On the glass partition between me and the driver were three signs; one asked for help for the blind, another help for orphans, and the third for relief for the war refugees. One does not have to look for distress. It is screaming at you even in the taxis of London." "Tom Driver in 'Columbia University Forum,'" in Graver and Federman, *Samuel Beckett: The Critical Heritage,* 221.
21. Vladimir's soliloquy ("To all mankind they were addressed, those cries for help still ringing in our ears! But at this place, at this moment of time, all mankind is us, whether we like it or not" [Beckett, *Waiting for Godot,* 51]) embodies the existential side of this dilemma, rather than the posthuman form it assumes in Beckett's later work.
22. Beckett, *Proust and Three Dialogues,* 121.
23. Beckett, *Three Novels,* 274.
24. Beckett's much quoted observation that van Velde is the "first to admit that to be an artist is to fail, as no other dare fail" is frequently taken as an exclusive description of the artist's goal or task. I take "dare" and "fail" to be transitive verbs. The artist dares the reader; we run the risk of failing that cry "made ill." *Proust and Three Dialogues,* 125.
25. Such late prose works as *Ill Seen, Ill Said* further develop this medical diagnostic of the call.

26. Samuel Beckett, "Intercessions of Denis Devlin," in *Disjecta*, 91.
27. Ibid.
28. Samuel Beckett, "Cascando," in *Collected Poems in English and French* (New York: Grove Press, 1977), 29.
29. Beckett, *Three Novels*, 311. "Décidement il semble impossible, à ce stade, que je me passe de questions, comme je me l'étais promis. Non, je m'étais seulement juré de ne plus en formuler. Qui sait? Je tomberai peut-être, d'ici peu, sur l'heureux arrangement qui les empêchera à tout jamais de se formuler, dans mon, ne soyons pas pédant, dans mon esprit." Beckett, *L'Innommable*, 41.
30. Adorno, "Trying to Understand 'Endgame,'" 264. "Beckett jedoch entziffert die Luge des Fragezeichens: die Frage ist zur rhetorischen geworden." Adorno, "Versuch," 308.
31. Gilles Deleuze, *Bergsonism*, trans. Hugh Tomlinson (Cambridge, MA: Zone Books, 1990), 17.
32. Gilles Deleuze and Félix Guattari, *What Is Philosophy?* trans. Hugh Tomlinson and Graham Burchell (New York: Columbia University Press, 1994), 1.
33. Martin Heidegger, "The Question Concerning Technology," in *The Question Concerning Technology and Other Essays*, trans. William Lovitt (New York: Harper Torchbooks, 1977), 35.
34. "Die genannte Frage ist heute in Vergessenheit gekommen, obzwar unsere Zeit sich als Fortchritt anrechnet, die 'Metaphysik' wider zu bejahen." Martin Heidegger, *Sein und Zeit* (Tübingen: Max Niemeyer Verlag, 1986), 2.
35. Roland Barthes, "The Last Word on Robbe-Grillet?" in *Critical Essays*, 202.
36. The essay concludes with an observation about the way Robbe-Grillet's characters frequently point to unspecified objects: "*This*, they say. But what is this—*this* what? Perhaps all literature is in this anaphoric suspension which at one and the same time designates and keeps silent." Ibid., 204. Barthes's assignation of an interrogative function to literature and theater continues his thinking in his introduction to *On Racine:* "To write is to jeopardize the meaning of the world, to put an *indirect* question that the writer, by an ultimate abstention, refrains from answering. It is each of us who gives the answer, bringing to it his own history, his own language, his own freedom. . . . There is no end to answering what has been written beyond hope of an answer: asserted, disputed, superseded—the meanings pass, the question remains." Roland Barthes, *On Racine*, trans. Richard Howard (New York: Performing Arts Journal Publications, 1983), ix.
37. Beckett's thirty-second play *Breath* features a light illuminating for five seconds a stage scattered with debris, a brief cry, a ten-second intensification of the light accompanied by an "inspiration," then "silence and hold for five seconds." Then there is a ten-second "expiration" with a decrease in light, followed by the same brief cry. (Beckett, *Breath*, in *Collected Shorter Plays*, 209.) Though clearly broken into segments, the constitutive elements are not easily separated. The breath, the cry, and the light are dependent on each other rather than in a hierarchical order: to quote the play, the play would have to be quoted in its entirety. The play is designed so that no element excludes any of the others, and to discourage any immodest interventions by the critic.
38. In *Allegories of Reading* Paul de Man focuses on the break between grammar and rhetoric. This break appears most visibly around the *rhetorical question*, notably Yeats's line, "How can we know the dancer from the dance?" One of the consequences of de Man's analysis is a radical questioning of questioning, an immersion in the rhetorical quandary of the question. Unlike Beckett's work, which produces active questions, de Man's analysis seems to register the ways in which the only proper reply to

Yeats's poem is *another rhetorical question*. "Confronted with the question of the difference between grammar and rhetoric, grammar allows us to ask the question, but the sentence by means of which we ask it may deny the very possibility of asking. *For what is the use of asking, I ask, when we cannot even authoritatively decide whether a question asks or doesn't ask?*" Paul de Man, *Allegories of Reading* (New Haven, CT: Yale University Press, 1982), 10 (emphasis added).

39. Beckett, *Three Novels,* 307.

40. For a discussion of *petitio principii* see John Woods and Douglas Walton, *Fallacies* (Providence, RI: Foris Publications, 1989), 29–42.

41. Brater, *Beyond Minimalism,* 128.

42. Hans Robert Jauss, *Towards an Aesthetic of Reception,* trans. Timothy Bahti (New York: Harvester Press, 1982), 43.

43. Beckett, *Waiting for Godot,* 55. Pozzo says to Estragon, "A moment ago you were calling me Sir, in fear and trembling. Now you're asking me questions. No good will come of this!" Ibid., 20.

44. Ibid., 21.

45. Ibid.

46. Samuel Beckett, *What Where,* in *Collected Shorter Plays,* 312.

47. "En réalité, le texte beckettien est hors des questions, au sens traditionnel: il n'en pose, ne s'en pose pas plus qu'il n'en laisse à l'écart." Bruno Clément, *L'Oeuvre sans qualités: Rhétorique de Samuel Beckett* (Paris: Editions du Seuil, 1994), 52.

48. Samuel Beckett, *First Love and Other Shorts* (New York: Grove Press, 1995), 60.

49. It is interesting to note that each novel of the trilogy isolates a list of questions, often numbered. These dissipate the force of the question by trying to bring the banal necessities to the level of knowledge. Often, it is not clear how some of the questions can be numbered among others. For example, in *Malone Dies,* Malone is bedridden and writes down a list of questions for a man who he believes visited him and hit him on the head with his cane. Among the questions for the man, if he is to return, are: "1. Who are you? 2. What do you do, for a living? 3. Are you looking for something in particular? What else?. . . . 7. It was wrong for you to strike me. 8. Give me my stick. . . . 12. Why has my soup been stopped? 13. For what reason are my pots no longer emptied? 14. Do you think I shall last much longer? 15. May I ask you a favour? 16. Your conditions are mine. . . . 18. You couldn't by any chance let me have the butt of a pencil? 19. Number your answers. 20. Don't go, I haven't finished." Beckett, *Three Novels,* 272. Such lists truly dissipate the form of the question by, as it were, tightening it. The stringency of the question contains the possibility of the answers that, Malone specifies, he wants the stranger to number. The greatest questions are truly asked by the bedridden, and this is possibly why Beckett's vagabonds usually flee from asking questions.

50. Ibid., 18.

51. Ibid., 218.

52. Lawrence Harvey, *Samuel Beckett, Poet and Critic* (Princeton, NJ: Princeton University Press, 1970), 249. See also Beckett's letter to Axel Kaun in which he writes, "Grammatik und Stil. Mir scheinen sie ebenso hinfällig geworden zu sein wie ein Biedermeier Badeanzug oder die Unerschütterlichkeit eines Gentlemans ("Grammar and Style. These seem to me to be as weak/invalid/outmoded as a Victorian bathing suit or the imperturbability of a true gentleman"). Beckett's choice of the word "hinfällig" brings his statement closer to law and order as it is also a legal term describing a law or an argument that is no longer valid or that is defunct. "German Letter of 1937," in *Disjecta,* 52.

53. A similar statement is found in *Malone Dies*: "A minimum of memory is indispensable, if one is to live really." Beckett, *Three Novels*, 203. Beckett's prose is "ambiguous" exclusively around the issue of the adequate and the minimum, which is to say that the ambiguity is not to expand our possibilities of reading but to make us question what minimum—and how small a minimum—is actually accorded a necessity by Beckett. It is not clear whether Malone is saying that "really" living requires some memory or, rather, next to no memory. This minimum is marked as much by its meagerness as by its ineradicability. The "indispensable" aspect of this minimum of memory is that which cannot be used, used up, but also dispensed with. It is this uselessness of the minimum that makes it necessary.

54. Israel Shenker, "An Interview with Beckett," in Graver and Federman, *Samuel Beckett: The Critical Heritage*, 148.

55. Ibid.

56. When the traveler reaches the immobile Pim, they press their bodies together. Here the traveler communicates with Pim through a series of physical signs (not unlike the system devised by Molloy with his mother): "table of basic stimuli one sing nails in armpit two speak blade in arse three stop thump on skull four louder pestle on kidney five softer index in anus. . . . " Samuel Beckett, *How It Is* (New York: Grove Press, 1964), 69. This then progresses to questions scratched in Pim's back with a nail.

57. Ibid., 7.

58. Christopher Ricks, *Beckett's Dying Words* (Oxford: Oxford University Press, 1993), 83.

59. Beckett's cultivation of weakened syntax led him to experiment with the meager structure of Western Union telegraphs. Toward the end of 1983, Beckett receives a query from the *New York Times* about his hopes and resolutions for the new year. Beckett telegraphed this reply: "RESOLUTIONS COLON ZERO STOP PERIOD HOPES COLON ZERO STOP BECKETT." Ibid., 87. Beckett's message dictates its own punctuation. He includes "colon" (twice) and "period" as punctuation to call attention to the incompleteness of his sentences. Beckett would not be outdone by the stop by which telegrams conventionally signaled the end of the sentence. The more one wants "colon" and "period" to function grammatically, however, the more they may acquire other connotations. "Period," for example, may mean, with finality, no hopes whatsoever, end of story. "Colon" may suggest where Beckett feels that hopes and resolutions may go.

60. Stanley Cavell, "Ending the Waiting Game: A Reading of Beckett's 'Endgame,'" in *Must We Mean What We Say?* (Cambridge: Cambridge University Press, 1976). 119.

61. Beckett, *Three Novels*, 67.

62. "Quaqua" is Beckett's neologism for blather. In *Waiting for Godot* Lucky speaks of "a personal God quaquaquaqua with white beard quaquaquaqua outside time without extension" (28). We can measure the distance between *Godot* and *How It Is* by noting that the narrator of this work must seemingly take dictation from Lucky's monologue. The quaqua has left the isolated space of monologue, something to be listened to and endured, and assigns inscriptions to the text we are reading. Lucky goes from being a critic thinking on the stage to the secondhand author of *How It Is*.

63. Bersani and Dutoit, *Arts of Impoverishment*, 60.

64. "Abandon all hope, ye who enter."

65. Bataille, "Molloy's Silence," 17.

66. In 1970 the artist Geneviève Asse asks Beckett if he has a text that she could illustrate. Beckett gives her the work that, five years later, would become *For to End Yet Again*. Beckett visits her studio and, as Knowlson describes it, "The text did not have

a title until she had finished her work. One day, he suggested 'Abandonné' and asked specifically that it should be printed as if the letters were carved out of stone." The inspiration for this title comes from a statue Beckett passes on the way to Asse's studio, a monument "to Ernest Rousselle, the president of the French commission for children who are abandoned and in need. At its foot is a bronze statue of a curly-haired, young child with no shoes, reclining with his eyes closed and his head on a traveling bag. Beneath the statue a single word, 'Abandonné!' is cut out of the stone." Knowlson, *Damned to Fame*, 513.

67. Samuel Beckett, "The Calmative," in *Complete Short Prose*, 61.
68. Samuel Beckett, "From an Abandoned Work," in *Complete Short Prose*, 163.
69. Cohn, *Beckett Canon*, 217.
70. Beckett, "From an Abandoned Work," 156.
71. S. E. Gontarski, "From Unabandoned Works: Samuel Beckett's Short Prose," in *Complete Short Prose*, xv.
72. Beckett, "From an Abandoned Work," 159.
73. Ibid., 163.
74. Beckett, *Three Novels*, 414; Beckett, "From an Abandoned Work," 162.
75. Beckett, "From an Abandoned Work," 160.
76. Ibid., 164.
77. Adorno et al., *Aesthetics and Politics*, ed. Fredric Jameson, trans. Ronald Taylor (London: Verso Press, 1977), 191.
78. Derek Attridge writes that Beckett's texts are so "self-deconstructive" that "there is not much left to do." *Acts of Literature* (New York: Routledge Press, 1991), 61. The greatness of Beckett's work, however, originates in the way it leaves us feeling, at the same time, that there is *everything* to do.
79. Beckett, *Endgame*, 49.
80. Beckett, *Three Novels*, 139.
81. My translation is a modification of the Muir version. Franz Kafka, *Diaries*, trans. Willa and Edwin Muir (New York: Shocken Press, 1975), 398.
82. Paul de Man describes this condition of language as part of an imperative of language. Speaking of a scene in *La Recherche* in which Marcel's grandmother orders him to stop reading and go outside, de Man comments, "It seems that the language is unable to remain . . . ensconced and that it has to turn itself out." De Man, *Allegories of Reading*, 70.
83. Immanuel Kant, *Foundations of the Metaphysics of Morals*, trans. Oskar Piest (Indianapolis: Bobbs-Merrill, 1959), 33.
84. "Everyone says: Hunger is the best sauce; and people with a healthy appetite relish everything, so long as it is something they can eat. Such delight, consequently, gives no indication of taste having anything to do with choice. Only when people's needs have been satisfied can we tell who among the crowd has taste or not." Immanuel Kant, *Critique of Judgment*, trans. James Creed Meredith (Oxford: Oxford University Press, 2007), 42.
85. Beckett, *Three Novels*, 87. The passage later continues, "And in this command which faltered, then died, it was hard not to hear the unspoken entreaty, Don't do it, Molloy. In forever reminding me thus of my duty was its purpose to show me the folly of it? Perhaps."
86. Adorno, "Trying to Understand 'Endgame,'" 265.
87. Beckett, *Three Novels*, 87.
88. This comes from Freud's description in *Interpretation of Dreams* of the reasonings of the unconscious, exemplified in the contradictory and excessive logic of the

man who, upon being accused of denting his neighbor's kettle, explained that (1) he did not dent the kettle, (2) there was already a dent in the kettle when he received it, and (3) he did not borrow the kettle. See Sigmund Freud, *Interpretation of Dreams*, standard ed., trans. A. A. Brill (New York: Norton, 1989), 120.

89. Kant's categorical imperative depends on the principle, "So act that the maxim of your action could become a universal *law*." Immanuel Kant, *The Metaphysics of Morals* (Cambridge: Cambridge University Press, 1991), 192. Beckett's minimalism and subtractive aesthetic interrogate the universality of the maxim and in this way take aim at Kant's ethical system. See Beckett's paratactic translations of the maxims of Sebastien Chamfort.

90. In *Company*, for example, Beckett writes about a murmur that a character hears in the second person: "A voice comes to one in the dark. Imagine. To one on his back in the dark. . . . Only a small part of what is said can be verified. As for example when he hears, You are on your back in the dark. Then he must acknowledge the truth of what is said. But by far the greater part of what is said cannot be verified. As for example when he hears, You first saw the light on such and such a day." Samuel Beckett, *Company* (New York: Grove Press, 1991), 7. This form of address has the effect of simultaneously describing a state of affairs that already exists and, through this description, of forecasting or informing a state to come.

91. Beckett, *Worstward Ho*, 9. Also see the first line of *The Unnamable*: "Where now? Who now? When how? Unquestioning. I, say I. Unbelieving. Questions, hypotheses, call them that. Keep going, going on, call that going, call that on." Beckett, *Three Novels*, 291.

92. The verb "say" is similar in this regard to the way "never" works in Beckett's text: "Never to naught be brought. Never by naught be nulled." Beckett, *Worstward Ho*, 32.

93. Richard Ellman, *James Joyce* (Oxford: Oxford University Press, 1959), 662.

94. Charles Baudelaire, *Oeuvres Complètes* (Paris: Gallimard, 1951), 884. "He makes it his business to extract from fashion whatever element it may contain of poetry within history, to distil the eternal from the transitory." Charles Baudelaire, *The Painter of Modern Life and Other Essays*, trans. Jonathan Mayne (New York: Da Capo Press, 1964), 12.

95. Beckett, *Worstward Ho*, 9.

96. Beckett composed but did not air this broadcast.

97. Samuel Beckett, "The Capital of the Ruins," in *Complete Short Prose*, 278.

98. The character Nagg tells this joke in *Endgame*, and it provides the title for Beckett's essay on aesthetics, "Le Monde et le Pantelon." In brief, the joke tells the story about a man who brings his pants to a tailor and gets a different excuse as to why they are not ready each time he returns to the shop. His impatience at a breaking point, he informs the tailor that it took God only six days to make the world. "That's right," says the tailor, "but look at the world . . . and look at my TROUSERS!" See Samuel Beckett, *Endgame*, 22.

99. Beckett, "Capital of the Ruins," 277.

100. My interpretation here differs sharply from Lois Gordon's. Gordon writes about this passage, "Beckett exalts both the comfort to be drawn from the inward human capacity to surmount circumstances of the utmost gravity and the sustenance to be given and gained in moments of camaraderie." Lois Gordon, *The World of Samuel Beckett* (New Haven, CT: Yale University Press, 1996), 201.

101. Beckett, *Worstward Ho*, 22.

102. Beckett, "Sottisier" notebook, 23.3.81.

103. Beckett's other inheritance from Shakespeare is the bard's observation that beauty "beggars description." The phrase is used in reference to Cleopatra: "For her own person, / It beggar'd all description." *Antony and Cleopatra* 2.2. *The Tragedy of Antony and Cleopatra*, ed. Jonathan Bate (Middlesex, UK: Echo Library, 2006), 33. Shakespeare suggests that beauty incapacitates or disemploys description, reducing it to tatters as it attempts to transform appearance into language. Much of Beckett's oeuvre is an exploration of what happens to this derelict and impoverished state of description not only in its encounter with beauty but with misery and the beggar as well.

104. Badiou, *On Beckett*, 89.

105. Beckett, *Worstward Ho*, 32.

106. Badiou, *On Beckett*, 94.

107. Beckett, *Worstward Ho*, 21, 43.

108. Walter Benjamin articulates the soldier's encounter with World War I in terms of impoverishment: "Wasn't it noticed at the time how many people returned from the front in silence? Not richer but poorer in communicable experience?" *Selected Writings*, 2:731.

109. In his poem "No Worst, There Is None," Gerard Manley Hopkins writes, "No worst, there is none. Pitched past pitch of grief, / More pangs will, schooled at forepangs, wilder wring." Through his disheveled grammar, Hopkins comes close to Beckett's vision of a text of the ever worsening. Through pain, Hopkins achieves a sense of the nontranscendent worst. Hopkins's text takes up Beckett's rhetorical hyperbole literally: he speaks about being pitched past pitch. (The word "hyperbole" comes from the Greek meaning "to throw wide"). *Pitched past pitch* of grief means to turn the worse into a type of excess of movement: Hopkins's poem struggles with pitch as a thing and pitch as a verb. Gerard Manley Hopkins, *Poems and Prose*, ed. W. H. Gardner (London: Penguin Books, 1985), 61.

110. Bataille, "Concerning the Accounts Given by the Residents of Hiroshima," 232.

Afterword

1. For Proust's narrator, art facilitates new vision and exerts its aftereffect within the spectator. When gazed upon long enough, for example, the figures within a Renoir leave the frame of the painting and begin to lend their qualities to people and vehicles seen in the street: "Women pass in the street, different from those we formerly saw, because they are Renoirs, those Renoirs we persistently refused to see as women. The carriages too, are Renoirs, and the water, and the sky." Marcel Proust, *In Search of Lost Time: The Guermantes Way*, trans. Christopher Prendergast (New York: Penguin, 2003), 325. Only by seeing Renoir in the world do we begin in fact to see what his paintings harbor. In like fashion, Proust's novel may sensitize us to Proustian moments in our world, to propagate the effects of his work through our own experience.

2. Of all the productions I've seen and been involved in, the setting that seems most fitting for Beckett's play would be a production on the Gaza Strip.

3. Harold Camping, an evangelist on the Family Radio Network, predicted that the world would end on May 21, 2011. When May 22 arrived without the righteous having ascended to heaven or the damned suffering fire, brimstone, and plagues on earth, Camping recalculated his prediction and gave the world an extended deadline until October 21, 2011. Between these two dates Camping suffered a stroke. Camping's followers had turned into Beckett characters, saddled with an expectation for something that not only did not arrive, but did not arrive twice, in two acts. One can

imagine a production of *Godot* staged outside Camping's radio studio, in which Didi and Gogo are two crestfallen apocalyptics who struggle with spirituality as a promise kept only at one end. The vagabonds would sweep up not after doom has arrived but after its prediction has failed.

4. Ross Douthat, "The Decadent Left," *New York Times*, December 4, 2011.

5. Quoted in Karen A. Frank and Te-Sheng Huang, "Occupying Public Space, 2011: From Tahrir Square to Zuccotti Park," in *Beyond Zuccotti Park*, ed. Ron Shiffman et al. (Oakland, CA: New Village Press, 2012), 8. On October 12, 2011, Michael Bloomberg, the mayor of New York City, came to Zuccotti Park to announce that the encampment would have to be temporarily removed in order to clean up the area. A concern for "sanitation" thinly concealed the politics behind the decision.

6. Samuel Beckett, *Three Novels*, 67.

7. The workers on strike in France in 1968 eventually refused to join the cause with protesting students.

8. Rebecca Solnit, "Civil Society at Ground Zero," in *The Occupy Handbook*, ed. Janet Byrne (New York: Back Bay Books, 2012), 297.

9. Chris Hedges, "A Master Class in Occupation," in Byrne, *Occupy Handbook*, 164–72. He writes, "The park, especially at night, is a magnet for the city's street population" (167).

10. Columbia University students protesting the Vietnam War occupied the president's office and other Columbia administrative buildings in 1968; ROTC headquarters have been occupied in Boston, New York, and Puerto Rico; the monument of Wounded Knee was seized in 1973 by Oglala Lakota protesting the US government's failure to fulfill treaties with Native American peoples.

11. Simpson, "First Dublin Production," in Cohn, *"Waiting for Godot,"* 34.

12. Todd Gitlin, *Occupy Nation: The Roots, the Spirit, and the Promise of Occupy Wall Street* (New York: HarperCollins, 2012), 109.

13. Judith Butler, "Bodies in Public," in *Occupy: Scenes from Occupied America*, ed. Astra Taylor and Keith Cessen (New York: Verso, 2011), 193.

14. Samuel Beckett, "Les Deux Besoins," in *Disjecta*, 56 (author's translation).

15. Beckett, *Waiting for Godot*, 21.

16. Ibid., 8.

17. Adorno, "Trying to Understand 'Endgame,'" 264.

18. Adorno, *Aesthetic Theory*, 39.

Bibliography

Abbott, H. Porter. "Samuel Beckett and the Arts of Time: Painting, Music, Narrative." In *Samuel Beckett and the Arts: Music, Visual Arts, and Non-Print Media*, edited by Lois Oppenheim, 7–24. New York: Garland Publishing, 1999.
Ackerley, C. J., and S. E. Gontarski, eds. *The Grove Companion to Samuel Beckett.* New York: Grove Press, 2004.
Adorno, Theodor. *Aesthetic Theory.* Edited by Gretel Adorno and Rolf Tiedemann. Translated by Robert Hullot-Kentor. Minneapolis: University of Minnesota Press, 1997.
———. *Negative Dialectics.* Translated by E. B. Ashton. New York: Continuum, 1973.
———. *Noten zur Literatur.* Frankfurt: Suhrkamp, 1974.
———. "Notes on Beckett." Translated by Dirk Van Hulle and Shane Weller. *Journal of Beckett Studies* 19, no. 2 (2010): 157–78.
———. *Notes to Literature II.* Translated by Shierry Weber Nicholsen. New York: Columbia University Press, 1991.
Adorno, Theodor, Walter Benjamin, Ernst Bloch, Bertolt Brecht, Georg Lukács, and Frederic Jameson. *Aesthetics and Politics.* Edited by Fredric Jameson. Translated by Ronald Taylor. London: Verso, 1977.
Agamben, Giorgio. *Homo Sacer: Sovereign Power and Bare Life.* Translated by Daniel Heller-Roazen. Stanford, CA: Stanford University Press, 1998.
Albright, Daniel. *Beckett and Aesthetics.* Cambridge: Cambridge University Press, 2003.
Anouilh, Jean. "'Godot' or the Music-Hall Sketch of Pascal's Pensées as Played by the Fratellini Clowns." In Cohn, *Casebook on "Waiting for Godot,"* 12–13.
Badiou, Alain. *On Beckett.* Edited by Nina Power and Alberto Toscano. Manchester, UK: Clinamen Press, 2003.
Bair, Deidre. *Samuel Beckett, a Biography.* New York: Harcourt Brace Jovanovich, 1978.
Bandman, C. "The Play's the Thing . . ." *San Quentin News*, November 28, 1957.

Barthes, Roland. *Camera Lucida.* Translated by Richard Howard. New York: Noonday Press, 1981.
———. *La chambre claire: Note sur la photographie.* Paris: Gallimard, 1980.
———. *Critical Essays.* Translated by Richard Howard. Evanston, IL: Northwestern University Press, 1972.
———. *On Racine.* Translated by Richard Howard. New York: Performing Arts Journal Publications, 1983.
Bataille, Georges. "Concerning the Accounts Given by the Residents of Hiroshima." In Caruth, *Trauma,* 221–35.
———. "Molloy's Silence." In *Modern Critical Interpretations: Samuel Beckett's Molloy, Malone Dies, The Unnamable,* edited by Harold Bloom, 13–24. New Haven, CT: Chelsea House, 1988.
———. "Le silence de Molloy." *Critique* 7, no. 15 (1951). 387-96.1970.
Bataille, George, Michel Leiris, Marcel Griaule, Carl Einstein, Robert Desnos et al. *Encyclopedia Acephalica.* London: Atlas Press, 1995.
Baudelaire, Charles. *Oeuvres Complètes.* Paris: Gallimard, 1951.
———. *The Painter of Modern Life and Other Essays.* Translated by Jonathan Mayne. New York: Da Capo Press, 1964.
Baudrillard, Jean. *Screened Out.* Translated by Chris Turner. New York: Verso, 2002.
Bean, Annemarie, ed. *A Sourcebook of African-American Performance: Plays, People, Movements.* New York: Routledge, 1999.
Beckett, Samuel. *Collected Poems in English and French.* New York: Grove Press, 1977.
———. *The Collected Shorter Plays.* Edited by S. E. Gontarski. New York: Grove Press, 1984.
———. *Complete Short Prose, 1929–1989.* Edited by S. E. Gontarski. New York: Grove Press, 1995.
———. *Company.* New York: Grove Press, 1991.
———. *Disjecta.* Edited by Ruby Cohn. London: Calder, 1983.
———. *Eleuthéria.* London: Foxrock, 1998.
———. *Endgame.* New York: Grove Press, 1958.
———. *First Love and Other Shorts.* New York: Grove Press, 1995.
———. *How It Is.* New York: Grove Press, 1964.
———. *Ill Seen, Ill Said.* London: Calder, 1982.
———. *L'Innommable.* Paris: Editions de Minuit, 1953.
———. "J. M. Mime." In *Samuel Beckett: An exhibition.* Edited by James Knowlson. London: Turret Books, 1971.
———. *Molloy.* Paris: Minuit, 1951.
———. *Murphy.* London: Calder, 1993.
———. *No Author Better Served: The Correspondence of Samuel Beckett and Alan Schneider.* Edited by Maurice Harmon. Cambridge, MA: Harvard University Press, 1999.
———. *Notes Diverse Holo.* Edited by Matthijs Engelberts and Everett Frost with Jane Maxwell. Amsterdam: Rodopi, 2006.
———. *Proust and Three Dialogues with Georges Duthuit.* London: Calder, 1991.
———. "Sottisier" Notebook, MS2901, *Beckett Collection,* University of Reading.
———. *Stories and Texts for Nothing.* Translated by Samuel Beckett. New York: Grove Press, 1967.
———. *The Theatrical Notebooks of Samuel Beckett.* Volume 1, "Waiting for Godot." Edited by Dougald McMillan and James Knowlson. New York: Grove Press, 1994.
———. *Three Novels: Molloy, Malone Dies, The Unnamable.* Translated by Samuel Beckett. New York: Grove Press, 1991.

―――. *Waiting for Godot.* New York: Grove Press, 1982.
―――. *Worstward Ho.* New York: Grove Press, 1983.
Benjamin, Walter. *Illuminationen.* Frankfurt: Suhrkamp, 1977.
―――. *Illuminations.* Translated by Harry Zohn. Edited by Hannah Arendt. New York: Schocken, 1969.
―――. *Reflections.* Edited by Peter Demetz. Translated by Edmund Jephcott. New York: Schocken, 1986.
―――. *Selected Writings Volume 1, 1913–1926.* Edited by Marcus Bullock and Michael W. Jennings. Translated by Edmund Jephcott. Cambridge, MA: Harvard University Press, 1996.
―――. *Selected Writings Volume 2, 1927–1934.* Edited by Michael Jennings, Howard Eiland, and Gary Smith. Translated by Rodney Livingstone et al. Cambridge, MA: Harvard University Press, 1999.
Bersani, Leo. *Balzac to Beckett: Center and Circumference in French Fiction.* Cambridge, MA: Harvard University Press, 1972.
Bersani, Leo, and Ulysse Dutoit. *Arts of Impoverishment.* Cambridge, MA: Harvard University Press, 1993.
Blanchot, Maurice. *La Folie du Jour.* Paris: Fata Morgana, 1973.
―――. *Le Livre à Venir.* Paris: Gallimard, 1959.
―――. *The Madness of the Day.* Translated by Lydia Davis. New York: Station Hill, 1981.
―――. *La Part du Feu.* Paris: Gallimard, 1949.
―――. *The Work of Fire.* Translated by Charlotte Mandell. Stanford, CA: Stanford University Press, 1995.
Blau, Herbert. *As If: An Autobiography.* Ann Arbor: University of Michigan Press, 2011.
―――. *Sails of the Herring Fleet: Essays on Beckett.* Ann Arbor: University of Michigan Press, 2004.
Boll, Andrea. "Puking My Puke of a Life in Waiting for Godot in New Orleans." In Chan, *Field Guide*, 239–41.
Boxall, Peter, ed. *"Waiting for Godot" and "Endgame": A Reader's Guide to Essential Criticism.* New York: Palgrave Macmillan, 2003.
Bradby, David. *Beckett: "Waiting for Godot."* Cambridge: Cambridge University Press, 2001.
Brater, Enoch. *Beyond Minimalism: Beckett's Late Style in the Theater.* Oxford: Oxford University Press, 1987.
―――. *Why Beckett.* London: Thames & Hudson, 1989.
Brecht, Bertolt. *Brecht on Theater.* Translated by John Willet. New York: Hill & Wang, 1991.
Bryden, Mary. "Gender in Transition: 'Godot' and 'Endgame.'" In Connor, *A New Casebook*, 151–63.
Burke, Edmund. *A Philosophical Enquiry into the Origin of Our Ideas of the Sublime and Beautiful.* Oxford: Oxford University Press, 2009.
Butler, Judith. "Bodies in Public." In *Occupy: Scenes from Occupied America*, edited by Astra Taylor and Keith Cessen, 192. New York: Verso, 2011.
Byrne, Janet, ed. *The Occupy Handbook.* New York: Back Bay Books, 2011.
Caruth, Cathy, ed. *Trauma: Explorations in Memory.* Baltimore: Johns Hopkins University Press, 1995.
Cavell, Stanley. *Emerson: Transcendental Etudes.* Stanford, CA: Stanford University Press, 2003.
―――. *Must We Mean What We Say?* Cambridge: Cambridge University Press, 1976.

Chan, Paul. "Provocation: Next Day, Same Place. After 'Godot' in New Orleans," *TDR/The Drama Review* 52, no. 4 (Winter 2008): 2–3.

———, ed. *Waiting for Godot in New Orleans: A Field Guide*. New York: Creative Time Books, 2009.

Chan, Paul, and Kathy Halbreich. "Undoing: A Conversation between Kathy Halbreich and Paul Chan." In Chan, *Field Guide*, 306–21.

Chion, Michel. *The Voice in Cinema*. Translated by Claudia Gorbman. New York: Columbia University Press, 1999.

Cioran, E. M. "Encounters with Beckett." In Graver and Federman, *Samuel Beckett: The Critical Heritage*, 334–39.

Clausewitz, Carl von. *On War*. Translated by J. J. Graham. London: N. Trübner, 1873.

Clément, Bruno. *L'Oeuvre sans qualités: Rhétorique de Samuel Beckett*. Paris: Editions du Seuil, 1994.

Cluchey, Rick. *The Cage*. San Francisco: Barbwire Press, 1970.

———. "My Years with Beckett." In *Theatre Workbook 1: Krapp's Last Tape*, edited by James Knowlson, 120–23. London: Brutus Books Limited, 1980.

——— and Michael Haerdter. "*Krapp's Last Tape*: production report." In *Theatre Workbook 1: Krapp's Last Tape*, edited by James Knowlson. 124–41. London: Brutus Books Limited, 1980.

Cohn, Ruby. *A Beckett Canon*. Ann Arbor: University of Michigan Press, 2005.

———, ed. *Casebook on "Waiting for Godot."* New York: Grove Press, 1967.

———. *From Desire to "Godot": Pocket Theater of Postwar Paris*. Berkeley: University of California Press, 1987.

———, ed. *Samuel Beckett's "Waiting for Godot": A Casebook*. London: Macmillan, 1987.

Connor, Steven. *Samuel Beckett's "Waiting for Godot" and "Endgame": A New Casebook*. Basingstoke, UK: Macmillan, 1992.

———. *Theory and Cultural Value*. Cambridge, MA: Blackwell, 1992.

Craig, George, Martha Dow Fehsenfeld, Dan Gunn, and Lois More Overbeck, eds. *The Letters of Samuel Beckett, 1941–1956*. Cambridge: Cambridge University Press, 2011.

Deleuze, Gilles. *Bergsonism*. Translated by Hugh Tomlinson. Cambridge, MA: Zone Books, 1990.

Deleuze, Gilles, and Felix Guattari. *Anti-Oedipus*. Translated by Mark Seem. Minnesota: Minnesota University Press, 1986.

———. *What Is Philosophy?* Translated by Hugh Tomlinson and Graham Burchell. New York: Columbia University Press, 1994.

de Man, Paul. *Allegories of Reading*. New Haven, CT: Yale University Press, 1982.

Derrida, Jacques. *Acts of Literature*. Edited by Derek Attridge. New York: Routledge, 1992.

———. *Negotiations*. Edited and translated by Elizabeth Rottenberg. Stanford, CA: Stanford University Press, 2002.

———. *Writing and Difference*. Translated by Alan Bass. Chicago: University of Chicago Press, 1978.

Diamond, Elin. "Re: Blau, Butler, Beckett, and the Politics of Seeming." *TDR/The Drama Review* 44, no. 4 (Winter 2000): 31–43.

———. "'The Society of My Likes': Beckett's Political Imaginary." In *Samuel Beckett: Endlessness in the Year 2000*, edited by Angela Moorjani and Carola Veit, 382–88. Amsterdam: Rodopi, 2002.

Douthat, Ross. "The Decadent Left." *New York Times*, December 4, 2011.

Driver, Tom. "Tom Driver in 'Columbia University Forum.'" In Graver and Federman, *Samuel Beckett: The Critical Heritage*, 217–23.

Duckworth, Colin, ed. Introduction to *En Attendant Godot*. London: Harrap, 1966.
Ellman, Richard. *James Joyce*. Oxford: Oxford University Press, 1959.
Erickson, Jon. "The Body as Object of Modern Performance." *Journal of Dramatic Theory and Criticism* (Fall 1990): 231–43.
Esslin, Martin, ed. *Samuel Beckett: A Collection of Critical Essays*. Englewood Cliffs, NJ: Prentice Hall, 1965.
———. *The Theatre of the Absurd*. New York: Anchor Books, 1961.
Fahy, Thomas Richard, and Kimball King, eds. *Captive Audience: Prison and Captivity in Contemporary Theater*. New York: Routledge, 2003.
Fazzone, Amanda. "Walls within Walls." *Washington City Paper*. http://65.79.227.222/articles/17051/walls-within-walls
Feldman, Matthew. "'Agnostic Quietism' and Samuel Beckett's Early Development." In *Samuel Beckett: History, Memory, Archive*, edited by Seán Kennedy and Katherine Weiss, 183–200. London: Palgrave Macmillan, 2009.
Foucault, Michel. *Ethics: Subjectivity and Truth*. Edited by Paul Rabinow. New York: New Press, 1998.
———. *The Foucault Reader*. Edited by Paul Rabinow. New York: Pantheon, 1981.
———. *The Order of Things: An Archaeology of the Human Sciences*. Translated by Mark Seem. New York: Vintage, 1973.
Frank, Karen A., and Te-Sheng Huang. "Occupying Public Space, 2011: From Tahrir Square to Zuccotti Park." In *Beyond Zuccotti Park*, edited by Ron Shiffman et al., 3–20. Oakland, CA: New Village Press, 2012.
Freud, Sigmund. *Writings on Art and Literature*. Stanford, CA: Stanford University Press, 1997.
Frost, Everett. "Letter to the Editor." *Beckett Circle* 16, no. 1 (Spring 1994): 5.
Gisleson, Anne. "Godot Is Great." In Chan, *Field Guide*, 214–17.
Gitlin, Todd. *Occupy Nation: The Roots, the Spirit, and the Promise of Occupy Wall Street*. New York: HarperCollins, 2012.
Gordon, Lois. "'No Exit' and 'Waiting for Godot:' Performances in Contrast." In Fahy and King, *Captive Audience*, 166–88.
———. *Reading "Godot."* New Haven, CT: Yale University Press, 2002.
———. *The World of Samuel Beckett*. New Haven, CT: Yale University Press, 1996.
Goytisolo, Juan. *Landscapes of War, from Sarajevo to Chechnya*. Translated by Peter Bush. San Francisco: City Lights, 2000.
Graver, Lawrence, and Raymond Federman, eds. *Samuel Beckett: The Critical Heritage*. New York: Routledge & Kegan Paul, 1979.
Griffin, Tim. "'Waiting for Godot': Paul Chan in New Orleans." *Artforum International* 46, no. 4 (December 2007): 51.
Hadžiselimović, Omer, and Zvonimir Radeljković. "Literature Is What You Should Re-Read: An Interview with Susan Sontag." *Spirit of Bosnia* 2, no. 2 (April 2007). http://www.spiritofbosnia.org/volume-2-no-2-2007-april/literature-is-what-you-should-re-read-an-interview-with-susan-sontag/.
Hardt, Michael. "Prison Time." In *Genet: In the Language of the Enemy*, edited by Scott Durham, *Yale French Studies* 91 (1997): 64–79.
Harris, Michael. "'Godot' Presented at Quentin." *San Francisco Chronicle*, November 24, 1957, 23.
Hedges, Chris. "A Master Class in Occupation." In Byrne, *Occupy Handbook*, 164–72.
Hegel, G. W. F. *The Philosophy of History*. Translated by J. Sibree. New York: Dover, 1956.
———. *Vorlesungen Über die Philosophie der Geschichte*. Stuttgart: Phillip Reclam, 1961.

Heidegger, Martin. *Holzwege*. Frankfurt: Vittorio Klostermann, 1950.
———. *Poetry, Language, Thought*. Translated by Albert Hofstadter. New York: Harper & Row, 1971.
———. *The Question Concerning Technology and Other Essays*. Translated by William Lovitt. New York: Harper Torchbooks, 1977.
Hill, Leslie. *Beckett's Fiction: In Different Words*. Cambridge: Cambridge University Press, 1990.
Hollier, Denis. *Les dépossédés*. Paris: Minuit, 1993.
Homan, Sidney. *Beckett's Theaters: Interpretations for Performance*. Lewisburg, PA: Bucknell University Press, 1984.
———. *The Embarrassment of Swans*. Unpublished memoir.
Hopkins, Gerard Manley. *Poems and Prose*. Edited by W. H. Gardner. London: Penguin, 1985.
Horne, Jed. "Is New Orleans Waiting for Godot?" In Chan, *Field Guide*, 242–47.
Houston Jones, David. *Samuel Beckett and Testimony*. London: Palgrave Macmillan, 2011.
Insdorf, Annette. *Indelible Shadows: Film and the Holocaust*. Cambridge: Cambridge University Press, 1989.
Iser, Wolfgang. "Counter-sensical Comedy in 'Waiting for Godot.'" In Connor, *A New Casebook*, 55–68.
Jauss, Hans Robert. *Towards an Aesthetic of Reception*. Translated by Timothy Bahti. New York: Harvester Press, 1982.
Kafka, Franz. *Diaries*. Translated by Willa and Edwin Muir. New York: Schocken Press, 1975.
———. "The Silence of the Sirens." In *Franz Kafka, The Complete Stories*. Edited by Nahum N. Glatzer. Translated by Willa and Edwin Muir. New York: Schocken, 1971.
———. *Tagebücher*. Berlin: Fischer Verlag, 1967.
Kalb, Jonathan. *Beckett in Performance*. Cambridge: Cambridge University Press, 1989.
Kaltenheuser, Skip. "The Prison Playwright." *Gadfly*, September/October 1999, 5.
Kant, Immanuel. *Critique of Judgment*. Translated by James Creed Meredith. Oxford: Oxford University Press, 2007.
———. *Foundations on the Metaphysics of Morals*. Translated by Oskar Piest. Indianapolis: Bobbs-Merrill, 1959.
Kenner, Hugh. *A Reader's Guide to Samuel Beckett*. London: Thames & Hudson, 1973.
———. *Samuel Beckett: A Critical Study*. Berkeley: University of California Press, 1973.
Kerr, Walter. "Oh Beckett, Poor Beckett!" *New York Times*, February 11, 1973, 146.
Knowlson, James. "Beckett's Production Notebooks." In Cohn, *"Waiting for Godot": A Casebook*, 52–53.
———. *Damned to Fame: The Life of Samuel Beckett*. New York: Simon & Schuster, 1996.
———. *"Krapp's Last Tape": Samuel Beckett's Production Notebook*. New York: Grove/Atlantic, 1991.
Knowlson, James, and John Pilling. *Frescoes of the Skull: The Later Prose and Drama of Samuel Beckett*. New York: Grove Press, 1980.
Koshal, Erin. "'Some Exceptions' and the 'Normal Thing': Reconsidering 'Waiting for Godot's' Theatrical Form through Its Prison Performances." *Modern Drama* 53, no. 2 (2010): 187–210.
Lambert-Beatty, Carrie. "Essentially Alien: Notes from Outside Paul Chan's 'Godot.'" *Parkett* 88 (2007): 76–81.
Lamont, Rosette C. "Letter to the Editor." *Beckett Circle* 16, no.1 (Spring 1994): 4.
"Letter to the Editor." *Le Monde*. February 2, 1953.

Levinas, Emmanuel. *Existence and Existents.* Translated by Alphonso Lingis. Pittsburgh: Duquesne University Press, 2001.Mannes, Marya. "Two Tramps." In Cohn, *"Waiting for Godot,"* 30–31.
McMillan, Dougald, and Martha Fehsenfeld. *Beckett in the Theatre: Volume 1, from "Waiting for Godot" to "Krapp's Last Tape."* London: Calder, 1988.
Mercier, Vivian. *Beckett/Beckett.* Oxford: Oxford University Press, 1977.
———. "The Uneventful Event." *Irish Times,* February 18, 1956, 6.
Moses, Gilbert, John O'Neal, Denise Nicholas, Murray Levy, and Richard Schechner. "Dialog: The Free Southern Theater." In Bean, *Sourcebook,* 102–13.
Munk, Erika. "Notes from a Trip to Sarajevo." *Theater* 24, no. 3 (1993): 14–30.
———. "Only the Possible: An Interview with Susan Sontag." *Theater* 24, no. 3 (1993): 31–36.
———. "Reports from the 21st Century: A Sarajevo Interview." *Theater* 24, no. 3 (1993): 9–13.
———. "Sontag Stages 'Godot' in Sarajevo." *Beckett Circle* 15, no. 2 (Fall 1993): 2.
Nancy, Jean-Luc. *The Birth to Presence.* Translated by Elizabeth Rottenberg. Stanford, CA: Stanford University Press, 1993.
Nietzsche, Friedrich. *Basic Writings of Nietzsche.* Translated by Walter Kaufmann. New York: Modern Library, 1980.
Nixon, Mark. *Samuel Beckett's German Diaries, 1936–1937.* London: Continuum, 2011.
Nussbaum, Martha. *The Fragility of Goodness.* Revised edition. Cambridge: Cambridge University Press, 2001.
O'Neal, John. "Motion in the Ocean: Some Political Dimensions of the Free Southern Theater." In Bean, *Sourcebook,* 114–20.
Oppenheim, Lois, ed. *Directing Beckett.* Ann Arbor: University of Michigan Press, 1994.
———. *The Painted Word: Samuel Beckett's Dialogue with Art.* Ann Arbor: University of Michigan Press, 2000.
———. "Playing with Beckett's Plays: On Sontag in Sarajevo and Other Directorial Infidelities." *Journal of Beckett Studies* 4, no. 2 (Spring 1995): 35–46.
Orgel, Stephen. "The Play of Conscience." In *Performativity and Performance,* edited by Andrew Parker and Eve Kosofsky Sedgwick, 133–51. New York: Routledge, 1995.
Proust, Marcel. *In Search of Lost Time: The Guermantes Way.* Translated by Christopher Prendergast. New York: Penguin, 2003.
Puchner, Martin. *Stage Fright: Modernism, Anti-Theatricality, and Drama.* Baltimore: Johns Hopkins University Press, 2002.
Rabaté, Jean-Michel. "Philosophizing with Beckett: Adorno and Badiou." In *A Companion to Samuel Beckett,* edited by S. E. Gontarski, 97–117. Malden, MA: Wiley-Blackwell, 2010.
Rank, Otto. *The Myth of the Birth of the Hero.* New York: Vintage, 1959.
Ricks, Christopher. *Beckett's Dying Words.* Oxford: Oxford University Press, 1993.
Roach, Joseph. "All the Dead Voices." In *Land/Scape/Theater,* edited by Elinor Fuchs and Una Chaudhuri, 84–93. Ann Arbor: University of Michigan Press, 2002.
———. "The Great Hole of History." In *Reflections on Beckett: A Centenary Celebration,* edited by Anna McMullan and S. E. Wilmer, 134–48. Ann Arbor: University of Michigan Press, 2009.
Robbe-Grillet, Alain. "Samuel Beckett, or Presence on Stage." In *For a New Novel: Essays on Fiction,* translated by Richard Howard, 111–26. New York: Grove Press, 1965.
Ronen, Ilan. "'Waiting for Godot' as Political Theater." In Oppenheim, *Directing Beckett,* 239–49. Ann Arbor: University of Michigan Press, 1994.

Ross, Ciaran. *Beckett's Art of Absence: Rethinking the Void*. London: Palgrave Macmillan, 2011.
Sartre, Jean-Paul. *Bariona, or the Son of Thunder*. In *The Writings of Jean-Paul Sartre, volume 2, Selected Prose,* edited by Michel Rybalka and Michel Contat, 72–136. Evanston, IL: Northwestern University Press, 1985.
Saussure, Ferdinand de. *Course in General Linguistic*. Translated by Wade Baskin. New York: Philosophical Library, 1959.
Schama, Simon. *Landscape and Memory*. New York: Dutton, 1995.
Shakespeare, William. *The Kittredge Shakespeare's King Lear*. Edited by George Lyman Kittredge, Irving Ribner, and Scott Foresman. New York: Blaisdell, 1968.
———. *The Tragedy of Antony and Cleopatra*. edited by Jonathan Bate. Middlesex: Echo Library, 2006.
Shenker, Israel. "An Interview with Beckett." In Graver and Federman, *Samuel Beckett: The Critical Heritage,* 146–49.
Shrdlu, Etaoin. "Bastille by the Bay." *San Quentin News,* November 28, 1957, 3.
Simpson, Alan. "First Dublin Production." In Cohn, *"Waiting for Godot,"* 33–37.
Smith, David. "In Godot We Trust." *Observer,* March 7, 2009, 8.
Solnit, Rebecca. "Civil Society at Ground Zero." In Byrne, *Occupy Handbook,* 294–99.
Sontag, Susan. *Where the Stress Falls*. New York: Picador, 2001.
States, Burt O. *The Shape of Paradox: An Essay on "Waiting for Godot."* Berkeley: University of California Press, 1978.
Strayton, Richard. "Inmates Waiting for 'Godot.'" *Los Angeles Herald Examiner,* May 8, 1988, 9.
Suvin, Darko. *To Brecht and Beyond*. Sussex, UK: Harvester Books, 1984.
Thompson, Nato. "Destroyer of Worlds." In Chan, *Field Guide,* 58.
Tretiakov, Sergei. "Bert Brecht." In *Brecht: A Collection of Critical Essays,* edited by Peter Demetz, 16–25. Englewood Cliffs, NJ: Prentice Hall, 1962.
Turan, Kenneth. *Sundance to Sarajevo: Film Festivals and the World They Made*. Berkeley: University of California Press, 2002.
Valéry, Paul. *Sea Shells*. Translated by Mary Oliver. Boston: Beacon Press, 1998.
Villiers, Sara. "Beware of the Snipers." *The Herald* (Glasgow), August 20, 1993.
Westerdorp, Tjebbe. "Catharsis in Beckett's Late Drama: A New Model of Transaction?" In *Samuel Beckett Today/Aujourd'hui 1,* edited by Marius Buning, Sief Houppermans, and Daniele de Ruyter, 106–13. Amsterdam: Rodopi, 1992.
Whitman, Alden. "In the Wilderness for 20 Years." *New York Times,* October 24, 1969, 32.
Zilliacus, Clas. "Three Times 'Godot': Beckett, Brecht, Bulatovic." *Comparative Drama* 4, no. 1 (Spring 1970): 3–17.

Index

abandonment, 2–4, 8, 33, 66–67, 73, 105, 110–11, 125, 131, 146, 161–65, 180, 183, 218n66; of buildings in New Orleans, 106–7; dialectical view of, 163–64; of hope, 161; to law, 131, 136; and myth, 214n62; nonlimited view of, 161–63; of words, 126–28; of works, 73–74, 162–63; and writing, 161–63. See also *From an Abandoned Work*
Abbott, H. Porter, 76
absurdity 12–14, in Eastern Bloc, 8; in New Orleans, 109–11; in prison, 12–14, 18, 24; in Sarajevo, 66–67; in Zuccotti Park, 181–82
Adorno, Theodor, 16, 29, 34, 38, 47, 65–66, 98, 108, 137. 143, 145–46, 150, 163–67, 186, 188, 193n14, 202n10, 205n89; on commitment 163–65; on rhetorical questions, 150–52
Agamben, Giorgio, 2, 16
Akalaitis, JoAnne, 18, 104, 106–7, 208n160,
Albright, Daniel, 195n41
animality, *see* vagabond thought; murmur

Anouilh, Jean, 16–17, 95, 194n16
aquilex (water gatherer), 75–77, 161
Arts of Impoverishment (Bersani and Dutoit), 146
Asmus, Walter, 53
Audiberti, Jacques, 53
author, *see* warden

Badiou, Alain, 133–34, 175–76, 209n171
Bandman, C., 19, 24–25, 43–47, 68, 199n108, 199n114, 200n119
Banksy, 86
Bardot, Brigitte, 23
Bariona, or the Son of Thunder (Sartre), 28–29
Barthes, Roland, 151–52, 192n8, 216n36
Belgrade, Godot performance in, 7–9, 188
Boussagol, Bruno, 34
Bataille, Georges, 11, 137–40, 161, 176–77. *See also* myth
Baudelaire, Charles, 170–71, 220n94
Baudrillard, Jean, 63, 74
Beckett, Samuel, challenge to readers, 143–46; directing *Godot*, 19–20,

95–96; dream of indigence, 143–45; estate of, 5–6, 192n13; on gender of actors of *Godot*, 33–34; physical confinement of his actors, 17, 194n22; stage directions, 5, 17–19, 144, 298n160; supervision of actors' movements, 17–20; symptomatic of our age of mass uprooting and detainees, 6–7; and televised *Godot*, 20–21; and theater of crisis, 6–9; as volunteer at Irish Red Cross Hospital, 171–73; as witness, 64–69. See also *Capital of the Ruins; Catastrophe; Eleuthéria; Endgame; From an Abandoned Work; Ill Seen Ill Said; Malone Dies; Molloy; Murphy;* "Sottisier" notebook, *Unnamable, Waiting for Godot*
begging, and charity 140–42, 171–73; and choosing, 126; and contingency, 139–41; and language, 221n103; and myth 136–42; questions, 152–57. See also *petitio principii*
Belgrade, *Godot* production in, 7–9, 188
Belgrade Drama Theater, 7
Benjamin, Walter, 2, 110, 116, 136–40, 191n5, 199n105, 210n177, 214n61, 221n108
Bernstein, Jonathan, 179
Bersani, Leo, 115–16, 130–31, 146, 160
Bibanovic, Dubravko, 79
Blanchot, Maurice, 101, 134–35. See also *La Folie du jour*
Blau, Herbert, 9, 30, 34, 36, 39–40, 96, 197n74, 198n80, 207n133
Blin, Roger, 42–43, 183, 193n15, 195n41, 197n73
Boll, Andrea, 88–91
Bomb Shelter (Bibanovic), 79
Bond, James Bond, 84
Bradby, David, 64–65, 105, 209n162
Brando, Marlon, 40
Brater, Enoch, 32–33, 152–53
Breath (Beckett), 216n37
Brecht, Bertolt, 2–5, 24, 39, 42, 45–46, 56, 58–59, 186–87, 191n5, 192n8, 192n9, 192n10, 215n5; and *Gegenentwurf* for *Waiting for Godot*, 3–5
Bryden, Mary, 33
Burke, Edmund, 37

Butler, Judith, 182
bystanding, 188–89

The Cage (Cluchey), 9, 47–53, 200n135
Camping, Harold,
Camus, Albert, 13, 18, 186
Capital of the Ruins (Beckett), 171–73
Catastrophe (Beckett), 32–33
catharsis, 9; in prison, 44–47; in a protest 188–89; in war 67–69
Cavell, Stanley, 159
Chan, Paul, 6, 9–10, 14–15, 23, 30, 64, 70, 84–97, 100–107, 109–11, 210n175; and Beckett's stage directions, 97; staging play near illuminated levee 89–90; and the uncanny, 84–87
Chaplin, Charlie, 53, 97
Chekhov, Anton, 87–88
Cioran, E. M., 76–77
Classical Theater of Harlem, 9, 64
Clément, Bruno, 154, 217n47
Clinton, Bill, 15, 23, 91, 95, 100, 111
closed system 5–6, 9, 35–38, 55–57, 63, 96, 118, 197n78; and closed space, 16, 19, 30, 36, 198n87; of prison library, 198n91
Cluchey, Rick, 9, 12, 15, 36–40, 47–52, 57, 68, 195n39, 198n87, 198n99, 200n121, 200n125, 201n135. See also *The Cage*, prison, San Quentin Drama Workshop, *The Wall is Mama*
Cohn, Ruby, 162, 193n15
Connor, Steven, 145
context, beyond the stage, 3–7, 14–15,146–48; and *Godot*, 3, 142–44; on stage, 4–5, 144–46. See also no-man's-land
Critique of Judgment (Kant), 219n84

De Man, Paul, 216n38, 219n82
De Saussure, Ferdinand, 82
defenselessness, 16, 67–68, 93–94, 136–38
Deleuze, Gilles, 150, 213n32
Derrida, Jacques, 145–46, 209n162
Diamond, Elin, 4
Dickens, Charles, 2
Dinulović, Prerag, 7

INDEX • 233

Dutoit, Ulysse, 115–16, 146, 160

Eleuthéria (Beckett), 28, 60–61, 196n50
Ellman, Richard, 169
Endgame (Beckett), 17–18, 23, 25, 29, 34, 49, 65, 80, 91, 93, 99–100, 104, 106, 108, 143, 146, 150, 164
Erickson, Jon, 201n150
Esslin, Martin, 6–7, 12–14, 18, 26–29, 38, 44, 60, 64
enough, 82–84, 205n87
exposure, and bare life, 2; of Beckett's prose, 149–50, 159, 170–71; of ear, 121–27; of vagabonds 16–17, 131–35, 184–86

Facebook era, 184
FEMA, 5, 15, 23, 64, 88–90, 94, 100, 111
Foundations of the Metaphysics of Morals (Kant), 166, 220n89
fourth wall, 56–58
Free Southern Theater, 70–72, 74
Freud, Sigmund, 85–86, 219n88
From an Abandoned Work (Beckett), 76, 161–63
Frost, Everett, 5, 78–79

Genet, Jean, 13, 29
Giacometti, Alberto, 81–82, 205n79
Gitlin, Todd, 182
Gontarski, S. E., 162
Gordon, Lois, 195n48, 196n56, 220n100
Gregory, André, 23, 195n36
Goytisolo, Juan, 67, 72, 93
Guattari, Félix, 150, 212n32

Hall, Peter, 194n23, 196n57, 207n133
Hamlet (Shakespeare), 44–45
Harvey, Lawrence, 1, 157
Havel, Václav, 32–33, 197n67
Hayles, N. Katherine, 197n78
Hedges, Chris, 181
Hegel, G.W. F., 47, 55, 211n30
Heidegger, Martin, 17, 66–67, 150, 209, 216n34; on destitute time, 66
Homan, Sidney, 22, 39, 52–54, 57–59

Hopkins, Gerard Manley, 221n109
Houston Jones, David, 35–38, 202n11
How It Is (Beckett), 154, 158–61, 168, 218n56, 218n62,
Hugo, Victor, 2, 92
hypothetical imperative,

Ill Seen, Ill Said (Beckett), 135, 137

Jakobson, Roman, 125
James, Harold Dean, 179
Jauss, Hans Robert, 153
Jönson, Jan, 19, 73
Jouanneau, Joel, 105
Joyce, James, 65, 75–76, 92, 114, 145, 158; dictating to Beckett, 169

Kafka, Franz, 2, 24, 51, 69, 73, 93, 99, 119, 145, 160, 163, 165, 191n6, 207n142
Kalb, Jonathan, 26, 65
Kant, Immanuel, 134, 166–67, 219n84, 220n89. See also hypothetical imperative
Katrina, 1, 3, 6, 64, 66, 84–89, 100–101, 106, 110, 178, 207n131; photographic depictions of, 110–11
Keaton, Buster, 40
Kelly, Emmett, 60
Kenner, Hugh, 35, 60, 80, 196n58, 199n109, 213n57
Knowlson, James, 29, 31–32, 42, 59, 81, 146–47
Koshal, Erin, 19, 56–60
Kumla Prison, 14–15

Lacan, Jacques, 129
La Folie du jour (Blanchot) 134
La Santé Prison, 13, 31–32
lavatory lights, 124–25
Lembke, K. F., 9, 12, 41–43, 48, 59, 68
Les Misérables, 2
Levinas, Emmanuel, 97–98
Lower Ninth Ward, 5–6, 11, 64, 85–96, 100, 103, 106, 121, 179; as stage set for Godot, 103–4
Lüttringhausen Prison, 3, 5, 12, 48;

performances of *Godot* in, 14–16, 41–43, 59

Malone Dies (Beckett), 118, 118–19, 148, 156–57, 211n18, 211n19, 214n63, 218n53
Mandell, Alan, 196n60, 198n88
Manzay, J. Kyle, 89
McComb, Mississippi, performances of *Godot* in, 3, 70–72, 206n116
Mercier, Vivian, 6, 92, 96
Miami Herald, 15
Molloy, 13, 116–39, 154–56, 160–62, 166–68, 181, 206n116, 210n12, 210n13, 213n38, 213n54, 214n72
Moses, Gilbert, 203n32
Munk, Erika, 68, 82, 204n67
murmur, 40, 123, 162–63, 211n30; and address, 211n16, 220n90; and animality, 118–20; heard with head, not ear, 116–18; on stage, 119–21; and hypothetical imperatives, 166–68, and vagabond thought, 116–21; between prison walls, 53, 132
Murphy (Beckett), 35, 197n77

Nagin, Ray, 103
Nancy, Jean-Luc, 131–32
New Orleans, 1, 3, 4, 6, 9, 14–16, 23, 27, 64, 207n146; post-Katrina impoverishment of, 92–94; response to *Godot*, 100–103; as setting for *Godot*, 64–67, 88–90, 101, 103, 106–7; surreal post-Katrina landscape of, 84–87, 205n91; waiting transformed in, 26–27. *See also* Ray Nagin; Lower Ninth Ward; Paul Chan
99% Theater Company, 11, 183
No Exit (Sartre), 18, 28
no-man's-land, 103–4; in New Orleans, 88–90, 96; and Beckett's stage, 8, 92, 104–6; in prison performances, 14, 50–52; in Sarajevo, 67–68

Occupy Wall Street, 11, 178–89; de-escalation of passive resistance, 179; merging with themes of homelessness and work in *Godot*, 186–88; strategy of demandlessness, 182–83; and intrusive police presence, 187–88; protest signs demarcating stage for *Godot*, 183–86; tactics and theatricality of, 179–82; transformation of spectators into bystanders, 188–89. *See also* bystanders; police; 99% Theater Company; Zuccotti Park
O'Neal, John, 70–71, 203n29
Oppenheim, Lois, 93, 96, 107–9

Palestine, 105, 208n161, 221n2
Pašović, Haris, 72, 204n53
pensum, 94, 128–31; 213n38
petitio principii, 2, 152, 155
Pierce, Wendell, 89
Plotnitsky, Arkady, 213n43
police, 16, 21, 31; handling stage props during San Quentin *Godot*, 34–35; importance to staging Beckett's plays, 8, 188–89; presence during Belgrade *Godot*, 7–8; presence during Zuccotti *Godot*, 186–88
poverty, and Beckett's work 1–3; and the reader,148–51; ascertaining Beckett's characters' condition of, 92–93; as disenfranchisement of means, 147–48; Beckett's dream of, 143–45; of Beckett's work realized in real world crisis, 3–6, 67–70; as helplessness, 164–65; homeless welcomed by Occupy Wall Street protest, 181–82; and hypothetical imperative, 166–70; as lessening and dwindling, 76–78; as minimum, 10, 318n53; as need and demandlessness, 1–2, 66–67, 181–83; poetics and ethics of, 146–47; and provisionality, 170–73; reader's unresentful relation toward, 144–46; and rationing, 51–52, 97–100; and theater, 48–49; as worsening, 173–77. *See also* closed system; vagabond thought
prison, Beckett's work addressed to, 32–33; and caged dynamic, 18–19; hierarchy renamed via Beckett's play, 30; latent image of in Beckett's

work, 30–31; life in, 13–14; as metaphor, 29–30, 196n56; study-object in Beckett's work, 59–60. *See also* closed system, Kumla Prison; Lüttringhausen Prison; Raiford Prison; San Quentin Prison; La Santé Prison
prisoners, articulation of powerlessness, 24; Beckett's Morse code with, 31–32; and boy in *Godot*, 197n74; concept of world, 43–44; destroyers of theater etiquette, 60–62; empathy with Beckett's work, 38–41, 43–47; experiencing *Godot* differently from other audiences, 14–15, 29–30, 55–56; 195n41; Godot as, 41–42; as non-captive audience, 60; pilgrimages to Beckett, 42, 48; and theatrical confessions, 44, 199n111; understanding restricted movements on stage, 20–21; indifference toward term "pseudocouple," 40; shouting at stage, 52–60, and transference, 57, 61. *See also* fourth wall
Proust, Marcel, 17, 93–94, 121, 135, 156, 178, 212n37, 221n1
provisionality , 66, 83, 101, 104–6, 141, 152, 153, 160; and Beckett's aesthetics 169–73; versus improvisation 16–17
Puchner, Martin, 17

Rabaté, Jean-Michel, 200n118
Raiford Prison, performances of *Godot* in, 3, 9, 15, 39, 52, 55, 188
Rank, Otto, 214n62
Realart, Ed, 27
Ricks, Christopher, 158–59
Rilke, Rainer Maria, 116
Roach, Joseph, 29–30, 196n57, 207n133

Sartre, Jean-Paul, 18, 28–29, 163
San Francisco Chronicle, 22, 24
San Quentin Drama Workshop, 9, 36–37, 49, 198n91, 200n122
San Quentin News, 19–20, 23–27, 43, 195n46,
San Quentin State Prison, performance of *Godot* in, 3–5, 7–9, 11–15, 21–37, 30, 33, 36–37, 40, 43, 46–47, 49–50, 53, 57, 59, 68, 179, 188
Sarajevo, 1–3, 6, 9, 11, 14–16, 23, 27, 63; addressed by *Godot*, 72–74; as living paraphrase of *Godot*, 67–68; effect of war on theater 4–5, 78–82; overlapping with poverty on Beckett's stage, 82–84, 91–100; and silences in *Godot*, 53; as waiting for Godot, 100–101
Schechner, Richard, 71
Schneider, Alan, 19
Schwarz, Katie, 188
Shakespeare, William, 174, 203n24, 221n103; world's stage versus Beckett's plays, 63–64
Shostakovich, 65
Shrdlu, Etaoin, 20, 23, 31, 199n114
Smith, Cauleen, 205n91
Solnit, Rebecca, 181
Sontag, Susan, 4–6, 9–10, 14–15, 23, 30, 53, 74, 87–89, 92–93, 95, 98–102, 106–16, 125–26, 129–30, 138, 140, 143, 146, 148–49, 151–53; decision to stage *Godot* in Sarajevo, 63–65, 72–73; on staging only half of *Godot*, 78–82; on utility of theater, 73–77
"Sottisier" notebook (Beckett), 66, 174, 203n19, 212n36, 220n102
States, Bert, 87–88
Suvin, Darko, 5, 6, 8, 35, 37, 192n17, 197n81,
syntax of weakness, 146, 157–61, 169, 218n59

Theatre Arts Magazine, 198n91
Tophoven, Elmar, 31
tramps, as the name for Beckett's characters, 96–98; cinematic versions, 97; namelessness of 135–39; nobody versus anybody, 87–91; and financial crisis, 179–81. *See also* Charlie Chaplin

uncanny, 15, 84–87, 125, 205n94
Unnamable (Beckett), 40, 128, 131–33, 138–40, 149, 152, 154, 158, 162 168, 210n4, 220n91

vagabond thought, 113–16; and animality, 116–19, 132–34; as axiomatic, 123–25; dispossessed, 115–16; and listening, 116–21, 210n12; and Lucky's monologue 113–14; as obligation, 128–31; and mindset of Occupy protesters, 179–82; as radio, 121–23; as endless supposition, 125–28; silenced on Beckett's stage, 112–13; and terror, 131–35; as wind, 118–19, 211n18. *See also* pensum

Valéry, Paul, 128

waiting, and crisis, 67–69; distinguished from expectation, 26–28, 29–31, 79–82; as helpless expenditure, 23–26; and residents of Lower Ninth Ward, 100–103; resolution of, 103–4; as theme to cons, 21–26; utilitarian waiting, 23–24, 100

Waiting for Godot (Beckett), amnesia in 65–67, 150; asymptotic and parabolic understanding of, 107–9; audiences leaving early from, 27, 59–60, 80–82; broken silences of, 52–60; and civil rights movement, 70–72; contexts for, 2–5, 103–7; demanding juxtaposition to reality, 4–6; dialogue from, resonating beyond the stage, 53–60, 90–91, 103–4, 187–88; empathy in, 44–46, 188–89; as inverted telescope, 178; as metaphor, 5; misery distinguished from *Les Misérables*, 2; misery distinguished from *Bariona*, 28–29; as music, 64–65; name and rename of Godot, 100–103; and Occupy Wall Street movement, 178–89; police and staging of, 7–8, 16, 21, 34, 46, 59, 187–88; and prison 16–21. *See also* Belgrade; Lower Ninth Ward; Lüttringhausen Prison; McComb, Mississippi; Raiford Prison; San Quentin Prison; Sarajevo; Zuccotti Park

Waiting for Guffman, 102–3

The Wall is Mama (Cluchey), 9, 48

warden, 33–34, 41, 49, 51

What Where (Beckett), 73, 154

Wigger, Stefan, 18–19

Williams, Cezar, 187

Worstward Ho (Beckett), 10, 167–75

Zilliacus, Clas, 4

Zuccotti Park, *Godot* performance in, 3, 11, 178–89, 222n5; as privately owned public space, 11, 181–83

www.ingramcontent.com/pod-product-compliance
Lightning Source LLC
Chambersburg PA
CBHW021139230426
43667CB00005B/190